STEWART GILL OWEN was born in Blackburn and grew up in Lancashire. After art school, his career was in design and advertising, and as a lecturer in further and higher education. He now lives in Somerset with his wife Jessie. Their two daughters often visit, bringing the five grandsons with them.

Stewart is a keen historian. It is the most immediate and 'living' history that has inspired *Two Sons*, which his first book. Many of us still have links with the First World War. Stewart lost an uncle in Flanders and one of his ancestors was the poet Wilfred Owen. Something that happened so long ago is in many ways still with us.

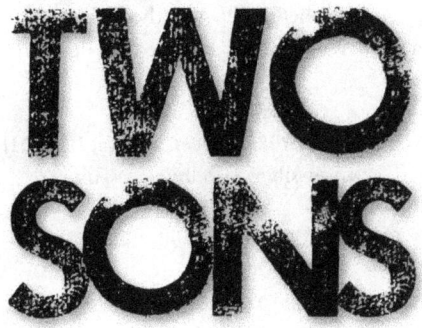

TWO SONS

STEWART GILL OWEN

SilverWood

Published in 2014 by the author
using SilverWood Books Empowered Publishing®

SilverWood Books Ltd
30 Queen Charlotte Street, Bristol, BS1 4HJ
www.silverwoodbooks.co.uk

Copyright © Stewart Gill Owen 2014

The right of Stewart Gill Owen to be identified as the author of
this work has been asserted by him in accordance with the
Copyright, Designs and Patents Act 1988.

All rights reserved. No part of this publication may be reproduced,
stored in a retrieval system, or transmitted in any form or by any means,
electronic, mechanical, photocopying, recording or otherwise, without
prior permission of the copyright holder.

ISBN 978-1-78132-252-9 (paperback)
ISBN 978-1-78132-253-6 (ebook)

British Library Cataloguing in Publication Data
A CIP catalogue record for this book is available from
the British Library

Set in Bembo by SilverWood Books
Printed on responsibly sourced paper

To Jessie

Passchendaele 1917

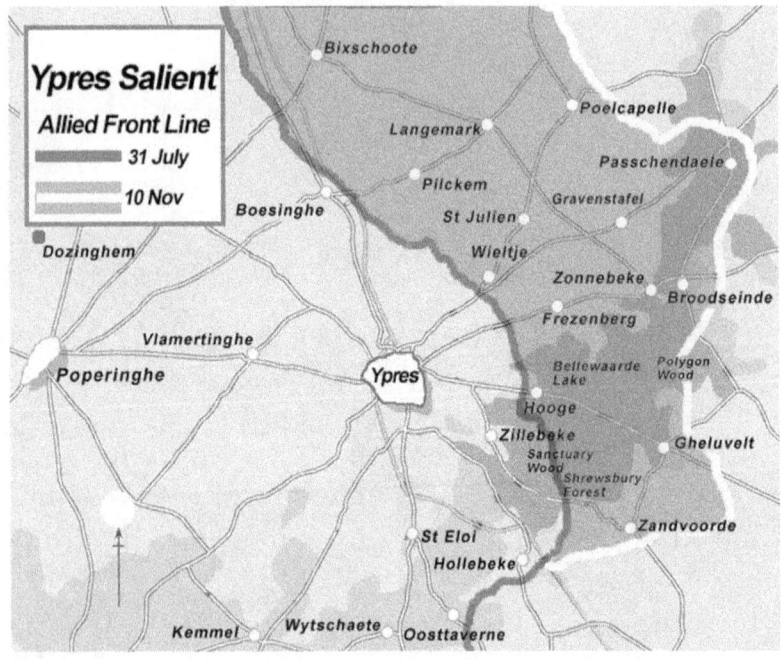

"There's a grave in Belgium with my name on it."
Herbert Edward Owen, 1918-2000

Preface

Herbert Edward Owen was my uncle and he was killed in Belgium in the First World War whilst serving with the Royal Garrison Artillery. My father, Herbert Edward Owen, was born in July 1918 and was named after the brother he never knew. He talked of a headstone that marked a grave in Belgium that had his name on it. In 1990, my wife Jessie and I travelled to Belgium with my parents to visit Dozinghem Cemetery to see Herbert's grave.

Some of my family history forms the basis of this book. I have changed some of the characters, added to the detail of events and changed the name of the family.

This is a story that refers to the battle of Passchendaele that took place in Flanders in 1917. However, it's not a detailed day-by-day account of how that notorious conflict took place. It's a story about the consequences of that campaign and how the lives of two families were dramatically changed following the battle.

This book is based on a number of encounters that took place between a British and a German family in Belgium in the summer of 1932. The date is significant because, in July of that year, Hitler and the Nazi party were threatening to take control of Germany and there was a growing fear in Belgium of the possibility of renewed hostilities. My view is that this is a story that has never been told in any depth before. It's about the victorious and defeated, and how the dead of each nation are remembered or forgotten.

As we travel along the journey of our lives we will experience joy, pride, despair, love, grief and the fear of loss. *Two Sons* is about the emotions, the passion and the feelings that many of us share, regardless of nationality, class, faith and status.

Chapter One

31 July, 1917 – Hooge, Belgium
2nd Battalion, The Royal Lancastrian Light Infantry

The artillery bombardment is thunderous and relentless. One flash after another illuminates the sky, creating strong and harrowing shadows on the faces of the soldiers in the trench. The white and blue light from the explosions glances off the glistening and drenched waterproof capes of the men. Corporal Herbert Williams looks up. Between the flashes of shellfire it seems to be getting lighter. 'I think dawn's coming, Sarge,' he says to Sergeant Davies.

'Well you've got better eyes than me, Bert, it still looks bloody dark from where I am; black as the grave.'

Sergeant Davies sits next to Corporal Williams on a small wooden bench. He takes off his steel helmet and rubs his short-cropped hair. Although he's in his mid-thirties, the war has clearly aged him with the almost visible scars of battle etched into his face. On the other hand, the recently promoted corporal looks younger than his twenty years; still fresh-faced even though he's served in the trenches for almost three years. The sergeant looks up towards the sky.

'It'll be a bit yet.' He pauses for a moment. 'Mind you, it's not a light I look forward to seeing, Bert. Not today.'

From his top pocket the sergeant produces a packet of Woodbines, takes out two cigarettes, puts one in his mouth and offers the other one to Corporal Williams. The sergeant lights his cigarette, inhales slowly and looks first one way and then in the other direction down the dark and gloomy trench. The rain, heavy and persistent, hammers down with a predictable and monotonous rhythm, adding to the large pools of deep brown muddy water that have settled around the feet of the anxious and fearful young soldiers. 'We've been here before, Bert, you and me. Most of this lot haven't. They're kids now and the ones that survive, well, they'll be all grown up by tomorrow.'

The corporal lights his cigarette. 'Best they don't know, Sarge, when you think about it, like.' He takes in the smoke and sighs deeply. 'We've been lucky to have got this far.'

'You'll be all right, Bert, just keep moving quick and don't forget to duck.'

'I'll have to. Mam told me to look after myself.'

'Under orders eh? Your mother wants you home in one piece,' says the sergeant as he looks down at his Lee Enfield 303 rifle, rubbing his hand down the barrel as if polishing it. He looks towards the nervous young recruits. 'All this lot, they're just boys. Their mothers want them home safe, nicely tucked up in bed.'

Corporal Williams draws on his cigarette. 'How many blokes do you think you've killed, Sarge?'

'That's a strange question, Bert. Where did that come from?'

Corporal Williams pauses for a moment while the sound of a heavy barrage subsides. 'I've thought about it quite a bit recently. I don't know why, though, it's never bothered me before.'

The sergeant thinks for a moment. 'I've lost count really. I might have killed more than I think or not as many. I remember at the Somme when I got in one of their trenches, this bugger fell back and put his hands up, he were shouting in English, *give up, give up*. He must have been practising saying it.'

'Thought he might need to say it sometime,' laughs the corporal.

'Aye, I thought that. I pointed my gun at him and thought, *what the fuck do I do now?* Then this other stupid German bastard came running at me firing his revolver all over the fucking place, so I shot him. I looked back and thought that the one who was trying to give up was going to pick up the gun that his mate had dropped. So I shot him as well. I'll never know if he were trying to pick that gun up. Thing is, I don't want to know.'

'I'm the same, Sarge. Last year I threw a grenade into a machine gun post and when I looked in, there were four dead or nearly gone. I thought their parents would be getting some bad news and I felt sorry for them.

The sergeant throws down the stub of his Woodbine. 'Bert, if you think like that, you might as well pack it in. Look after yourself and bugger the rest.'

'Captain's coming,' announces the corporal.

The two soldiers stand as if to attention as the captain approaches them. Captain Charles Johnson, although young, at the age of twenty-eight, is a veteran of command. His handsome features are finished off by a distinctive and well-groomed dark moustache.

'Well, Sergeant?' asks the captain. 'Here we are again. Your men ready?'

'Yes, Sir. They're ready as they are and as they can be.'

The captain moves closer to the sergeant and speaks in a hushed tone. 'Make sure they all go, Sergeant. It's down to you – you know that.'

'Aye, Sir. They'll go. I won't let them think about it. I'll be last out. I won't leave anybody behind, you can rely on it.'

'Thank you, Sergeant. We don't want any embarrassment. I'm sure you understand and get my drift so to speak?'

'It'll all be done as you expect it, Sir.'

'As always, Sergeant.'

A soldier carrying a large jar of rum walks carefully through the trench. As he passes a group of soldiers he stops and pours the thick dark liquid into each of the tin mugs that they're holding in front of them. Corporal Williams puts his mug up to his lips and slowly drinks the small amount of liquor on offer. The captain takes out a hip flask and takes two quick gulps of a very fine brandy and offers the flask to the sergeant.

'Something with a bit more quality, Sergeant, I think you'll find.'

'Thank you. Decent of you, Sir.'

The captain looks at his watch; he ignites his cigarette lighter to light up the face of the timepiece. '3.30 and a bit,' he says.

'What time do we go, Sir – 3.50, isn't it?' asks Corporal Williams.

'Spot on, Corporal. 3.50 it is.'

A young lieutenant joins the three men. Both officers check their watches again.

'3.31 I make it,' says the captain. He looks across at a private soldier and shouts out an order. 'Soldier!'

The startled soldier stands to attention, 'Yes, Sir.'

'Tell Warrant Officer Sims, Staff Sergeant Perkins and all corporals from B Company to join us here immediately.'

The soldier acknowledges the order and moves quickly down the trench.

'3.32, now. That's correct as far as I'm concerned,' confirms the lieutenant.

Warrant Officer Sims, Staff Sergeant Perkins and five corporals walk quickly through the trench, they push past the waiting troops and are careful to keep to the wooden duckboards to avoid stepping into the puddles of water. The captain acknowledges their attendance. 'Good, thank you for joining us, gentlemen, there are a few things we need to briefly discuss about this particular operation.' The captain looks at his senior soldiers. He's aware of their considerable battle experience, he knows that they'll perform competently and will carry out their duties as a well-trained and courageous unit.

He starts his briefing and talks in a loud voice to ensure that he's heard over the intense and loud thud of the bombardment and the clatter of the rapid discharges. 'I know you're very aware of the drill but there are a few other things that you need to know about. Once we've secured their first line trenches we need to push them into a retreat, keep a sword at their backs, you know how it is, if they run we keep at them and don't let them stop and regroup.'

The captain checks his watch again. '3.35 now. Getting closer.' He produces a map, takes a lamp off one of the corporals, illuminates the document and points to a blue line drawn on the plan. 'This is our first objective. The first trench is on the way to the ridge. We've got to be in there and sorting them out. I want to be ready to advance as soon as the second wave is ordered out.'

'From there on will we get artillery cover?' asks Sergeant Davies.

'Of course, from there on we'll be covered by a creeping barrage,' replies the captain. 'It'll be very important to keep up with the pace of the artillery. We can't afford to get behind, you understand?'

The men nod in agreement before their briefing is temporarily interrupted by another round of explosions that shake the trench and send out almost visible sound waves that reverberate from one ridge wall to another. Many of the soldiers attempt to block out the deafening roar of destruction by pushing their fingers into their ears. When the excessively high volume of pounding subsides, the warrant officer shouts, 'Is it true that we'll have the tanks with us, Sir? I haven't seen or heard them yet.'

'That's because they're not here, sadly,' answers the captain. 'Well, not immediately in our sector, too muddy I'm told. They're right of course and we'll just have to manage without them. Anyway, bit too tempting for the chaps to shelter behind them and that could slow us down. I keep saying it but we've got to keep up the momentum and get out of the line of fire. It's those damn machine guns that I'm worried about. When our chaps go down or are caught on the wire, they have to be left, let the stretcher bearers see to them.'

'Prisoners, Sir,' asks Sergeant Davies. 'How do we deal with them?'

'What's that, Sergeant?' asks the captain, struggling to hear him over the sound of the artillery discharges.

'How do we deal with any prisoners, Sir?' shouts the sergeant.

The captain pauses for a moment until the deafening sound of the artillery explosions diminishes. 'You must use your discretion, Sergeant, but don't take any nonsense from them or put up with any funny business; if they don't play the game, well, you know what to do. Get the corporals with some new recruits to ferry them back, but tell them to watch them like hawks, understand?'

'Understood, Sir,' bellows the sergeant.

The captain looks at his watch. '3.43 now.' The lieutenant nods in agreement. Captain Johnson refers back to the map. 'Now, we've got the Worcester and the Northants chaps on our left, with the Sherwood Foresters and the East Lancs on the right, so we're in safe hands. Field artillery will smash some of the wire but as you know it's not always that successful and we'll have to deal with it. Make sure we've got enough cutters and spread the openings because we don't want any funnels for their machine gunners to aim at. General Gough's got a lot riding on this, his reputation's on the line, so he won't want to see us coming back with our tails between our legs.'

Captain Johnson lights another cigarette and points the lamp at the map. 'We've got to push through Chateau Woods, pass Bellewaerde and onto the ridge; I'll be happy when we've taken the ridge. We've got to get to their machine guns. If we can keep them quiet we've got a good chance. They've got a lot of concrete boxes and well-fortified positions in their lines, and we can only sort them out with Mills bombs, so we've got to get up close. Can't help thinking we've drawn the short straw with this one – bit of a compliment really, I suppose. As they said at the briefing, if anybody can do it, the Royal Lancs can.'

'Same as always, Sir,' asks the staff sergeant. 'If the other units that are close by have lost their officer command, do we help out like?'

'That's it, Staff Sergeant. If we're in good shape, then yes take them under your wing and drive them on. Like our chaps, don't let them shelter in the shell-holes, they'll want to when those machine guns start up. You know the score. This artillery will have done a lot of damage but there'll still be plenty of the Bosche who'll be ready for us.'

Captain Johnson pauses and takes a good look up and down the trench. He nods in approval. 'Well, men, we look set and ready. Now, to your stations and get those ladders in position.'

The captain checks his watch again. 'There we are, 3.47,' he confirms. He unfastens his holster and takes out his Webley revolver. He carefully loads some bullets into the chamber of the gun and loudly declares, 'All in order now, men, let the Bosche see what the Royal Lancs are made of.'

Sergeant Davies checks the position of the men and shouts one way down the trench. 'Fix!' then barks his order the other way. 'Fix!' Although the trench is filled with the booming and intense sound of the artillery bombardment, the silence of the men can still be heard. He pauses for a moment, then holds his head back and with one loud gasp he shouts, 'Bayonets!'

The familiar sound of metal scraping against metal is heard as the soldiers remove their bayonets from their belts and attach them to the end of their rifles. To some, a few, it's a welcome sound because it means that the waiting is over. To others it's a sound that they dreaded to hear. In a moment, a very brief moment, they will have to face the possibility of pain and death. The veterans of The Somme and other campaigns know that despite what they are told, their chances of surviving the coming battle are not good. The trench that they have come to hate is now a place of sanctuary and safety. It's a place they have to leave.

'Now, boys,' barks the sergeant. 'I don't much like my own company and I'll be pleased to climb out of the trench because...' he stops briefly to scan the faces of his men, 'because when you buggers have all gone, I'll be lonely, being on my own, won't I?'

A slight ripple of laughter is heard. The captain nods approvingly at the sergeant. He smiles at the lieutenant and checks his watch again.

Corporal Herbert Edward Williams holds his rifle in his right hand and grips a rung of the ladder with his left. He puts his foot on the ladder and turns to Sergeant Davies. 'See you on the ridge, Sarge.'

'Aye, good lad, Bert, show these young-uns how it's done.'

The captain looks intently at his watch, puts the whistle in his mouth, takes a long deep breath and creates a long, piercing, shrill sound. The soldiers climb out of the trench and advance across the muddy shell-scarred terrain. Corporal Williams leads the way and moves swiftly around the rim of the shell craters. Then the distinct and dreaded sound of machine gun fire is heard, faint and in the distance at first but increasing in volume and intensity.

Corporal Williams looks around to check on the soldiers behind him; he feels reassured, none down yet. Then a murderous burst of fire and the young corporal falls into a large water-filled shell-hole and there he lies. He tries to move but can't... he feels his chest and then the side of his head... he looks at his blood-soaked hand and watches as the deep red liquid drips off each of his fingers. He knows it's bad, as bad as it can be. 'Sorry, Mother,' he says and closes his eyes.

Chapter Two

30 July, 1932 – Poperinge, Belgium

The motor coach pulls up outside a large, impressive-looking house located on a busy dusty street in the centre of the town of Poperinge. It's a warm and sunny afternoon. The motion of the coach's wheels has whipped up some clay dust from the road and it swirls around as it's carried by a gentle breeze. Most of the passing traffic is horse-drawn and there are many pedestrians walking by. The driver steps down from his driving cab, walks to the other side of the coach, opens the passenger door and holds out his hand to assist his customers as they step down from the vehicle.

The first to be seen is the slightly portly figure of John Williams, who's dressed in a smart grey check three-piece suit and is sporting a dark flat cap. He politely waves the driver's hand away. 'No assistance required on this occasion, thank you, driver, but a different story with the ladies, no doubt. If you would be good enough to see to their needs, I would be grateful.'

John stands and admires the view. He stretches and rubs his index finger over his large and drooping moustache. He's a man in his mid-fifties; he looks well, appears to be in fine health and retains a good head of hair for his age. Although, in his younger years, his hair colour was dark brown, it's now clearly turning grey. The expression on his face shows that he's pleased with himself because once again he's successfully managed to transport his family from Lancashire in the north of England to the Flanders region of Belgium with very little trouble and inconvenience. The success of the outward part of their journey has been achieved by detailed planning, negotiation and persuasion. One by one the passengers alight and step down from the coach.

First to stand next to John is his wife, Annie; she's a sturdy and handsome-looking woman and appears to be of a similar age to her husband. Annie's dressed in what she describes as her *Sunday best*, which is a smart cream-coloured jacket over a long floral-patterned dress. Her head and face are shielded from the sun by a large straw hat that's decorated with flowers made of felt.

John points up to a sign that's positioned on a post by the large house. 'There it is, Annie,' he announces. 'Madame De Vos Hotel. It's still here, looking in pretty good nick and as grand as I remember.'

'Well I'm glad about that, John,' replies Annie. 'I wouldn't have fancied sleeping on that old charabanc.'

John looks directly at his wife and smiles, 'Now, Annie, it'll be twelve years we've been coming here and ten to Madame De Vos's place; have I ever let you down on any occasion concerning these trips of ours?'

Annie can't resist teasing him. 'No, John, another expedition successfully carried out and completed…' She pauses for a moment. 'Mind you, we've got to get home yet.'

'Well, Annie, these things don't just happen. Nothing should be left to chance. That's my policy and it works, every time.'

The couple becomes aware of the presence of a large woman who's standing at the top of the steps of the decorative and ornate-looking veranda at the front of the hotel. They immediately identify her as Madame De Vos, the owner of the establishment. The lady, who's dressed in black and wearing a pure white apron, walks down the steps. She has her arms open in the form of a greeting. It's as if she's about give the couple an affectionate hug.

'Mr Williams and Mrs Williams, how good to see you.

It is that time of the year again,' she says. The welcoming woman takes hold of John's hands, looks him in the face and smiles warmly at him. John removes his cap and acknowledges her greeting. For a woman who John knows to be in her early forties, she looks remarkably youthful, her round face free of the telling lines that display age and physical maturity.

'And how are you both?' Madame De Vos enquires.

Annie smiles back at her, 'Rather travel weary but on the whole in good health, thank you, Madame De Vos.'

'As Annie says, we are both thriving, thank you, Madame De Vos,' replies John. 'And how are you and your family?'

'We are as well as we can be,' she replies. 'My mother-in-law, if you remember her, is finding walking difficult these days, as you will see. My boy Hugo is growing very well, they say that it is because I feed him too much. Perhaps they are right and soon he will be taller than me. I can see that you do look a little tired, but that can be remedied. As you English say, *we can fix that*. Your rooms are ready and tomorrow you will be, as you might say, *tip-top*, is that right?'

'Oh yes, well done, Madame De Vos,' replies John. 'We'll be as right as rain tomorrow. You do make us welcome and I know we'll be very comfortable with you – recuperation and recovery is guaranteed when we're in your hands, Madame De Vos.'

Madame De Vos stares beyond John and Annie. 'Now, who have you brought with you this time?'

The other passengers, having left the coach, assemble behind John and Annie. Before John can begin his introductions, Annie's sister, Mary, pushes her way forward. She clutches the rim of her hat to secure it against a sudden gust of wind and holds a handkerchief up to her face as if she's negotiating her way through a sandstorm. Mary is almost two years younger than her sister and although she's of a smaller build, she does resemble Annie in facial appearance. However, her facial expressions on the other hand are very different. Like her sister, she's wearing a long, floral dress that she keeps for special occasions.

'I'm sorry, Madame. What's your name?' Mary asks hurriedly. 'I need to get inside. This dust's getting on my chest and that won't do at all.' She looks at Annie, and her sister's disapproving look makes her realise that she might have been rude and disrespectful in not introducing herself.

'Oh,' she says. 'I'm Mrs Reynolds. We haven't met before. Well we wouldn't have, would we?' She looks round and adds, 'Behind me is my husband, Henry.' She steps closer to Madame De Vos. 'He's a bit confused, no change there.'

Madame De Vos looks at the gentleman who Mary's referring to. She sees a slim-built, middle-aged man of average height. He's wearing grey flannel trousers and a red and dark blue striped blazer. He nervously removes his cap to reveal a head of hair that's almost white in colour, which is in stark contrast to his small, dark and well-trimmed moustache. Mary summons Henry and orders him to accompany her into the hotel and he takes her arm to assist her in climbing the steps.

A slightly embarrassed John coughs and composes himself. 'Sorry about that, Madame De Vos. She's a bit fatigued.' He pauses and beckons to his daughter to step forward. An attractive young woman who's of a slim build steps forward and stands next to her father. Her long dark hair is appropriately tied up and secured under a plain but tastefully-designed broad-brimmed hat that's dark red in colour. The hat complements and goes with a slim-fitting, light pink, knee-length dress that her father thinks is a little too short, although he knows that it's the fashion of the modern era. John places his arm around his daughter's shoulders and proudly proclaims, 'This is our Emma, she's twenty-one years of age.'

Emma corrects her father. 'Twenty-two.'

'Aye, twenty-two, that's right' agrees John. 'She's going to be a teacher, before she's wed, like.'

'And after Dad, if I decide to get married.'

'Aye, we'll see,' says John. He summons a young, good-looking, fair-haired, teenage boy to stand in front of him. He places his hands on the boy's shoulders, removes the youth's cap and announces, 'This is our youngest, it's Herbert Edward, and I know he's fourteen, we call him Bertie and he's going to be an engineer, he's interested in the subject and he's working towards it.'

Madame De Vos smiles at Emma and Herbert. 'But Emma, we have met before, when you were quite small.'

'I remember you, Madame De Vos,' replies Emma.

'You remember her then,' adds John. 'It were a number of years ago, about eight or nine. Fancy that – with all the people that you have to deal with.'

'I do not forget nice and pleasant people, Mr Williams, and Emma is also *my* given name,' says Madame De Vos.

'That's very good of you to say that. It's very reassuring,' replies John.

Madame De Vos invites the family to enter the hotel and leads the way. Annie puts her hand around John's arm as they walk. 'I suppose you mean it's reassuring that Emma created a good impression.'

'Well, you know it's a good thing when folk tell you that they appreciate the way your children are,' explains John.

'Well, she's certainly impressed with you, John,' adds Annie. 'I'll have a word with her later and put her right on a few things.'

They walk up the steps and onto the veranda. John and Annie acknowledge the presence of an elderly lady who's sitting in a rather antiquated wheelchair that's positioned in the corner of the porch. She's dressed in a dark grey frock and is wearing a deep burgundy-coloured shawl around her shoulders. She wears a delicate white lace bonnet on her head and on her face is a small pair of round metal-rimmed spectacles. They recognise her as being Madame De Vos's mother-in-law, Mevrouw De Vos. As John and Annie pass by, they smile at her and politely nod. The elderly lady greets them with a smile and a wave. Behind the family, the coach driver carries some of the cases. He's clearly struggling, having underestimated the weight of the luggage, and is relieved when Hugo, Madame De Vos's young son, approaches him and asks if he needs assistance. The driver gratefully accepts the offer and although the youth is of a small build and only thirteen years of age, carrying cases is something that he's used to doing. He applies himself to the task with considerable confidence and enthusiasm.

The family gathers in the well-appointed reception room where the interior decoration and furnishings reflect a bygone age more associated with the British Edwardian period. The furniture comprises an ornate and decorative chaise longue that has been positioned by the large bay window and two large, well-padded settees, which are both covered in a dark green material that displays a decorative paisley pattern. In the rest of the room there are a number of comfortable easy chairs and hard-backed, upright seats that are described by Madame De Vos as being *something firmer for the back*. In the corner of the room is a small but adequate writing desk with an oil lamp strategically placed to assist in the process of putting pen to paper and composing. Heavy, floral, tapestry curtains are drawn back to make use of available exterior light and yet still manage to restrict over-intrusive illumination. The old-fashioned decorative theme is maintained and promoted throughout the hotel.

Madame De Vos enters the room where other guests are now starting to congregate. 'Now, please sit down. It has been a long journey for you, I think. You are so brave. I don't like to travel on the water. I never learned how to swim you know.'

Mary shakes her head and complains, 'I didn't think we were ever going to get here. We were supposed to sleep on the boat, but of course you can't.'

'That is a shame,' says Madame De Vos and adds, 'some tea, I think, I'm sure that it will refresh you.'

'That will be very nice, Madame De Vos,' replies Annie. 'Very welcome and much appreciated.'

'And how was the sea crossing?' asks Madame De Vos.

'A bit choppy,' replies Henry, 'or lumpy as the sailors might say.'

'But we've known worse,' adds Annie.

'We're not very nautical as you know, Madame De Vos,' says John, 'but we managed it. We coped because it's a means to an end.'

Madame De Vos clasps her hands together. 'And I'm very glad you did and I hope you have a nice stay with us.'

The ladies sit down by the window and John takes out his pipe. Annie looks at him with a disapproving stare and points to a door leading to the foyer and outside. She turns to Mary. 'I don't mind myself but it's not to everybody's liking,' she says.

'Filthy habit,' says Mary, 'I find it disgusting.'

John acknowledges his wife's agitation and stands up. 'Not wanted here, Henry, you and me as usual. You'll join me, won't you?'

'Aye,' replies Henry as he checks his pocket to ensure that he has his tobacco with him, 'glad to keep you company, John.'

The two men leave the room and walk through to the veranda. They both fill their pipes and light up; they enjoy a moment's peace as they taste the spiced flavours of the smoke. Herbert joins them and his father puts his arm across his son's shoulders. 'Best leave them to it, gentlemen,' remarks John. 'Let them enjoy their tea in their smoke-free room.'

John turns to see that the elderly lady is still seated in the corner of the veranda. He raises his pipe and nods towards it. 'I'm sorry, Mevrouw De Vos. Do you mind?'

Mevrouw De Vos smiles and nods her head to indicate that she has no objection.

'How are you?' asks John.

'As well as I am, *danku*,' replies Mevrouw De Vos.

'Oh,' he says, forgetting that she hasn't been introduced to Henry or Herbert. 'This is my brother-in-law Henry and this fine young fellow is my son Herbert.'

Henry slightly bows and respectfully says, 'Pleased to meet you, Madam De Vos.'

John coughs slightly and corrects his brother-in-law, 'It's Mevrouw De Vos, Henry. That's because we're in Dutch – or, as some would say, Flemish-speaking Belgium now.'

Henry looks confused, 'But Madam, Madam De Vos, the owner, how is it that she's…?'

'It's Madame De Vos, Henry. You see, she is the owner of this establishment and she's Mevrouw De Vos's daughter-in-law.'

'I see, but…'

'Now look,' continues John. 'It's complicated and a bit confusing, Henry, you have to remember we're in Belgium. It's not like us in England; things are very straightforward with us and that's how we like it.'

The youth who had helped the coach driver with the cases passes by Mevrouw De Vos. She stretches out and holds his arm. 'Hugo… *kleinzoon*,' she announces.

'Grandson,' adds Hugo. 'I am her grandson.'

John immediately recognises the slender, dark-haired youth. 'Yes, I know and how you've grown, young man.'

Mevrouw De Vos looks at John but speaks in Dutch to Hugo for her grandson to translate. Hugo listens intently, pauses for a moment and says, 'My grandmother asks if you have been making those special clothes again, for the men?'

John displays a broad smile, he's pleased that she's remembered. 'Ah, the funeral orders. So your grandmother recognises me and recalls my trade, how kind.'

Mevrouw De Vos talks in Dutch again and nods towards John. Hugo listens and speaks again to John, 'She says that you work hard to come here. It must be very important to you.'

John nods in agreement. 'You're right, Mevrouw De Vos. It means a great deal for us to come here and the extra money gets us here.'

A further conversation takes place between grandmother

and grandson, then it becomes obvious that the mood of the dialogue changes. Their talk takes on a more serious form and the discussion is clearly about a subject that's of concern to the elderly lady. Hugo says, 'My grandmother asks if you are worried about the possibility of another war?'

John is somewhat taken aback by Mevrouw De Vos's question, pauses for a moment, composes himself and replies, 'Another war, who with?' he smiles slightly because he can see an opportunity to promote his opinion. 'Tell your grandmother not to worry, Hugo. Trust me that will never happen.' He raises a finger in a gesture of defiance and adds, 'We put an end to that; the Germans were taught a lesson and they won't be back for seconds, you can rest assured.'

Hugo translates what John has said, his grandmother shakes her head, clearly she does not agree. '*Ik hoop...*' Mevrouw De Vos starts to say. She becomes more agitated and speaks to Hugo again in Dutch.

Hugo bows his head and listens. When she's finished talking he looks up and says, 'She hopes that you are right, but she says that she thinks that you are wrong...'

Mevrouw De Vos interrupts her grandson. She has identified something in his translation that she does not agree with, she speaks abruptly to him, 'I think, *nee,*' she says. '*Ik denk dat, nee, Ik weet.*'

Hugo is a little embarrassed. 'My grandmother corrects me and insists that I tell you that she knows that you are wrong and some time the Germans will come again.'

Mevrouw De Vos looks defiantly at John, as if she feels that there is now no need for further discussion because her point has been made. John shakes his head. 'Tell your grandmother not to get so worked up, Hugo. She won't benefit from it and it's not good for her.'

Hugo passes on John's comments. Mevrouw De Vos starts to reply. However, John wants to bring the conversation to a close. He raises his hand. 'We must be excused now. Our ladies will be wondering where we've got to. Thank your grandmother, Hugo, for… well, should we say, our interesting conversation.'

John and Henry extinguish their pipes, say goodbye to Mevrouw De Vos and enter the house. The elderly lady is still frustrated and clearly troubled.

'Another war?' says Henry. 'Where does she get that from?'

'It's this Hitler business, that's what it is,' explains John, 'I've read about it, Henry, take no notice, she's an old lady and gets a bit confused like, I should think'.

Henry's still concerned, 'She's a bit upset though and in a bit of a state.'

John puts his hand on Henry's shoulder, 'You're right, old chap, she needs telling and put right. She could do herself some harm, woman of that age getting all worked up like that.'

'Perhaps you could have another word with her, John, when she's a bit calmer.'

'No, Henry, that won't do because she's set on it. I'll have a word with Madame De Vos and she'll put her right. Once it's explained to her, things will be better.'

Henry isn't convinced, 'Well, it'll take some doing, she might know a bit more about it than we do, I mean living here like.'

John stares directly at Henry. He's now serious. 'Now look, Henry, I don't know if you remember – perhaps you weren't there at the time.'

'Where?' asks Henry.

'In the Lion. That time in the Red Lion when we talked about it.'

With the limited amount of information supplied, Henry remains confused. 'Talked about what, when were that?'

'Oh, a few months back,' says John. 'Anyway, it were this thing with George Howarth. You know George?'

Henry thinks for a moment, 'Oh yes, I know George – butcher isn't he?'

John's pleased that progress is being made. 'That's him. Well, he started on about this another war business, said things like *those Germans, they're not finished with it.*'

'He must have read something about it like,' says Henry.

'Well, we put him right,' says John triumphantly. He moves closer to Henry to make his point, 'Now look here, George, I said, when those Germans strutted their way through Belgium, bullying and threatening as they did, it were easy for them. Then they came across our lads and they soon realised they'd more than met their match and that were it.'

'That's right, John, we taught them a lesson they wouldn't forget.'

'That's what I told George, it took a time but, in the end, they knew they had to give up because we weren't going to. That's why it were the war to end all wars.'

'That told him, then.'

'I told him,' says John. 'It were complicated and he had to look at all the facts, you see. They're not allowed to build any more battleships or tanks and things like that, you know.' John feels that their conversation is at an end and to demonstrate that time is going on, he removes his pocket watch from his waistcoat and looks at the time. 'Now, let's re-join the ladies.'

The reception room is quite busy because the hotel is almost full and polite conversation is taking place between the guests who are mainly from Britain. Most of them are visiting war graves and the battlefields. As well as the British guests, there's a Dutch family staying and also a newlywed French couple from Paris. Although the reception room is not small, it feels like it's a confined space due to the number of people who are meeting and socialising. The hotel staff have provided tea, coffee and cakes. As they pass through the room carrying jugs of apple juice and water, the waiters respond to individual requests from the guests and they go back to the kitchen to seek out alternative food and drink. A smiling Madame De Vos enters the room and walks directly towards John.

'Mr Williams, I have made your arrangements,' she announces. 'It is with the local garage to provide you and your family with a small coach to take you to the cemetery in the morning. Your driver will be Paul, he's a nice, polite boy and I know his mother well. He will be here to pick you up at ten o'clock in the morning and as you might say, *on the dot*.'

John is obviously pleased to receive confirmation of the arrangements. 'Thank you, Madame De Vos, very much appreciated. Another piece of this very complicated jigsaw is in place.'

Madame De Vos only hears part of John's reply due to the high level of noise in the room, 'I'm sorry, Mr Williams. Did you say that you wanted a jigsaw?'

John laughs. 'No, no, Madame De Vos, just my way. An expression and not to be taken literally.'

Madame De Vos then moves over to a couple who appear to be on their own. She invites them to meet the other guests and ushers them to the centre of the room to where the Williams family and the Reynolds are in conversation. The gentleman is dressed in a very expensive-looking, dark blue suit. He's slim and reasonably tall in build, a small dark brown moustache matches the colour of his hair and, just above his ears, grey streaks give him a rather distinguished appearance. The lady's facial features present her as being a fine-looking woman who's of average height and slender in build. Her pale skin tone makes her dark red hair appear to be very prominent and promotes it as being a very distinctive feature. Like her husband, no expense has been spared with her outfit, which is a dress that's light green in colour with a subtle, delicate striped pattern. Around her neck she wears a string of pearls that are definitely not artificial or paste. 'Mr and Mrs Williams and Mr and Mrs Reynolds,' says Madame De Vos. 'May I introduce Colonel Aspinal and Mrs Aspinal who are en route to Geneva for a holiday.'

Madame De Vos then looks at the Aspinals for confirmation. 'Is that correct, Colonel – or was it Zurich?'

'Major, it's Major Aspinal, replies the major, 'and that's right, Geneva, bit of a holiday, never been before, thought we'd see it, mountains and lakes. Really looking forward to it.'

'That is nice,' says Madame De Vos, 'and you thought you would *break your journey* as you might say, here in Poperinge. If you don't mind me asking, you were or perhaps are still a military man and were you here in the war?'

'Yes, retired from the army, barrister by profession now,' the major answers. 'And yes, served in Flanders. Thought I'd just stop off and see the place again. I remember Pops very well, fond of the place, Toc H and all that.'

John steps forward and more formally introduces himself. 'My name is John and this is my wife, Annie.'

Mary waits for Henry to take the lead and when this doesn't happen immediately, she takes matters into her own hands. She glares at her husband and says, 'I'm Mary, Mary Reynolds and this is my husband, Henry.'

'Very good,' replies the major. 'As Madame De Vos said, I'm Major Aspinal and this is my wife, Mrs Aspinal.'

'We, that's me and my wife, Annie,' says John, 'come here every year on the anniversary of our son's death. I'm proud to say that he were with The Royal Lancastrian Light Infantry.'

The major stares at John for a moment, he looks him up and down. 'Every year? My goodness. It's a long way to come, and costly I should think.'

John moves closer to Major Aspinal and talks in a hushed tone. 'When I started out in employment, I began as a commercial cloth cutter and as time went on I trained to be a tailor. I work for Mr Webster now in the town and every now and then I do a bit of tailoring on the side like. When there's a funeral, some of the men ask me to make them a new suit for the occasion. I do this in my spare time and I save this money. That funeral order pays for the trip.

'I'm so sorry for the loss of your son,' says Mrs Aspinal. 'So sad for you, but you must have been very proud of him.'

Annie appreciates Mrs Aspinal's comments. 'Very proud, as proud as we can be, thank you Mrs Aspinal… he were a corporal, you know.'

'Was he really,' says the major. 'Corporal eh? Jolly good, well done, good chaps the Royal Lancs.'

John acknowledges the respectful statement made by the major. 'Aye, they were good chaps, my–' he looks at Annie. 'Sorry, I mean, *our* boy. He were wounded at Passchendaele and died two days later near here.'

'*Were wounded,*' repeats the major. 'Of course you mean *was wounded*. You northern people have your own language.'

'It's the way we are, Major,' answers John, indignantly.

'Quite right,' says the major. 'I had to take a platoon of East Lancashire chaps on field manoeuvres once during the war. They would finish their sentences by saying *like* and *over yon*, very amusing. It's the odd word, but it makes us different, good fellows though and very willing.'

Henry is eager to participate in the conversation. 'Barrister eh, that's a grand job, isn't it?'

'Well, it is, on the whole,' replies the major. 'Bit tedious at times but it pays well enough and of course there's the estate to maintain. It's a family affair, our chambers, never gave it much thought really. It was always expected that I would study law. After school, I went for a little chat at my father's old college at Oxford. They asked if I was interested in any sports. I told them that I did some shooting and a bit of rowing. They said that that was splendid and that was it.'

'This estate,' asks Mary, 'is that where you live?'

'Family estate,' replies Mrs Aspinal. 'Not far from Lewis in Sussex. We visit some weekends and we live in Kensington. Do you know it?'

'No, where is it?' asks Mary. 'Is it nice?'

'London,' replies Mrs Aspinal. 'We like it. I like it. I don't dislike the country but it's nice to have a good social calendar to be able to attend, you see. Then there are the children. It's important that they're appropriately and suitably married of course.'

'And they can do that in London better than anywhere else, like?' asks Henry.

Mrs Aspinal gives Henry a questioning look. 'Well, of course, where else would you suggest?'

Henry is unsure as to how to respond, so he shrugs his shoulders and Annie comes to his rescue. 'We obviously live in different worlds, Mrs Aspinal,' she laughs. 'Our social calendar amounts to Friday nights at the whist drive at the church hall.'

Mrs Aspinal stares back at her. 'I'm sure that's very nice for you, Mrs Williams. We prefer bridge, but only when we're entertaining of course.'

'Must be nice having an estate though,' says John. 'Somewhere to go, like.'

'Well it is,' replies the major, 'but it's a headache you know, paying off death duties, upkeep and then of course there are the staff. It's always a question of getting the right staff and people you can trust.'

'You must have a busy time of it, with all your court stuff as well like,' says Henry.

'Keeps me busy, Harold,' replies the major.

Henry is slightly embarrassed and a little irritated, 'It's Henry, Major, not Harold.'

'Sorry, Henry,' replies the major. 'What's your occupation? What do you do to while away the hours and put food on the table?'

'Well,' replies Henry. 'I'm a drayman, and I work for a brewery.'

'A drayman,' says the major. 'Is that delivering alcoholic drinks?'

John steps slightly forward to offer some support. He places his hand on Henry's shoulder and proclaims, 'One of the finest draymen in Lancashire is our Henry, in my view. When I see Henry driving those impressive shire horses up the streets, stopping off and carefully delivering his precious cargo, which is ale of the most excellent quality. I get a warm feeling inside.'

'Ale of the most excellent quality,' repeats the major. 'Sounds impressive. Not my tipple of course.'

'Not keen on ale, Major?' asks John. 'Perhaps not partial to the brew in your local, it varies you know, especially in the south, I've heard.'

'You mean the local public house, near to where we live, in Sussex perhaps? Not been there too often, when we're on a shoot on a few occasions, I've sampled local beer.'

'Oh,' says John, 'where do you normally sup, like?'

The major seeks clarification. 'Sup? You mean drink, well, a quality single malt at home at times, mostly at my club but I don't think they have any ale there. Perhaps bottled porter beer, do you think?'

Their conversation is interrupted by Madame De Vos who announces that dinner is now served. John excuses himself and approaches Annie, he offers her his arm. 'Will you join me, Mrs Williams?'

Annie responds, 'I'll be pleased to accompany you, Mr Williams'.

John leans closer to Annie and quietly says, 'Dinner this week at this time… tea when we get home.'

Chapter Three

31 July, 1932 – Dozinghem Military Cemetery, Belgium

A canvas-topped charabanc coach slowly splutters and shakes its way down a narrow dirt road. It pulls up outside the gates to a military cemetery. Paul, the driver, a well-built young man of rugged appearance, applies considerable strength to pull up the lever that engages the handbrake. Paul takes his duties very seriously and is wearing a suit that he's clearly grown out of some years before. He proudly wears a grey, chauffeur-style hat which his mother gave him for his twenty-first birthday. The young man eagerly jumps down from the driver's seat and trots round to open the door to allow the passengers to safely step off the coach. First to take Paul's hand and step down is Mary.

'Thank you, young man. Paul isn't it?' she says. 'My sympathies for having to negotiate these unmade roads. I'm feeling very unsettled now with all that shaking about, not blaming you, course I'm not, but I'd get in touch with the council if I were you.'

One by one the passengers step off and walk towards the gates. They talk as they walk. Annie and Emma are holding flowers. John hands Henry a small Brownie box camera. 'We'll have a nice picture later, Henry,' he says. 'If you wouldn't mind, your expertise and skill will be greatly appreciated.'

Henry is quite surprised and taken aback by his brother-in-law's request. 'Aye, right John, as long as it's not too complicated and technical mind, I'll work to your instructions.'

'Then I have no concerns there, Henry, I trust you without

question, it'll be a nice addition to the family album.'

John and Henry lead the family through the gates, they pause for a moment to take in the view; before them are the rows of light grey, almost bleached white headstones laid out in neat and aligned rows. Between the rows of headstones, there are vibrant green avenues of well-manicured and closely-cut grass. Flowers of many different colours have been placed at the base of some of the stones by relatives and visitors who have wanted to pay their respects. Part of the perimeter wall displays red, pink and white roses that are attached to the terracotta brickwork. Central to everything is the tall white cross of remembrance that stands proudly at one end of the cemetery. The family follows a path that leads past the first row of headstones and, as they pass one of the cemetery gardeners, John nods to him. He turns to Henry with a satisfied expression on his face. 'They like to see us here, Henry, because they know that we're appreciating their work.'

Henry looks back at a gardener who's busily tending one of the graves. 'Labour of love I should think, John.'

Annie approaches the two men. She holds a parasol in one hand and some red roses in the other. John stops walking and views the cemetery. 'When we first came here, Henry, it were just a field of wooden crosses, nothing special were it, Annie? Now look at it, gets better every year.'

'Beautiful,' replies Annie. 'It looks especially nice on a pleasant day like today, all those white headstones set against the green of the gardens and the blue sky.'

John points at the entrance gate and talks in a loud voice as if he's making an announcement of some great importance and insists on being heard. He also talks directly to another group of people that is standing close by and he welcomes them to become part of his proclamation. 'When we entered through those gates we came onto British soil.' He then points to the ground and continues, 'This land has been given to our country by a grateful nation.'

His audience, including the group of people he doesn't

know, nods in approval. 'Every year,' he says. 'I'm reminded of the sacrifice that these dear boys made, when General Kitchener made his request and demanded a response, they came and obeyed without hesitation, they gave up their lives so we can walk proud.'

The invited guests begin to applaud and John's family feel obliged to join in. John's obviously flattered; he looks pleased with himself and raises the trilby hat that he's wearing. He smiles. He feels a performance coming on and gestures for his audience to follow him and leads the small crowd in a procession. As he passes each headstone he comments on the inscription.

'Black Watch,' he announces. 'Two Yorks and Lancs boys here, oh these chaps were with the Worcesters and these three were with the East Lancs, they fought with our boys, the Royal Lancs at Passchendaele...'

John continues his talk. An elderly man in the party steps forward to speak to Annie. 'He knows a bit about it,' he says in a broad Scottish accent. 'Is that gentleman your tour guide, or can we listen in?'

Annie laughs. 'Tour guide, oh he'd like that, likes the sound of his own voice, my John.' She can see that the man's looking confused. 'No,' she says, 'bless you, he's my husband, just a visitor like you. He does this every year and he likes an audience.'

The man looks embarrassed. 'I'm sorry that we intruded. I just thought...'

Annie interrupts him, 'No, no listen to him, please, you're right, he does know a bit about it, he's studied it in some depth. He'll be more than happy for you to listen to him.'

John continues his guided tour, providing a detailed account of some of the battle history of the regiments and the sacrifices that were made. After a time, the crowd thanks him and disperses. John places his hand on Herbert's shoulder and smiles at him. 'Now Bertie, let's see how our Bert's doing.'

Father and son walk on. Annie hands the parasol to Emma

and takes hold of Mary's arm to slow her pace. 'Let them be for a bit, Mary, some time on their own.'

Emma understands the delicate situation and elects to stay with her mother. They watch as John and Herbert walk towards the large cross which is close to where Bert has been laid to rest. When they reach the grave John stands with his arm around Herbert's shoulders. They look at the inscription on the headstone and for those few precious moments they're silent and thoughtful.

'Herbert Edward Williams,' reads John. 'Your brother's in a good place here, Bertie. Just look at that stone, they really look after him, it couldn't be better.'

Their meditation and contemplation is interrupted by Henry who wanders up to them, 'Here he is, Henry, 'says John. 'When Annie puts her flowers on there, it'll just set it off nicely, it'll look a real treat.'

'Aye you're right,' replies Henry, 'they do keep it nice, no more than your boy deserves though, John.' John nods in agreement. He obviously approves of Henry's endorsement.

At some distance away Annie, Emma and Mary view this emotional scene. Mary becomes agitated when she sees Henry standing with John and Herbert. She tries to attract his attention by waving at him,.'Just look at him! Oh come away, gormless. He's got no idea, so insensitive.'

Henry spots Mary beckoning to him, for a moment he's a little puzzled. 'What's our Mary going on about?' Then he begins to understand, excuses himself and walks slowly away to re-join his wife.

'At last!' says a somewhat exasperated Mary. 'The penny's finally dropped, wonders will never cease'.

Emma comforts her mother by putting her arm around her. 'Dad's really been looking forward to this, hasn't he, Mum, showing Bertie his brother's grave.'

'You're right there, Emma,' replies Annie, 'as I've often said, he feels that our Bertie is a replacement, if you know what

I mean. He'd always told him that there's a grave in Belgium with his name on it and one day he'd bring him here to see it.'

'And here we are, Annie,' says Mary.

'Yes, and here we are, Mary, as you say,' replies Annie thoughtfully.

'Don't you want to join them, Annie?'

'I will, in a bit, let them have this moment together. As I said, it's their time, I can wait.'

Back at the grave, Herbert asks his father, 'I wonder what he'd be like now, Dad?'

'Oh, much the same as he were. Liked a joke, came with me to the Lion when he were on leave and enjoyed a pint. Good at dancing and had a bit of an eye for the ladies. He were a handsome lad, took after his mother,' John winks at Herbert and smiles broadly.

After a moment Herbert says, 'I suppose he'd be married by now?'

John's enjoying his conversation with his son, it's an opportunity to re-visit, to ponder and to remember. 'Aye, more than likely, he'd be... he'd be about thirty-four now. Married, oh I should think so, and kids no doubt, your nephews and nieces they'd be.'

John once again puts his hand on his son's shoulder. 'You'd have liked him, Bertie, and he'd have got on with you. He got on with most folk, it's the way he were.'

'He was good at football wasn't he, Dad?'

'Good at most things, Bertie, in sport like. I wanted him to work with me as a tailor, as you know. Whatever he did he would have been good at it. Good with cloth, had a feel for it.' John raises his hand as if to indicate an imaginary sign, 'I could see it, Bertie, J. WILLIAMS & SON, Tailors of Distinction.'

John looks up at the cross and says quietly to himself, 'He can be anything that we want him to be. They can't disappoint when they've gone and they're no longer with you.'

'What's that, Dad?'

'Just a thought, Bertie, just my thoughts,' replies John, who then wipes his eyes with his hand. He looks round to see Annie, Mary, Emma and Henry approaching them.

John composes himself. 'I think a picture would be nice now.' He addresses his brother-in-law and issues something of an order. 'Time for a photograph, Henry, as I requested, thank you.'

Annie laughs. 'Henry, make yourself useful, take a picture, you've had your instructions, under orders now.'

Henry steps forward, 'Right, I've been looking at the camera, I think I know what to do, now, Annie do you, would you like to…?'

Annie looks at Henry. He appears to be gesturing towards the grave and pointing in the direction of John and Herbert, she understands what he's suggesting. 'No, Henry, thank you, just John and Bertie for now.'

Henry responds to Annie's instructions, walks to the front of the grave, and John and Herbert move behind the headstone. Henry moves one way and then the other and stares into the small viewfinder on top of the camera. He places his hand in front of the opening to make a shield and block out the sun's intrusive light, 'Now,' he says. 'If you could move to your right a bit, it'll be a good deal better.'

John sighs deeply, 'No, Henry, we can't. We can't move the headstone can we, you move to your left a bit and change the direction of the camera.'

Henry assesses the instructions that John has issued, realises that they make sense and he's rather embarrassed because the solution to the problem is very simple and easily rectified.

'Oh, oh…y…yes,' he stammers, 'that's it, now, that's just right, very nice.'

John needs to confirm that the picture will now be taken to his specific direction, 'Now, Henry, you've got all three of us in it, haven't you?'

'No, John,' replies Henry, 'Annie doesn't want to be in it.'

John sighs deeply, what should have been a straightforward and uncomplicated procedure seems to have presented a range of unforeseen difficulties and problems. 'I don't mean Annie, Henry, it's me, Bertie and our Herbert, do you see.'

'Of course I see what you mean. Now keep still, nearly there.' Again he stops looking into the viewfinder, looks up and says, 'Oh, John.'

Another sigh from John. 'What now, Henry?' he says abruptly, using a tone of voice that suggests he's becoming frustrated and losing his patience.

'Smiling,' asks Henry, 'or a bit sombre like?'

John looks down at his son. At last Henry's asked a practical and useful question. 'Now, that's not such a daft question is it, Bertie? Smiling I think, don't you son?' Herbert nods in agreement. John looks towards Henry and speaks quietly to Herbert out of the side of his mouth. 'We live in hope, Bertie, we might get a picture out of this yet.'

Henry takes the picture and looks pleased with himself. 'That's it. I'll just take one more to be on the safe side.'

The ladies have been watching this comical series of events. Annie and Emma find it to be quite amusing. Mary, on the other hand, is becoming increasingly irritated. 'Oh, he makes such hard work of it, we'll be here till Christmas at this rate.'

Henry winds the film on and eventually takes another picture, puts the camera into the case and places the strap over his shoulder, 'Fingers crossed,' he says.

John wipes his eyes again, and he and Herbert are joined by Annie, Mary and Emma. Mary removes the top from a small bottle and pours water into a vase that Emma has placed in front of the headstone. Annie then bends down and positions the red roses in the vase and arranges the display. When she's satisfied with the composition, she stands back and bows her head. This is a signal for Mary, Emma and Henry to take their leave and they quietly walk away. Annie takes out a handkerchief and hands it to John and he blows his nose very loudly. She stands between her husband and son and puts her arms around both of them. After a long pause Herbert leaves his parents and joins his sister, 'Now, John,' says Annie, 'you've become a bit upset. You'll get me going now, I don't think I've seen you this troubled before, not since the first time we came.'

'It's just come to me Annie, having our Bertie here. I don't want to see that name HERBERT EDWARD WILLIAMS on another headstone like this. Not in my lifetime.'

'Or our other boys' names, John, don't forget them.'

Annie looks directly at John and puts her hand on his shoulder. 'Anyway, John, where did that come from?'

'Oh just me being a bit silly, Annie, something that were said earlier, made me think a bit.'

Annie looks around the cemetery and softly sighs, 'Well, this place certainly makes you think, no doubt about that.'

John looks down at the bunch of roses that now adorn the grave, 'Look at that, Annie, red roses for a Lancashire lad.'

'Well they certainly wouldn't be white would they, John, that would never do.'

John chuckles, 'Perish the thought, Mother.'

Chapter Four

31 July, 1917 – Pilckem Ridge, Belgium
German Fourth Army, Eingrief Division

My dear Mother and Father, writes Lieutenant Kurt Lehmann. *When you receive this letter the worst of the battle will hopefully be over and it is my dearest wish that I shall be able to discuss these events with you when I next return home. I should also like to be able to say that the battle was not as bad as we had feared and that very few of my comrades had been killed or severely wounded. Sadly, I know from my experiences of the conflict in these fields of slaughter and carnage that this will not be the case. We have been in the bunker for five days now while the British and French artillery have relentlessly shelled us without a break and they do not grant us any respite. The advance of their infantry will surely follow shelling such as this. We know they will come and we must be ready for them. Again, I am preparing to meet our enemy, to once again take life, to meet my God, or suffer pain and dreadful injury…*

Lieutenant Lehmann puts down his pencil and with his finger and thumb squeezes and rubs the bridge of his nose. He screws his eyes tightly together, leans back, stretches and yawns. Leaning forward, he stares into a small shaving mirror that's propped up on the corner of the desk. Under the dim light provided by an oil lamp he studies the detail of his reflection; a firm square jaw and strong cheekbones identify him as the person that he knew. However, the once handsome face has now started to develop disturbing features which can be described as being almost skeletal. On the top of his head is the small amount of blond hair that the company barber has allowed him to keep.

The rest of his hair from around the side and the back of his head has been brutally and efficiently shaved off. 'Twenty-two and looking more like forty,' he says quietly to himself. 'This damn war has stolen my youth.' His thoughts are interrupted by two loud explosions which are heard close by, and loose earth falls from between the cracks in the boards that support the roof of the bunker.

'Coffee, Sir,' says the cadet soldier as he brushes the soil from his head. Lieutenant Lehmann acknowledges him and takes the metal mug of hot steaming liquid from him.

'Real coffee,' says the lieutenant. 'You are a genius, Thomas, it has been so long since I have had *real coffee*, thank you.'

The young cadet's embarrassed, he looks rather sheepish and admits, 'It's only really the same as you have had before, Sir.'

Lieutenant Lehmann smells the steam from the mug. 'I thought that we had a miracle here, Thomas, but now I smell acorns, some sort of bean, and corn perhaps.'

Sergeant Scholz sits down in a chair next to the table, lights a cigarette, inhales and blows the smoke out slowly. 'Leave the poor boy alone, he does the best he can with what he has to work with, don't tease him.'

Very much a veteran, the sergeant is popular with his men; his jocular manner matches his portly, short frame and his ruddy complexion and round face present him as being affable and sociable.

'I know,' replies the lieutenant. He turns to the cadet. 'Sorry, Thomas, just a little humour, a joke, you are dismissed, thank you.' He picks up the letter that he's been writing, puts it back down on the table, drums his fingers on it and says, 'Ah, it won't do, it is too real, too grim, too honest.' He screws up the document and skilfully throws it into a container on the other side of the table. 'In any case, it will probably be censored and altered.'

'We must be very careful not to tell it as it is, Sir,' replies the sergeant. 'Anyway, your parents should not need to worry, thin chaps like you, you are difficult to hit.' He laughs. 'Now, we of a more bulky shape, we're a bit too much of a target.' The sergeant removes a small photograph from his top pocket and holds the picture up for the lieutenant to see. 'My good lady wife Anna said to me, *when you go off to war, Lukas, do not eat so much, then you might lose some weight. The size you are now, somebody with a gun will be able to see you coming miles away and he will shoot you because you will be a big target.*'

Lieutenant Lehmann smiles fondly at the sergeant, they've served together for nearly two years and they're comrades in every sense of the word. The lieutenant takes out a new sheet of paper, puts the end of his pencil into his mouth, thinks for a moment and writes: *Dear Mother and Father, we are in good spirits, although we have been subjected to a lot of artillery fire lately, we are safe underground. We are hopeful that we will soon have the final victory that will bring us all home. There are many new recruits in our trenches and...*

The movement and the sound of soldiers standing to attention distract the lieutenant. Captain Vogt steps down the ladder, quickly returns the salutes of the men and strides towards the lieutenant and the sergeant. Sergeant Scholz puts on his cap, stands and salutes, as does Lieutenant Lehmann. The officer sits in the chair vacated by the sergeant, removes his helmet and, with his pocket-handkerchief, wipes the sweat and the dirt from his face. The lieutenant looks at the officer's sleeve and is horrified to see that it's covered in blood.

'Sir,' he says in an alarmed voice. 'You're bleeding. You've been wounded.'

Captain Vogt looks down at his arm and shakes his head. 'I'm bloody, but not bleeding,' he says. 'I had an escort, a junior soldier, he was behind me, there was an explosion and he was hit by some shrapnel. He took the full force of the blast and saved me from getting hit, I suppose.'

Kurt is not surprised by the officer's matter of fact way of telling of a fatality, after all, two and a half years at the front has taught him that life was now cheap and another death is just that, another death.

Captain Vogt takes out his pocket watch and holds it to the flickering light. '3.46,' he says.

Lieutenant Lehmann looks at his watch and agrees on the time. 'Could it be this morning?' he asks. 'Do you think it could be?'

'I don't like to wager,' he answers, 'but I would bet on it. Yes, I think they will come today. It's overcast out there, it will get light later than it should and it is very dark at the moment.' The officer looks at a small map and points to some of the detail on the plan. 'Our trenches here will be their first objective, if it's like before, they'll move beyond our first lines with a creeping barrage and using mortars. We have got to cut them down with our machine guns. We can stop them, and we have to.'

The captain checks his watch again. '3.49,' he confirms. He turns to Sergeant Scholz and orders him, 'Increase the flares to every two minutes and tell the lookouts to report immediately any movement or sign of activity. Even if they think that they have seen something, I want to know.'

An almighty blast shakes the bunker and much more earth falls from the cracks. The soldiers cough and splutter, they brush themselves down, a cloud of dust fills the chamber.

'That was close. I do not think that they like us!' shouts the sergeant and some of the men laugh.

Suddenly a lookout from outside shouts into the bunker, 'Alarm!' he screams. 'Alarm!'

The bunker becomes a scene of frantic activity; soldiers put on their helmets and grab hold of machine guns and rifles, they rush towards the ladder and hastily and nervously climb into the uncertain and exposed arena of combat. Captain Vogt holds out his hand to Lieutenant Lehmann. The young officer shakes his senior commander's hand. 'Come and see me and my family in Koblenz,' says the captain, 'when this is over. We will sit by the river, have a drink and remember what we did in the war and how we won it.'

'And in Mainz, where I live,' replies the lieutenant. 'We'll do the same with my family.'

Captain Vogt climbs the ladder and Lieutenant Lehmann follows him, *Damn, why*, he thinks, *why did he say that?*

The trench is a very busy place, soldiers are shouting and rushing to their posts, flares light up the sky and the sound of machine gun fire reverberates all around. Lieutenant Lehmann holds back his head and after the close, stale and oppressive atmosphere of the bunker, for a brief moment he enjoys the refreshingly cool air, even though it's impregnated with the stench of cordite and sulphur.

A soldier who's firing a machine gun from one of the ramparts is hit, cries out in anguish and slides down into the trench. The lieutenant rushes forward and climbs up the ladder, takes hold of the machine gun and with the aid of another soldier who feeds the ammunition belt into the chamber, begins firing. Light is coming and with the help of flares, no-mans-land is fully illuminated and the oncoming soldiers are left exposed and openly vulnerable. Then, one blinding light, an unimaginable and deafening roar and, for Lieutenant Kurt Lehmann, the gathering morning light is extinguished and will never be seen by his eyes again.

Chapter Five

31 July, 1932 – Poperinge

The coach drops the party off. They thank Paul and, apart from John, enter the hotel. John stays by the coach to discuss with Paul the possibility of making a trip to Ypres to view the evening ceremony of remembrance at the Menin Gate, and then perhaps a day out at the site of the battlefield at Hooge. Once the arrangements have been made, John shakes Paul's hand. 'Thank you, young man, safely taken and returned. I'm a bit of a seasoned traveller myself, you know, and I recognise a skilful operator when I see him in action.' He puts his hand in his pocket, takes out a coin and hands it to Paul. The grateful young driver, appreciative of his patron's well-meant comments and the financial return, takes his leave. John walks up the steps, turns and stands outside the entrance, lights his pipe and watches the charabanc coach move slowly down the dusty road. He looks at the busy scene. People are walking and enjoying the warm afternoon sunshine, they're obviously a mix of visitors and local residents. Emma, who's been looking for her father, joins him.

'Been a nice day, Emma, very satisfying. We'll have a lovely little walk this evening, just to finish it off like.'

'That will be very pleasant, Dad, and perhaps some refreshments at one of those nice cafés by the park.'

'You've read my thoughts, Daughter. Although there's a reason for us coming here, which is sombre in its way, there's no reason why we can't enjoy ourselves; your mother deserves it, a bit of pampering and the like.'

Emma smiles at her father. 'Our Bert wouldn't have minded us making a holiday of it, Dad.'

'Far from it, Emma. He'd have said, thanks for visiting, now you lot go off and have a drink for me.'

John breathes in slowly and points with his pipe towards an expensive-looking, smart car that's parked at the side of the hotel. 'Someone's got some money, very posh, worth a bob or two I should think.'

'It's lovely, be nice to have a motorcar like that, Dad.'

John's not convinced. 'A lot of trouble I should think, more trouble than they're worth, they tell me.'

John ensures that his pipe is no longer alight and places it in his pocket. He follows Emma into the hotel. They walk by a family that is checking in at the reception desk. John politely pushes past them but inadvertently nudges the lady. 'I'm very sorry,' he says. 'Very clumsy of me.'

The lady smiles back at him and replies, '*Entschuldigen Sie bitte.*'

John walks into the reception room and stops. Something has dawned on him. He's clearly shocked. Henry approaches him. 'Have you seen...?' he asks.

'Aye, I've heard. Germans. They're Germans.'

Annie joins in with the conversation. 'Well, I suppose it's unusual we haven't met their sort before, I mean we've seen them in Ypres sometimes, at a distance though.'

'Mind you,' says Henry, 'I should think it's a lot easier for them to get here than for us, can't be too difficult, not having to get on a boat like.'

John stares at his brother-in-law. He's becoming increasingly more angry. 'Well they didn't find it too difficult in 1914 did they? They bloody well didn't.'

Annie shakes her head and chastises her husband. 'Language, John, there's no need for that sort of talk.'

'Well, I'm not going to apologise, it's going to spoil it; this is our time, Annie, not theirs.'

'John, you'll be as polite as you have to be,' replies Annie. 'I don't want an upset and any bad feeling.'

Madame De Vos enters the room and can immediately see that John's troubled. 'Are you all right, Mr Williams? You don't look well.'

John sits down and looks up at her. 'Who are they, Madame De Vos?'

Madame De Vos realises that he's referring to the new guests, she smiles. 'Oh, a charming couple – Dr Lehmann and his wife, with their son, Peter.'

John is feeling very uneasy and stutters, 'B...but, they're from...'

'From Mainz, on the River Rhine, I believe.'

'Well, what are they doing here?'

'The same as you, Mr Williams. Visiting their son's grave.'

John shakes his head. 'Germans don't come here much, Madame De Vos, do they? I mean. I haven't seen them in your hotel before, not when we've been here.'

'We don't get that many German tourists. Many of their war graves are to the north and the east of here, but from time to time they do visit. Now, if you will excuse me I have some arrangements to make for our new arrivals.'

Madame De Vos leaves the room to arrange for the Lehmann family to be shown to their rooms. John and Henry sit, they're silent for a moment. 'I can't understand Madame De Vos taking them in,' says Henry. 'She lost a brother in the war didn't she, you told me that didn't you, John?'

'That's right, he were with the French Army and he were killed at Verdun.'

Henry leans over to John and says quietly, 'That's their posh car by the side of the hotel.'

'Aye, showing off, 'replies John. 'That's typical of their sort, took a beating in the war and still arrogant.'

Chapter Six

3 June, 1931 – Blackburn, Lancashire

Although the weather in mid-afternoon is potentially unsettled with the risk of showers, John and Annie decide to take a stroll through the Corporation Park and take advantage of any sunshine that could be on offer. The tune of *The Flag of Freedom* is being played professionally and competently by the Salvation Army Brass Band.

The couple have put on and are showing off their Sunday best. Annie's dressed in a long blue, two-tone coloured coat; she's wearing a narrow-brimmed, maroon hat which is finished off with a bow made of black ribbon. Friends who meet them comment on the quality and the look of her outfit. She's quick to inform them that her husband made it for her and that she's fortunate to be married to a man who has such skill and creative ability. John's wearing his best suit and sports a splendid black trilby hat, and he carries a rolled-up umbrella which he uses as a walking stick. He smokes his pipe and proudly marches on, and Annie keeps pace with him by holding onto his arm. John's eager to reach the bandstand before the Salvation Army finish for the day.

Once they've reached their destination, they settle into two vacant seats that are conveniently located side by side. Each well-known tune is very ably performed and the audience is given the opportunity to show its appreciation by placing coins into a tin that a female officer carries around each row of seats. John gladly makes a contribution. 'I'm not much of a Salvationist as you know, Annie, but they do play a nice tune.'

The afternoon entertainment continues and the threat of rain seems to have disappeared. They sit in the warm sunshine and as a result of consuming three pints of the most excellent Thwaites' ale and having enjoyed a very satisfying roast beef dinner, John's eyes start to close. His slumber is disturbed when Annie gently taps him on the shoulder. 'Come on, sleepyhead, we'd best be off. Didn't you say that Mr and Mrs Partington were coming round to talk about that funeral order?'

John reaches into his waistcoat pocket and holds his watch, he studies it for a moment. 'Do you know, Annie, I'd almost forgotten about them. You're right, we won't be late, but we'd best be off.' The couple leave their seats and head for the main entrance that leads out onto Preston New Road. They walk at a quick pace to ensure that they arrive for their appointment in good time. 'I were going to make some sandwiches,' says Annie. 'I've got some potted meat put by.'

They arrive at home and are relieved to see that Mr and Mrs Partington have not yet turned up. 'That's all right, Annie, not here yet. I don't like to see folk waiting on't doorstep, especially clients.'

They take off their coats and walk into the back room. Annie puts on her apron, takes the potted meat from the larder and cuts some bread. 'Shall we have some pickle, Annie?' asks John. 'I thought of lighting the fire in the front parlour. What do you think?'

Annie's busy. She fills the kettle and puts it onto the stove. 'Is it cold enough do you think and have you got time to make one up? I don't want them to find you in your waistcoat and shirtsleeves, with mucky hands.'

'No problem, Annie, I made it up this morning and it just needs a match putting to it. I think I'll light it because it might get a bit parky later.'

'If you like, John. Just have a quick look in there and make sure it's tidy. Emma were in there with her friend Dorothy. She's usually careful when she's in the front parlour, but just check to be on the safe side.'

John follows Annie's instructions and confirms that the room is fit for purpose. The loud tap of the doorknocker is heard and John opens the door. On the doorstep and dressed in black are Mr and Mrs Partington, who are a couple in the later stages of middle age. John invites them in. 'Come on in, Sam, and you, Martha.' Sam steps aside to allow Martha to enter first. John gives her a formal kiss on the cheek and then shakes Sam's hand. He takes their hats and coats and hangs them on the hall stand. 'A wise precaution,' he says. 'It's a bit chilly for June, but at least we didn't have any rain, although they said we would.'

John guides them into the front parlour and invites them to sit down. Annie, carrying the tea and sandwiches on a large tray, walks into the room. John takes the tray from her and puts it on a small table in front of the couple. 'You shouldn't have gone to all this trouble, Annie,' says Martha.

'No trouble at all,' says John. 'Nice bit of potted meat; we were going to have a bit of tea anyway.'

Annie pours the tea and passes round the sandwiches, there's silence while they drink and eat. John then adopts a serious facial expression. 'Can I just say, we were sorry to hear about your mother, Sam, will you accept our condolences? How old were she?'

'Eighty-six, thank you, John,' replies Sam.

'Were she really?' says John thoughtfully. 'Good age, that, eighty-six.'

'Nearly eighty-seven,' adds Martha. 'Would have been at the end of June.'

'Still, she did well to get to eighty-six,' adds Annie. 'How long were she a widow?'

'Twenty-four year ago, that's when my father died,' answers Sam.

There's a short period of silence, and their contemplation is interrupted when John claps his hands together. 'Now,' he says, 'to more practical matters. Let's see if we can give her a good send-off, two new suits isn't it, Sam?'

'Aye, that's right,' says Sam. 'One for me and one for our son, Arnold. Will that be all right?'

'No problem whatsoever,' replies John. 'Now, when's the funeral, how long have we got?'

'It's a week on Tuesday at St Silas's Church on Preston New Road,' answers Martha. 'Do you think you can manage it, with having to work during the day as well?'

'No problem at all,' says John, reassuringly.

'He's like a man possessed once he gets going,' adds Annie.

'So,' says Sam, 'the extra work is to get some money together so that you can go to visit your boy's grave in France, is that right?'

'Aye,' replies John, 'but it's Belgium, Flanders region. You lost a lad didn't you, where's he buried, Sam?'

Sam takes hold of Martha's hand. 'North Sea, Jutland, went down in the Invincible in 1916.'

John's embarrassed. He knew that their son had served in the navy and had been killed at sea but had forgotten. 'I'm sorry, Sam. I remember that now.'

'Why would you remember, John?' says Sam. 'You've got your own grieving to get on with. It doesn't matter where they are now, thing is they're no longer with us, although I must admit it would be nice to have a grave to visit.'

Chapter Seven

1 August, 1932 – Poperinge

It's the morning and the dining room is full of residents having their breakfast. Annie, Mary and Emma are discussing whether to buy some lace that they've seen in a small gift shop. They want to take some home as gifts for the family. There's also a family wedding to consider for next year. Annie is planning some detailed needlework for a dress that she's making for her cousin's daughter.

'That one particular ribbon will just finish off the dress perfectly,' she says.

'Well, if anyone can make a feature of it, you can Annie,' adds Mary. 'You've always been good with your hands. I can do it when I have to, but I don't have the patience most of the time.'

Their conversation continues. By contrast, John and Henry are subdued and eat in silence. Erich and Martina Lehmann, with their son Peter, enter the dining room. As they pass by the table occupied by John's family, Erich stops, bows his head a little and politely says, 'Good morning. It is another fine day, I think.'

John ignores Erich. 'I think that somebody is trying to rudely interrupt us while we're eating, Henry. Now what were you saying?'

Henry wasn't saying anything and struggles to create the impression that they were having a conversation. 'Aye, that were it, as you were saying, John,' he splutters. Annie's embarrassed and she reluctantly but politely nods to the Lehmann family.

They go to sit at a table in the corner of the room and pick up the small card menus. A young waitress approaches them and takes their order.

John looks over to them and leans over to speak quietly to Annie. 'They look a bit dour to me, very stern indeed, especially him, not at all friendly.'

Annie discreetly looks across the room and sees a good-looking family. Erich's dressed in a smart, light brown three-piece suit which complements his slender build. His high sculptured cheekbones and full head of grey hair supports a man of handsome appearance for his age, and Annie estimates him to be in his late fifties. His vision is improved and aided by him wearing small, round, metal-rimmed spectacles.

Annie raises her napkin to the side of her mouth and speaks to her sister. 'Very good-looking I think. Sophisticated, like.'

Mary glances over to the Lehmann's table. 'Looks a bit arrogant to me, Annie. A bit stiff like.'

Annie then looks at Martina and sees a slim, well-dressed, elegant lady of a similar or perhaps on second look, a slightly younger age to her husband. Her attractive facial features tell of a woman who was obviously a former beauty. Peter is very much his father's son in appearance; he's the same build and of a similar height. However, the hair is blond and he isn't wearing spectacles.

John turns to Annie. 'I'm going to light my pipe, Annie. The atmosphere has become distinctly unpleasant in here. It doesn't suit me and it's put me off my breakfast. I've lost my appetite.' John looks at Henry and cocks his head in the direction of the door leading to the rear garden. Henry flusters a little, puts down his knife and fork, and removes his napkin from under his chin. 'Right-o, I'll join you, John.' And then adds apologetically, 'No offence, ladies. Duty calls.'

John and Henry walk into the garden. As they stroll by the flowerbeds, they light their pipes and enjoy a smoke. They stop to admire the floral display.

'I'm not much of a horticulturalist as you know, Henry. That's Annie's department, but I do like the look of a nice bloom.'

After a short time, they're joined by Major Aspinal, who greets them. 'Good morning, gentleman, lovely day.'

'Morning, Major,' says John.

'You chaps enjoying this fine morning air?' the major asks.

John looks directly at the major. 'Nicer air out here.'

Henry's keen to explain. 'We've encountered some rather unpleasant people inside.'

Major Aspinal thinks for a moment and then identifies the problem. 'Oh, of course, you mean the Germans?'

'Aye,' replies John, 'that's it, you've got it.'

The major takes out a cigarette from an expensive-looking case, taps it on the box and lights it using a well-finished and ornate silver lighter. He takes a long and satisfying draw on the cigarette, holds back his head and blows out the smoke with a long breath. 'Yes, bit awkward, I suppose.'

'You must have come across Germans before though, Major,' asks John, 'in't war I mean.'

'Oh yes, prisoners, lots of them from time to time. Not all bad chaps of course, most of them plucky. Bit like our boys, really, to look at and the way they behaved.'

John feels uneasy about the comparison that the major's making. 'Yes but what you call plucky, I call mindless obedience. That could be it, couldn't it?'

Major Aspinal looks at John. 'Quite,' and after a moment's pause adds. 'As you say.'

Once this is confirmed in John's mind he asks. 'Were you involved at Passchendaele?'

'My baptism was at the Somme,' replies the major. 'And yes, the Third Battle Ypres – call it what you like. I was there 31 July, 1917, right at the start.'

'It must have been quite a show?' says Henry, eager to be involved in the conversation.

'Yes, our artillery pounded their lines for a few days to soften them up a bit.'

'Where were you?' asks John. 'What were your regiment?'

'Guards, I was with the Grenadier Guards. Captain at the time. We were up facing Pilckem Ridge, looking onto Langemark where the Bosche were really dug in.'

Henry becomes more and more interested in what the major's saying. 'Shelling must have hurt them, I mean really done some damage, didn't it?'

'Oh, we hurt them, but we didn't finish them off, you see. We knew they'd still be there no matter what we were told. Resilient chaps the Bosche.'

'But you had a go, Major,' says John. 'You did your duty, did what was expected.'

'Oh yes, we had our orders, you see, that's the way of it, no choice. Over the top and hope for the best.'

Henry asks, 'Everyone must have been ready for it like, and really up for it, I should think, after the waiting.'

'Well, as you say, the waiting was over, a bit of light in the sky, a tot of whisky, checked the watch, one long blow on my whistle and off we went.'

'I bet your chaps were keen,' says John.

'Older fellows, very tense, done it before, knew what was coming. Now, the young chaps, they seemed to be keener, a bit edgy and nervous mind you, which was very understandable. They were a bit raw and didn't quite know how bad it could be.'

'Were there a lot of young blokes in your trench?' asks Henry.

'We'd lost a lot at the Somme, needed some new blood. Bit too young really and wet behind the ears. Just before the shelling stopped I remember one of these new recruits saying that there wouldn't be any Bosche left alive. My company sergeant looked at him and said, *They'll be deep, the Hun, we won't get them all, not by a long way.*

'You knew they'd be ready for you, then?' asks John.

'Anyone who'd fought at the Somme knew the Bosche would be deep. *No need to worry them,* I said quietly to the sergeant, *they'll find out soon enough.*'

John is now totally engrossed in the story. 'And they did?'

'Yes, yes they did, one of them asked why we were going so early. Zero hour was 3.50am, you understand. *Well,* I said, *it's a long way to Berlin and it would be a good thing to get there before dark.* They liked that sort of talk. It took the edge of it, you see.'

'So how did it go?' asks Henry.

'As I said, just before full light we set off. We had the French on our left. Never a good thing that.'

'What do you mean?' says John.

'Having the French on your left, or on the right for that matter. As I said, not a good thing.'

'You didn't trust them?'

'Well, John… you don't mind if I call you John do you?'

'No, that's all right, Major, please do.'

'Not a question of not trusting, just needed to be kept an eye on. It's all about flanks, you see, in battle, John. If your flank isn't solid and it turns, you've got problems, could be in trouble.'

'And did they hold?' asks Henry.

'Bit slow, but they held, although it was touch and go and we had to keep our eye on them, you understand. Not bad chaps, the French, but never the same after Verdun in sixteen.'

'Took a pasting didn't they?'

'Yes, quite a mauling in fact, John. Course, chaps in the front line, not their fault, their generals and high command were a bit past it. Rather out of touch you see.'

The major lights another cigarette, inhales and looks up to the sky. He blows out the smoke and then turns to John and points at him. 'Now, John, your boy's regiment, different matter altogether.'

John pushes out his chest and breathes in deeply.

'Ah, the Royal Lancs.'

'First rate chaps. We had some of their boys with us but

the Second Battalion was fighting with the Sherwood Foresters further south. I understand they made a good show of it. Was that where your boy was, John?'

'Aye, that's right. He were at Hooge.'

'Lost a lot down there, as we all did. We started off all right, took ground, got through the wire, and achieved our first objectives. Made good progress, despite there being a lot of mud. It was easy to get bogged down you see. The Bosche counter-attacked and after a few days, normal service was resumed.'

'Normal service?' questions John.

'Stalemate. The breakthrough didn't really happen. Oh we carried on throwing more men at it, but it was over, lost cause, another false dawn I'm afraid to say.'

Henry looks uneasy. 'All for nothing then, is that what you're saying?'

'More or less, mind you, it may have had an effect in the end, you just don't know. After all, they'd lost an awful lot of chaps.'

John ponders on what the major has said. 'Well I'd like to think that it had some effect and helped finish the war, in the end like.'

'Maybe, John, I'm sure it did,' replies the major.

'I'd like to think that for my boy's sake.'

'Thing is, John. He did his duty and you couldn't have asked for any more than that.'

'I suppose you've visited the cemeteries to see where your old pals are,' asks John.

'Yes, pals, you mean fellow officers and the men of course. Artillery Wood, Cement House and Sanctuary, and so on. Where's your boy, John?'

'Dozinghem, Major.'

'Ah yes, casualty clearing. Yes, we've been there. Few of my chaps resting there; nice spot and well-kept.'

John nods in agreement. 'Aye, they keep it very nice.'

'Least they can do, John,' says the major.

'It's very moving when you visit,' adds John. 'Timeless and respectful.'

The major looks up to the sky then faces John. '*Some corner of a foreign field, that is forever England*, eh John, just about sums it up.'

'Well said, Sir,' says John.

Major Aspinal looks back at the hotel. 'Better look out for my good lady wife, don't want her to think I'm neglecting her. Won't hear the last of it, cheerio chaps.'

'Well,' says John. 'Goodbye, Major, I enjoyed our talk, very interesting.'

'Yes, so did I, glad to put you in the picture and all that.'

'Yes, bye Major,' adds Henry.

The major leaves the garden and John and Henry reflect on what they have heard.

'He didn't seem to think that Passchendaele was much of a success, did he, John?'

'It's complicated and a bit confusing, Henry. I think you'll find that he agreed that on reflection it had an effect on bringing the war to an end, in the end, in eighteen.'

Chapter Eight

10 May, 1916 – Mainz, Germany

Although the rations of food and drink are limited and the fare is somewhat meagre, Hans Friedel, the proprietor of the attractive café/bar, idyllically located on the banks of the River Rhine, has managed to put on a very creditable spread. The Lehmann family are enjoying their get-together and welcome the opportunity to catch up on all the latest news. All who are in attendance are wearing their best outfits, the men in either light cotton or more formal dark suits. The women look splendid, dressed in long, light-coloured summer dresses, slim at the waist, with billowing sleeves. Young family members, becoming bored with having to sit at the formal tables, break free and play on the grass area at the front of the café veranda. Their parents warn them to be careful and not to get grass stains on their best clothes.

In the corner of the main bar area, Uncle Sebastian is skilfully playing the upright piano. The tune is *The Piano Concerto No 20*, by Mozart and it adds a delightful audible backdrop to the event. The main purpose of the agreeably relaxing afternoon's function is to celebrate the engagement of Kurt Lehmann to his fiancée, Mariel Schneider. At the top table, Kurt, dressed in his smart dress uniform, talks quietly with Mariel, and the Lehmann family look on approvingly. The proposed new member of the family is a handsome girl, slim, with golden blonde hair that's neatly tied up on the top of her head. As she smiles, her bright blue eyes sparkle and shine out, she has a very fair and almost fragile-looking, delicate complexion. As well as Martina and

Erich, also seated at the top table are Erich's elderly parents, Martina's recently widowed mother, and Mariel's parents.

Erich Lehmann stands up and taps a spoon on a ceramic jug in front of him. The room quickly goes quiet and Uncle Sebastian stops playing the piano. 'Dear friends and family,' he says, 'what a day. Very pleasant for the time of year, I think.' There's a slight ripple of polite laughter. Erich continues, 'When we first met Mariel, I told Kurt that under no circumstances was he to allow her to slip out of his grasp.' Again more laughter. 'I also said that if he could persuade such a girl to consider spending the rest of her life with him, then he should consider himself to be the most fortunate of young men. Now, here we are and the great day has arrived and we can look forward to an even better day when they are married.' Erich raises his glass and announces, 'To Mariel and Kurt.'

All in the room stand and raise their glasses. 'To Mariel and Kurt,' they say as one.

General talk continues and Uncle Sebastian continues to play, this time it's a tune by George Fredrick Handel. Erich sits down and takes hold of Martina's hand, he moves his head closer to his wife and quietly says, 'He now has a good reason to survive this war, if God wills it, they will be very happy together.'

Martina looks at him.

'It is not a good time to make these plans but we must hope, be optimistic and pray for them both.'

Erich stands up and indicates that he would like to enjoy a smoke. He leaves the bar and stands on the veranda. He enjoys this time of the year, the winter is well behind them, the days are bright and warmer, and there's a light in the sky that continues well into the evening. Mariel's father, Franz Schneider, joins him, takes out an impressive-looking large cigar, and Erich strikes a match and holds it in front of him. Franz sucks in the smoke with quick short breaths and slowly the cigar becomes lit. He blows out the smoke and looks at the cigar.

'From Havana,' he says thoughtfully. 'Very few left now.

I'm having to ration myself and when they have all gone, I'll have to put up with a substitute, made from God knows what. I only smoke these on special occasions now and today is a very special occasion.'

Erich nods in agreement and he looks at Franz. He sees a man that, although heavily built, has an elegance about him. His hair-colouring and dark complexion are in noticeable contrast to his daughter's fair appearance.

'I meant what I said, Franz. Kurt is a most fortunate young man, she is a credit to you.'

Franz draws on his cigar.

'Thank you for that, Erich. Sorry, you don't mind me calling you by your given name? Or should I say Christian name, which is more in keeping with your Catholic persuasion?'

'Not at all, Franz, given or Christian. Please call me Erich – after all we will be related at some time.'

'Perhaps, when the war is won, that would be a good time for them to be married, do you think?'

'It would, if only we knew when that will be. As you know, I work at the hospitals close to the front and see so many dead and severely wounded. You wonder how long we as a nation can continue to bleed in this way.'

'But the government tells us that we are winning and that there will soon be the victory that we have been promised.'

'I expect that the British government tell their people that soon they will win the war, what else can a government say?'

Franz looks again at his cigar and then gives Erich a stern stare.

'I'm sorry, Erich, but isn't that defeatist talk? You should be careful about what you are saying and where you say it. Our brave boys are risking their lives every day and the least they can expect is our support and loyalty. The Kaiser has given his assurance that the sacrifices that are being made will be worth it; the British have to be stopped.'

Erich is surprised at Franz's comments. He had always

taken him to be an educated man and as a senior lecturer at a university, highly intelligent and well-read.

'I'm sorry, Franz. I am as loyal as any good German, but I have to be realistic. If the slaughter continues on both sides, it will mean that a generation of young men will be lost and we will be left as a nation of daughters. I joined the Medical Corp to help. I have seen the suffering at first hand and witnessed hopeless despair. Of course, I keep my thoughts to myself but when the generals come to visit the wounded and tell them that one more push will do it, well, I must admit I lose heart. I have heard the same said so many times. Call me disloyal if you like, but I will always do my duty. However, you must know, Franz, that it is hard on the western front because the scale of the slaughter is unrelenting.'

Franz replies in an abrupt tone, 'Things are not easy here at home, we have had such shortages: food, drink, clothes and medicine. Queues now form outside the shops in Frankfurt and every day there is news of more dead and wounded, lost sons and fathers to grieve for.'

Erich stares at him and after a moment's thought says, 'Shortages of medicine, that must be difficult, we also have a shortage of medicine. Many times I have had to cut into a young soldier's body to remove the shrapnel that I know will certainly kill him if it is not removed. On many occasions I do not have anything to anaesthetise him with nor am I able to give him morphine for his immense pain. When this happens, then yes, I find it difficult.'

Franz, although clearly not accepting Erich's point of view, is nevertheless somewhat embarrassed.

'Now look, Erich, perhaps we will not agree, but on a day such as this we should put our differences to one side and think of the future.'

Erich agrees. 'We must be positive for our children's sake and hope for the best outcome.'

'We should go back inside and drink to that,' says Franz.

'Now, in looking to the future what will Kurt do when he leaves the army, will he train to be a skilful doctor like his father?'

'No, he has never shown any aptitude for it, his interests are in architecture and building; he was studying the subject before he went into the army. I think he will go back to college to complete his training. That is what he tells me.'

'You are not disappointed when he tells you that he does not wish to pursue a medical career and join you in your practice?'

'Not really, I didn't go into medicine because my father was a doctor; I followed such a career because I genuinely thought that it would be rewarding, not financially but emotionally. Of course my father was pleased but he would have been satisfied if I would have pursued any career. I feel the same about Kurt. He must find what he wants to do. He has made a good start and fortunately, found an excellent partner for life.' Both men smile, the tension between them has lifted.

'The concern that I have,' says Franz, 'is that college is expensive and with little income and education fees, well, how will they manage?'

Erich laughs. 'There are those who think that I married Martina because her family left her financially well-provided for. When, on that spring day in 1894 I sat on a bench in the main square in Frankfurt, romance was the furthest thing from my mind. I was still working in London and I had come home to see my parents and other family members. I found myself talking to two very attractive young ladies who were sat on the same bench. One of the ladies was Martina and she was such a vision of beauty that any inheritance that she had was of no interest. I'm not saying that money has not been useful, especially in supporting the practice while I am away at the front. We will help Kurt to complete his studies, but it will only be when he really needs our support because he will have to learn to make his own way and I am sure he will.'

'But first he has a war to win,' says Franz. 'We have a lot of toasting to do, Erich, I suggest we make a start.' Both men laugh, Franz checks that his cigar is no longer alight and they return to the interior of the bar.

Close to the door there's a table and on it is a tray with glasses of wine. Erich stops, selects a glass and hands it to Franz. He picks up another glass and raises it to his eye level. Franz does the same. 'To the future.'

'To the future,' repeats Franz, 'and victory.'

The day has gone well, better than they could have hoped for, the horrors of war are almost forgotten. Uncle Sebastian is having a rest from playing the piano, so Hans Friedel has dusted off the wind-up gramophone player and he plays some waltz music by Strauss. This proves to be very popular and some of the couples start to dance and display a wide range of physical ability and well-practised skills. Erich sees that Kurt is sitting by himself on a bench down by the riverside. He takes a bottle and two glasses, and walks down to where his son is seated.

'Do you mind if I join you, or do you wish to be by yourself?'

'I will enjoy your company, Father, and appreciate the wine that you have brought with you.'

Erich sits down, hands Kurt a glass and pours in the clear white wine.

'Only a rather poor Riesling but it is drinkable.' He fills his own glass and raises it up. 'To you and Mariel.' Kurt raises his glass and acknowledges the toast. 'Now,' says Erich, 'I suppose the next question will be, when will you get married?'

Kurt thinks for a minute. 'I thought that we would marry when the war is over but I just don't know when that will be, it won't be soon I know that.'

'Does it matter to wait, Kurt?'

'It is not that I may be killed but that I may return having been badly wounded. I might be a cripple, been blinded, disfigured or having to face the rest of my life as an imbecile. I want Mariel to be free to decide if she would still want to be with me.'

'But you underestimate her. I think that you don't give her the credit she deserves.'

'Unlike many sons who talk to their fathers about the war, you are involved in it, you know the reality and the true horror.'

Erich nods, in his heart he can't disagree about the horrific injuries that he's seen and has had to deal with. He's also more aware than most about the struggle to finish the conflict and the enormity of the task of finally winning the war.

'I know we can't continue to bleed our country dry. We are destroying a whole generation of men such as you, Kurt.'

Kurt turns and looks at his father.

'Do you know what I find to be the most depressing thing about this war?'

'The killing?' says Erich. 'The maiming?'

'Oh yes, all that,' replies Kurt, 'but it is the way in which we as humans can invent the most hideous ways of killing.'

'You can't have war without killing, Kurt. It is what happens; the beast in man rises to the surface. At his worst, the human species becomes aggressive and reverts back to being a wild animal again.'

'We shoot them, we shell, we hurl grenades, we send out fire, dig under their trenches and blow them up and swamp them in gas. A week or so ago an officer who was also a chemist came to one of our trenches with his assistants. He was very enthusiastic and told us that he had a new type of gas. We were told, by him, that before the next attack and if the wind was in the right direction, we should release the canisters. Of course I told him that the enemy was well-practised in how to deal with gas and would be prepared for it. His response was to tell us that this was something new and it would win the war for Germany. He seemed to be so pleased with himself.'

'So, what was so new about the gas?'

'Well, he told me that the gas will drift over to the enemy trenches as normal. The enemy will see it, they will put on their gas masks and when the mist clears, they take off their protection, thinking that they are safe.'

'But they won't be safe,' says Erich, starting to understand what he's being told.

'The gas will settle on the soldiers, on the floor of the trenches and on anything that they touch. They will step on it and when they go into their bunkers for a rest, they will take the gas with them and in the close confinement of the bunker they will die. That chemist clapped his hands together and laughed, and I thought that we are now living in a world that has gone completely mad.'

Erich shakes his head and stands up.

'Come, Kurt, let us go and join the others and enjoy the rest of the day.' Father and son walk slowly up the grass slope. 'I agree with you, Kurt. It is depressing. Hopefully the chemist will one day be involved in research that will help humanity.'

'One day, but when?' says Kurt.

Chapter Nine

1 August, 1932 – Poperinge

It's a fine day and in many ways can be described as a glorious afternoon, if not a little too warm. In a well-kept municipal park in the centre of the town, many families are socialising and taking advantage of the open spaces where children can run and play. Emma Williams walks slowly along a path, and twirls the decorative, white canvas parasol that she's using to shield herself from the dazzling and bright rays of the sun. She passes a bench and fails to see that the lone occupant of the seat is Peter Lehmann. Peter senses an opportunity to talk to her and quickly extinguishes the cigarette that he'd only just lit. He walks after Emma and quickens his pace to ensure that he catches her up.

'Good morning, Miss Williams,' he says, when he's alongside her.

Emma is slightly startled and taken by surprise. 'Oh, good morning, Mr, um, Mr Loh...?'

'Lehmann, Peter Lehmann, but please, it is Peter. It is a lovely day, isn't it?'

'Yes it's very nice. I suppose you must call me Emma, but I'm surprised.'

'Why are you surprised, at what?'

'We had a teacher at our school and he went on a holiday to the Rhine. He said that he enjoyed it and most people were friendly enough.'

'But, I think there is a but.'

'Well, what he found to be strange was the formality of

relationships in your language, even the way that you refer to people.'

'Your teacher was right. I should think that this would be strange for you. You would have to know my parents well and over a long period of time before they might ask you to call them by their given name, or what you might call a Christian name. They are senior to you and it is their, should we say, gift, to allow you to refer to them in such an informal way.'

'I see, but you asked me to call you Peter and we hardly know each other.'

'But we are equals and I think that this is not a problem for me.'

'Hmm, I like to think of us as equals.'

'We are.'

Emma thinks for a moment. 'My teacher also said that there was a formal and an informal language.'

Peter laughs. 'Again he is right. When in German I ask what your name is and we do not know each other particularly well, I will say, *Wie heißen Sie* and if we are acquainted already I will ask, *Wie heißt du*. For us this is normal. Again, it is the responsibility of the senior person to give permission, if it is to be *Sie* or *du*. There are many examples of how we are formal or informal, it makes us different to you I think. It is the way we are brought up.'

'So how do I ask, *how are you*?'

'I hope you will ask, *Wie geht es dir*? This is the casual form and I hope that you will feel comfortable in asking in this way because it would mean that we are friends.'

'And if we aren't friends?'

'Then I will expect to hear you ask, *Wie geht es Ihnen*? But I hope that this will not be the case.'

'Well, I'm feeling well, thank you.'

'*Danke*, that is thank you and you would say, *Ich bin gut, danke*.'

'So I will ask you, *Wie geht es dir*?'

'And I will happily reply, *danke, mir geht es gut* because I am with you.'

Emma looks around to ensure they are not seen by her family. 'Look, I'm not sure that we should be…'

'Seen together?'

'Well yes, if my father…'

'No, you are right. If it makes you feel uncomfortable perhaps we should go our separate ways.'

Emma looks around again to be absolutely sure that there are no family members who can see them.

'Your English is very good. Did you have lessons at school?'

'Yes, some tuition at school, but mostly my father taught me. I was very young when he started teaching me and I found it to be quite easy. When you are young it is more natural, I think that your first language does not, what you might say, get in the way.'

'So, your father must speak English very well?'

'He studied in England and spent two years working at a hospital in London. Do you know any other languages?'

'A little French, from school.'

'But no German?'

Emma shakes her head and laughs. 'Oh no, my father would have a fit if I started speaking German!'

The young couple laugh and slowly walk along an unplanned route, only changing direction when something of interest takes their attention. The park is starting to become busy with visitors and local residents taking advantage of all that a balmy sunny day has to offer: warmth, colour and bright light. They stop by a small pond and Peter places his elbows on the railings, rubs his hands together and looks into the crystal clear water. Emma holds onto the top of the railings and views the tranquil and peaceful scene.

Peter turns to look at Emma. 'I'd heard from Madame De Vos that you come here every year. Is that true?'

'This is my second time but my parents have been here

every year since 1921 or it might have been 1920.'

Peter starts to walk, he puts his hands in his trouser pockets and looks at Emma as if to say, *will you join me?* Emma gladly accepts the invitation to continue with their liaison.

'How strange,' he says, 'every year.'

'Is it? Doesn't seem strange to me. It's something they've always done; we're used to it, most other families where we live go to Blackpool or Scarborough for their holidays, or places like that.'

'I'm sorry, not strange but unusual, I think. So you and your brothers do not have a holiday every year?'

'Well yes, we go with other members of our family, aunties and uncles to the seaside for a week.'

'And you find that this is to be enjoyable?'

Emma stops for a moment. 'Well, there are aunties and aunties, and there are uncles and uncles.'

Peter's puzzled. 'Meaning?'

'Well, when we go with Uncle George and Auntie Hilda, they tend to be rather strict: no dancing, early to bed and if I unwittingly invited the attention of a young man…'

'An admirer?'

'Yes, if you like, an admirer. Well you can imagine the problem. They take their guardianship very seriously.'

'But other aunties and uncles are different?'

'If my father tells us that Uncle Victor and Auntie Ethel would like to take us on holiday that year, we try not to be disrespectful to Uncle George, but we know that we'll have a very enjoyable time.'

'More fun, you might say?'

'Oh yes, more laughter, Uncle Victor is a bit of a comedian and Auntie Ethel is very relaxed, she laughs all the time at his jokes.'

'My family is much the same; some I like, others I have to like.'

Emma spots a bench that's suitably located under a tree that potentially could provide a welcome, shaded retreat. Before it's taken, she walks purposely towards it, sits and pats the available seat area next to her to invite Peter to join her. Peter happily accepts her invitation.

'How often have you been here?' she asks him.

'This is my second visit as well. Eight years ago I came here, and my parents have been three times. Your brother, Herbert – that is his name isn't it? Is it his first visit?'

'Yes it is. Bertie was named after my elder brother and my father always said that he would bring him here to see the grave. It's a grave with his name on the headstone.'

'And yesterday was the day,' says Peter.

'He wanted to take him when he felt that he was old enough to fully understand.'

'Of course, it makes sense to do so.'

'I heard from my mother that you live in a town called Mainz, in Germany, is that right?'

'Yes, Mainz, you know it?'

'Not really but I remember the name from geography lessons at school, near Frankfurt on the River Rhine?'

'Yes, that's right, and where in England do you live?'

'In Lancashire, a town called Blackburn, have you heard of it?'

'No, I'm afraid not. Is it nice?'

'We like it. It's what we've always known.'

'That's what matters. I know nothing of Black Bourne.'

'Black...burn,' says Emma very deliberately.

'Blackburn,' says Peter very slowly and deliberately.

'That's right.'

Peter thinks for a moment. 'Ah Blackburn, I know that they have a football team.'

'Yes, the Rovers, they're called Blackburn Rovers.'

'I'm sorry but sadly that is all I know of Blackburn.'

'Please, don't apologise, the Rovers are probably all that most people outside Lancashire know about Blackburn.'

'So, you know little of Mainz and my knowledge of where you live is limited. We are the same and are equal in that I think.'

Emma smiles at him. 'Yes, but your parents do have a very nice motorcar and we're not equal in that.'

The couple laugh. 'This is a nice place, Peter, very relaxing, I'm enjoying the day.' They continue to talk about their lives and what they would like to do in the future.

'How old were you when your brother died?' asks Emma. 'Do you remember him well?'

Peter thinks for a moment. 'I was eight years of age and you do remember a lot at that age. People say that I have the appearance of my father and that I take after him, you might say. Kurt took after my mother as far as I can remember and I recall that he was friendly and kind. He was very patient with me. I must have annoyed him at times because that is what little brothers do, but he did not get angry. Also I recall that he was very popular and he was engaged to be married. He would have been a good husband and father, I am sure of it.'

'He sounds very nice.'

'He was a good man. I think you can say that with some confidence. What about your brother, do you remember him well?'

'I was only six when he was killed. I remember that he would read to me when he was home on leave. A book called *The Tale of Peter Rabbit* by Beatrix Potter was my favourite story. I was having tea at a friend's house the day the news came telling us that Bert had died. When I walked in and went into the back room I saw Mum and Dad sitting on the kitchen chairs. They were holding hands and I knew that they had been crying. I didn't ask them why they were so upset because I knew what had happened. I ran upstairs to my bedroom, lay on the bed, took hold of the book and cried.'

'He was a good brother to you.'

'He was, a very good brother, and I still miss him.'

'Do you believe in ghosts?' asks Peter.

Emma gives Peter a slightly bewildered look, 'No, I don't think so, do you?'

'Well, I don't mean a headless horseman or a figure that seems to be wearing a white sheet. I think that ghosts are very much in our minds; they are friends, family members and lovers even. It is a case of unfinished business, people who have gone before their time. Do you see what I mean?'

'In a way,' says Emma. 'If somebody's older and although you're very fond of them, they die and you grieve, but you accept it.'

Peter turns towards Emma. He puts his hand on the back of the bench and leans forward. 'That is it exactly, of course we mourn for anybody that we care about, we miss them and continue to think of them, but as you say, we accept it. Although Kurt was taken from us, he remains with us and most days I think of him. He had so much more living to do, so much more to give and so many more things to enjoy and experience.'

'I know what you mean. Often Dad would say, *I wonder what Bert would have said about it,* or *if our Bert was here now, I know what he'd have done.* Dad says it more than anybody, but we all think it.'

They continue to sit and talk. Anybody looking at them would think that they had been acquaintances for a long time. Peter rises from the bench and holds out his hand to Emma to assist her in standing. The couple continue their walk and as they stroll along, Emma slips her hand through Peter's arm. He looks down at his arm and smiles. 'Well, Emma, where do we go from here?'

Chapter Ten

4 March, 1916 – North of Mons, Belgium
German Army, Bavarian Infantry Camp

Newly promoted Second Lieutenant Lehmann follows the long line of tents until he reaches one where he knows that Colonel Ristler is conducting his official duties. He informs the sentry on duty that he's received orders to meet with the colonel. The sentry puts his head into the doorway of the tent, speaks briefly to the colonel, and stands aside to allow Lieutenant Lehmann to step inside. Colonel Ristler looks up and acknowledges the young lieutenant's attendance. He points to a chair and carries on reading a document that he's holding. Lieutenant Lehmann realises that the pointing to the chair is an order for him to be seated. He removes his peaked cap and sits down.

He looks at the colonel but no eye contact is made. Eventually the colonel puts the paper down and stares at the lieutenant. He strokes his well-groomed, waxed moustache and then runs his hand over the top of his bald head.

'Now, Lehmann, I understand that you have an understanding of the English language and it is very good, is that right?'

Lieutenant Lehmann nods in agreement. 'Yes, my father taught me, you could say that I am fluent, and I also stayed in England with a family in Sussex for one summer in 1913.'

'You had friends in England?'

'My father worked as a doctor in London after he qualified. He and a colleague called Dr Payne became good friends and that is how I came to stay with the Payne family in southern England in a county called East Sussex.'

'That is very good; not only do you have a good grasp of their language, you also know how they think perhaps?'

'What is this leading to, Sir?'

The colonel stands and walks towards the doorway of the tent, he briefly looks out. 'Not raining at last, I hope we are in for a dry summer so we can push on and end this madness.' He turns to look directly at the lieutenant. 'I have an important job for you to do. It will require skill and some cunning.' He pauses for a moment, takes out a cigarette case and offers one to Lieutenant Lehmann who declines the offer by shaking his head. The colonel lights his cigarette and goes back to his seat. 'We have taken many prisoners and now we need intelligence. I want you to talk to some of the British soldiers, befriend them and get some information, as much as you can.'

'What sort of information?'

'You know, troop movements, regiments, specialist teams such as miners, supplies and so on. See what you can get. I'm assigning a young soldier to work with you. He is Private Myers.' The colonel checks his paperwork. 'Yes, that is right, Myers, and he can speak English quite well. You may find him to be useful.'

'And now, Sir?'

'Now you must report to Captain Becker. You will find him at the East Barracks.' The colonel hands the lieutenant a paper. 'Give him this and he will take it from there, he is expecting you.'

Lieutenant Lehmann stands, salutes and leaves the tent. He walks towards the East Barracks, which is a grand title for a number of industrial sheds which have been hastily converted for use. Eventually he finds the office of Captain Becker and after a brief introduction the two soldiers leave to find Private Myers and begin the task to which they have been assigned.

As they walk, Lieutenant Lehmann notices that the captain has a pronounced limp and a gloved hand is an indication of a wound to his lower arm. He has an unusually pale and sallow complexion and on the whole, presents a sickly appearance.

After meeting Private Myers, they retire to a secluded and quiet area to discuss tactics. The lieutenant has already started to formulate a strategy and is eager to discuss his plan. The reason for his enthusiasm is that if he is successful, he'll have extracted information from selected prisoners who may be unaware that they have betrayed their country. The lieutenant considers that the welfare and well-being of the prisoners is to be the priority, and the interrogation will be painless and conducted without force and brutality.

'Now, Private Myers,' says the lieutenant, 'you will be my assistant, and you cannot speak English.'

'But I can, I speak it very well,' he protests.

The young soldier is very confused. Private Myers is old enough to serve but looks as if he should be at school. His upper lip shows signs of the early growth of a moustache, but due to his age it has ceased to develop further. He's small in build and the company barber has done his best to remove all traces of hair from his head.

'No, you don't speak English, you will listen. I will only speak German to you, when I talk to the prisoners I will speak English, then I will deliberately translate what I am saying into German to help you.'

Private Myers realises what the lieutenant is planning and he grins. 'I understand, if you leave the tent or where we are talking to them, I will stay and their guard may be down. I will listen and report to you.'

'That's it exactly, well done, Myers. I think we will work well together.'

The captain nods his approval for the plan. 'When would you like to start, Lieutenant?'

'As soon as we can. Tomorrow morning, perhaps?'

'Your first appointment will be at a camp near Metz where non-officers are housed, and then you will travel to Trier to interview officers. I will arrange for transport to leave in the early hours of the morning.'

The captain wishes them well and leaves. Lieutenant Lehmann turns to the private. 'What is your given name?'

'Hans.'

'A good German name and it is what many British call us Germans. It could prove to be useful.'

The next day, the two soldiers approach the gate of the compound at a camp situated to the north of Metz. After showing the approval documents to the sentry on the gate, they're let in and wait while an officer approaches them. After a brief discussion they're shown to a large wooden hut. At the door, they stop to make sure that they both understand how their plan of action is to work.

'I will ask each soldier in turn if they are being treated well,' says the lieutenant, 'and ask if there is anything I can do for them. You will take notes, but remember to only write in German and not English.'

The weather's dull and the temperature very low, almost down to freezing. In the hut it's reasonably warm, a log burning stove at the far end of the building is well lit and many of the soldiers are sat around it. Lieutenant Lehmann sits on a bench by a large wooden table where three soldiers are seated. He greets them by introducing himself and in turn he presents Private Myers to them. The soldiers' replies are rather mumbled responses that are barely audible because they're clearly wary and suspicious. The lieutenant looks at the soldiers' uniforms; two of them are wearing tam-o-shanter berets and he quickly confirms, by analysing the tartan pattern of their kilts, that they are from the Black Watch regiment. The other soldier is from an English battalion, although the lieutenant can't quite make out the identity of his shoulder insignia.

The soldiers are drinking what is some form of inferior tea that resembles a grey-coloured cup of dishwater. He offers them some cigarettes; two accept, the third, one of the Scotsmen, refuses. Their talk is about the conditions of their imprisonment, the quality of the food and how well they are being treated.

Private Myers, under the direction of the lieutenant, writes down the information and he's careful to speak and write in German.

The three soldiers tell them their names, and they start to become more relaxed because they feel that the two German soldiers are genuinely concerned about their well-being. Lieutenant Lehmann focuses more on the two Scottish soldiers, he knows that there is sometimes a difficult tension between the two British nations and this could work to his advantage.

'I've never been to Scotland,' he says. 'I hear that it is beautiful, scenic and dramatic.'

One of the soldiers called Robertson, who's stoutly built, rugged in looks and abrupt in manner, coughs and laughs loudly. 'Dramatic you say, aye, well it's certainly dramatic where I come from, I take it you've never been to Glasgow, to the Gorbals, that's where I live. Now, that's not scenic, and there's no way it's beautiful.' The Scottish soldier inhales the smoke of his cigarette, coughs and shakes his head. 'Christ,' he says, 'is this what you smoke? They're shit; there'd be a bloody mutiny if we had to put up with this crap.'

The other Scottish soldier, who's named Kean, is slimmer and younger than Private Robertson and speaks with an accent that is very harsh and quite difficult to understand. 'It's more bloody scenic in here than where Robbo lives,' he says. Both the Scots look at each other and laugh.

The conversation continues and slowly the lieutenant gains some information, some of it insignificant, but occasionally an item of intelligence that just might prove to be useful is disclosed. Slowly a picture concerning troop movements and supply systems is being built up. Occasionally, the lieutenant leaves them on the pretext of answering a despatch and carrying out other duties. The three men talk more freely in front of Private Myers who they're convinced has a very limited, if any, understanding of their language.

'I think we've said too bloody much,' says Private Kean.

'He seemed very interested in what we had to say about the new field artillery guns and that practice we went on, with the radio wires that we used for listening for artillery placements.'

The English soldier, Private Bryant, a small man with sharp features, looks around to ensure that the German officer has not returned. 'Nothing they don't fucking know about already. The Hun know more than our top brass think they do.'

Private Myers does his best not to let the men know that he understands every word that they're saying. He needs to memorise the detail because he can't be seen to write it down. Now the men are off their guard, they start to confirm what they have told the lieutenant and question the content of what has been said. Lieutenant Lehmann returns and sits back down. This time he gives the English soldier more attention. 'Where are you from, not Scotland I think?'

'No,' replies the Private Bryant. 'Heathfield in Sussex, do you know it?'

'I know the area,' says the lieutenant. 'I stayed with a family in Rye one summer, I know Sussex reasonably well, are you with a Sussex regiment?'

'I am, I'm with the Royal Sussex and I'm proud to say it.'

'And so you should be, I hope one day I will be able to go back to Rye, when this madness is over, but I think that it will take a long time for the war to be finished.'

'Oh, not so long,' replies Private Bryant, 'not when the Americans join us.'

The lieutenant deliberately laughs. 'I've heard these stories, there is nothing in it, they won't get involved, it is not in their interests to do so.'

Private Bryant drinks what's left of his tea.

'A couple of weeks ago, the higher-ups, a couple of generals they were, came down through our trench with some other officers. At first, I didn't know where they were from because I'd never seen their uniforms before. Then my mate Frank told me they were Yanks and I asked our captain why they were here. He said that it was to see how we were doing things and that when they're in the war, they'll be ready.'

'Aye,' says Private Robertson, 'those bastards will swan in when all the fucking work's been done and take over. Then they'll tell us where we've been going wrong.'

'Where was it that the Americans visited you and why was it your trench?' asks the lieutenant.

'Our first line at...' Private Bryant's account of events is suddenly interrupted. 'Watch it!' he says to Private Robertson who's obviously kicked him under the table.

Lieutenant Lehmann realises that he's gone as far as he can on this occasion, stands, wishes the three soldiers well and leaves. Private Myers stays for a moment and, speaking in German, indicates that he would like to stay in the warm for a little longer. The soldiers ignore him and carry on talking. The German private looks elsewhere, but listens to them.

'What's your name?' Private Robertson asks the German private, who pretends not to understand. Private Kean points at his own chest. 'Gordon,' he says. Then he points at the German. 'You are?'

'Ah,' says Private Myers, 'Hans.'

The soldiers continue to talk and every so often they speak directly to Private Myers, 'What do you think, Hans, you stupid sod?'

The conversation continues in this vein and when they refer to the German private, Hans smiles and nods, but listens. 'Christ, Hans,' says Private Robertson, 'if they're all like you I don't know why it's taking us so bloody long to win this fucking war.'

After a short time Private Myers leaves and once out of the door he walks towards Lieutenant Lehmann who's standing a short distance away. The lieutenant's smoking a cigarette.

'Where was the trench that the Americans visited, Hans?'

'Mametz Wood,' replies Private Myers.

The lieutenant offers the private a cigarette but his young

assistant refuses to take one. 'I do not smoke,' he explains, 'never tried it, my chest is not strong.'

'That's very unusual, Hans, I'm not sure how I could manage without a smoke, no matter how bad it tastes. What do you think of the British soldiers?'

'My mother would not like their blasphemous language, but I hear as bad in our trenches. They are very similar to our soldiers, could be German.'

'You're right, Hans, but I've yet to see a German in a tartan kilt.'

For the next three weeks Lieutenant Lehmann and Private Myers continue to gather information. After they exhaust what's on offer with the soldiers at Metz they move on to employ the same tactics at the officer's camp at Trier. The exercise proves to be reasonably successful and the intelligence service is able to gain some useful information. However, Lieutenant Lehmann is pleased when the assignment comes to an end and he's given permission to return to some *honest* combat duties. He'd found the deception to be somewhat difficult to cope with and not in keeping with the standards that he'd been brought up with. During his final debriefing he sits on a chair opposite the desk that's occupied by Colonel Ristler. He waits to give his final report and the colonel keeps him waiting. The senior officer's smoking a large drooping pipe, the smoke gives off a rather unpleasant aroma and Lieutenant Lehmann wishes that he could finish his duties and leave. Without looking up, the colonel holds out his hand to take the written report off the lieutenant. He studies some of the detail, puts the report down and leans back.

'Not to your liking, Lieutenant, this mysterious and darker side of warfare?'

Lieutenant Lehmann is a little embarrassed. 'It has been interesting, Sir, and I'm sure that there are those who have a more natural ability to extract information.'

The colonel shakes his head. 'You do not do yourself any

justice. The exercise has been very useful, and Intelligence is generally well-pleased.'

'Generally?'

'We can always do better, can we not?'

Lieutenant Lehmann leans back and sighs heavily. 'The ordinary soldiers talked more, but you have to question how much they really knew. The officers had more knowledge but were more guarded and didn't give much away.'

'Brighter, more intelligent,' says Colonel Ristler. 'I have had many conversations with enemy officers. I often thought that at a different time and in another place, I could be sharing a glass of very expensive brandy with them, having enjoyed a fine dinner in their company. We aren't that much different. This war has made us different and the wounds that we have inflicted on each other will take a long time to heal.'

Lieutenant Lehmann is dismissed and he leaves the tent. Waiting for him outside is Private Myers. 'We are finished now, Sir?'

'Back to the grim reality of war, Private Myers, and in a strange way I'm looking forward to it.'

Chapter Eleven

1 August, 1932 – Poperinge

As the day moves on, the summer sun increases in intensity and many walkers seek the sanctuary and shelter of the shade offered by the awnings and large parasols located outside the numerous street cafés and bars. At one such café, Annie and Mary are sitting by a table and enjoying a very refreshing cup of tea. They reflect on their visit so far, they agree that despite the German family having had the audacity to lodge in their hotel, things have gone reasonably well, especially because they've been blessed with such glorious weather. The theme of their conversation returns to matters at home. In the early part of next summer, in June, John's nephew Wilfred is getting married. Wilfred is the eldest son of Hilda who is John's sister. She's a widow; her husband was killed a number of years ago in an accident while working as a mechanic, maintaining the machinery in a foundry. Since the death of her husband, Hilda has made a point of relying on the help and guidance that John provides. The wedding will be managed by John, and Annie is to be called upon to assist him.

'What's she like, this girl that Wilfred's planning to wed?'

'She's quite nice really,' says Annie, 'She's a bit, well, you know, a bit cotton mill.'

'Common, you mean.'

'I prefer to say that she comes from a humble background, Mary. She's very polite though and must have been well brought up, but she's not had much in the way of education. They live on Ivy Street.'

'What, down near the canal? I've always thought it must be a bit damp down there. Is there any money? Who'll pay for the do?'

'We all will, we'll help out with baking and cooking. We've got the hall under the church on Montague Street. We'll make it nice and do him proud.'

Annie sips her tea. 'I'm not sure what this tea is but it's quite nice.'

'When we first sat down and you went to pay a call,' says Mary, 'I gave the waiter our order and asked him to make sure that it were Indian tea and not Chinese. I told him to make sure it's black, nothing fancy I said. He told me that more people were starting to drink Chinese with a slice of lemon, and green tea was becoming very popular. I said, *we're not having any of those fancy ways, we're milk and two sugars, and proud of it.* I told him we were English and that we hadn't come to Belgium to learn how to take our tea.'

'I often think of the tea that our Bert had to put up with in the trenches,' says Annie. 'We used to send him some food parcels with biscuits, chocolate and things like that in it. I also put in some tea; he appreciated that because he and his friends had a little stove once where they could make a brew. He told me that they used to bring tea round in an old petrol can and although they scrubbed it as best they could, you could still taste the petrol. Most of the time the tea they were given had a type of condensed milk in it and it made the brew thick. It were a bit like cocoa and it were very sweet. I don't think that Bert would have minded a brew of green tea with a slice of lemon in it.'

Annie looks across the street and sees a person who she recognises; it's Martina Lehmann. Annie deliberately turns her head to avoid making possible eye contact. However, Martina has seen the two ladies and after waiting for some traffic to pass by, she walks across the road and approaches them. 'Good afternoon. May I join you?' she asks.

Mary is obviously very hostile to this unwelcome intrusion

and turns her back on Martina. Annie, although she feels the same, begrudgingly and reluctantly offers Martina a chair and their uninvited guest sits down. 'Please yourself,' Annie mumbles.

Mary gives Martina a dismissive glance. 'Do what you like, I'm going to pay a call then I'm going. I were enjoying it here as well.' She leans towards Martina and stares directly at her. 'We were planning our Wilfred's wedding, it were important.'

Mary stands, adjusts her sunhat and walks into the café. Martina sits, aware of the difficult and awkward situation that she feels responsible for creating. 'I'm very sorry, I have upset your friend and it was not my intention to do that.'

'Sister,' replies Anne in a very curt and abrupt tone of voice. 'She's my sister.'

Martina stands and prepares to leave. 'I shall go and leave you in some peace and you can continue to make the plans for the wedding.'

Annie thinks for a moment and realises that she's been unduly discourteous and seeks to make amends. 'Oh, she gets a bit tense, always has done. It's her way, please. I've been rude. Would you sit down? Wedding plans can wait.'

Martina feels relieved and sits once again. 'My sister, she is the same, sometimes, she is heated, is that right to say heated, hot-headed perhaps?'

'Fiery, you might say. I'm sorry, you must understand it's difficult for us.'

Martina looks out onto the street. 'Nice day. Nice and warm.'

Annie sighs and starts to feel more relaxed. 'Yes we're fortunate, and it does lift your spirits.'

Mary re-joins them and stares at Annie as if to say, *have you lost all reasoning?* Then, surprisingly, she pulls out a chair and sits down.

Martina smiles at her. 'I'm glad that you felt you could come back, I'm sorry that I upset you.'

'I didn't finish my tea and I'd paid for it so I might as well finish it!'

'As you might say,' says Martina, 'waste not.'

Mary shrugs and without looking at their unwelcome guest says, 'Well, we're not all made of money you know. Some of us have to watch the pennies.'

Annie addresses her sister, 'We were just saying what a nice day it is.'

Martina leans more forward to be sure that she's heard. 'My husband once lived in England, he said it rained a lot and when at home it rains, he says it is British weather again.' Martina laughs, but only a little.

The sight of Martina laughing annoys Mary. 'Well, I don't know about that because we have very nice days in the summer where we live, British weather indeed!'

Annie seeks to defuse a potentially unpleasant argument. 'Your English is very good, I hardly know a word of German, it's a mystery to me.'

'As I said, my husband lived in England. He was in Cambridge, do you know it?'

'Cambridge, I know of it,' replies Annie. 'What were he doing there, was he a student?'

'Yes, for three years, he had family connections there and then later he was in London.'

'Cambridge,' says Mary, 'very la-de-da, there are a lot of English boys who would have liked to have gone to Cambridge. Course they can't afford it and I suppose it's a case of who you know.'

'So, obviously my husband learned to speak English and then taught his family. Of course I am not as good at it as my Erich.'

Mary is still hostile. 'Good at everything is he, your husband?'

Martina thinks for a moment as she's clearly considering her husband's abilities and skills. She realises that she needs to placate and win over Annie's sister. 'Not so good at cooking and sewing.' Martina and Annie laugh. However, Mary doesn't.

'Can I ask, did your husband fight in the war?' Annie asks Martina.

'No, he was a little old for that, but he did join the army and worked as a doctor, his rank was as a medical officer.'

'That must have been hard.'

'Harder than he thought it would be, so many wounded with dreadful and terrible injuries.'

'Still,' says Annie, 'the army, your army I mean, must have been very grateful for his help.'

'Yes, he felt that he could help the soldiers, but he also knew that he could have done more. It changed him.'

Annie stares directly at Martina. 'How? how changed?'

'Before the war, he had strong Christian beliefs, we were, I mean, we are Catholics. I still go to mass and attend every week and I think you would call us devout.'

'And you and he changed?'

'I didn't change my views that much but Erich, well, I noticed the changes.'

Annie sits back in her chair. 'Not surprising, I suppose, considering. My John has never really been that bothered about religion. He reads about it and if he were asked what his faith were, he would say that he were a member of the Church of the Wensley Brethren. That usually stops the conversation because nobody has ever heard of them. In fact, what he doesn't tell them is that their meetings take place in the public bar of the Red Lion on Wensley Road.'

'The Red Lion?'

'It's John's local, a pub, a place where he meets his friends for a drink.'

'I understand,' says Martina. 'In Germany it can be the same. I have not heard of this pub.'

'It's a short name for a public house.'

'I see, it is clearer, we have bierkellers and bars, but my husband does not attend much.'

'It seems that men have to have places to go and drink

and talk,' Annie says. 'Now, before, you were saying that your husband were a believer and then lost his faith?'

Martina welcomes the opportunity to share her thoughts with Annie and with Mary, who now seems to be taking more notice of the conversation. 'As the war went on, he talked less and less of belief and hardly attended mass. As well as losing our son, I'll never know what he saw when he worked as a medical officer. He said very little but I knew that it was terrible and it affected him deeply, and now he does not go to church at all. I wish that he could rediscover his faith but I do not think that he will. Do you and your husbands attend church?'

'We're Church of England,' says Annie. 'I like to go to morning service on most Sundays. John comes with me sometimes but if he doesn't feel like it, he says *you go, Annie, I'm not feeling very religious today.*'

Martina and Annie smile, and Mary stares at the two women. She slowly shakes her head and still retains a somewhat solemn and sober expression.

'I go,' she says. 'Not keen on our vicar though, got funny ideas he has, modern thinking they call it. I make sure that Henry comes with me and he does, under sufferance though.'

This time the three women smile.

Martina catches the attention of one the waiters who's clearly struggling to attend to the large number of customers that has suddenly descended on the café. The fine weather has brought out what seems to be the majority of the population of the town, who are seeking refreshments and a place where they can rest. Martina orders a coffee with a slice of cake and although the waiter explains that there's a considerable waiting time, he tells her that he'll do what he can to hurry the order through.

Martina smiles at the waiter and thanks him for his attention, she compliments him on the way in which he's clearly committed to his work in the hope that her order will arrive sooner rather than later. She turns to continue with the theme of the conversation. 'I do get a lot of comfort from my religion. The belief that I have, that I might see my son again, has helped me through the dark times, soon after he died and even today.'

Annie agrees with her and fully empathises with Martina's thinking. 'Well, there's a lot of consolation in that.'

'You have the same thoughts, Mrs Williams?' asks Martina.

'I suppose I do, I mean I have my doubts from time to time, we all do, but yes, comforting most of the time.'

Martina focuses on Annie and speaks directly to her, 'My goodness, we are very grim. Let us talk of a possible better future. Your children are called Emma and Herbert, is that right?'

'Yes, our Emma and Herbert, we call him Herbert but he prefers to be called Bertie.'

'Have you any other children?' asks Martina.

'Oh yes, two more boys, James and Harold. We also had another girl but she died of diphtheria when she were five, it was a long time ago. The boys are all grown up and our James, we call him Jim, is married.'

Martina smiles and clasps her hands together in a gesture of delight and happiness. 'Ah, soon you may have grandchildren, it will be a blessing and it will be a great comfort for you.'

'Of course, I'm sure it will help, but you see, our Bert was the first and that's something a bit special.'

'I know what you mean and I agree with you, we have Peter of course, only Peter.'

'Still,' says Annie, 'you may have grandchildren one day.'

The waiter interrupts them when he puts a cup of coffee and some cake onto the table. Martina thanks him, lifts the cup and sips the coffee. 'I do hope so, I really hope so,' she says thoughtfully.

Mary starts to feel that she's being left out of the conversation. 'Well, I don't think I'll have any grandchildren. I've got two girls, not married yet and nothing but trouble when it comes to boys.'

Annie laughs. 'She's exaggerating of course. Lizzy and

Clare are delightful. They're good company and they brighten up our lives.'

'That's easy for you to say, you don't have to listen to the rubbish they talk about women's rights and the like. I told them, *you keep on spouting that nonsense and you'll never find a man to take you on.*'

'Take you on?' asks Martina.

'Marry,' explains Annie.

'Ah yes,' says Martina, 'it is what you wish for your children, it is somebody who will care for them and I think that it is natural.'

Annie agrees. 'Well it is, but it's the same with our Emma. I mean, these women's rights, that's what it's like today and it's a different world.

The café seems to be busier than ever, more potential customers arrive and look for available seating. Most of them are disappointed and leave. 'This place seems to be very popular,' says Annie.

'Must be making a fortune,' adds Mary. 'They know how to charge here.'

Annie turns to speak to Martina again. 'What's it like, the place where you live in Germany.'

'We live in Mainz, which is in the Rhineland District. You know the River Rhine?'

'Heard of it, a big river isn't it?'

'It is a very attractive river, it is a feature of the region, you might say, and we enjoy it.'

'We've got a river in the town where we live,' says Mary. 'It's called the Blakewater.'

'And is it nice? Do you enjoy walking by it and taking a boat trip perhaps?'

'Dries up some of the time,' replies Mary.

'Do you like living in Mainz?' asks Annie.

'Yes, I do, we think that it is nice. I was born in Frankfurt so I am used to where we live but my husband came from

Hamburg and he still has something of a northern accent.'

'Was it his work that brought him to Mainz, or did he fancy somewhere a bit warmer?' asks Annie.

'No, his father was also a doctor and he had family living in Mainz. He set up a health practice in the city and my husband, of course before he was my husband, came home from England and worked with him. My father-in-law died a number of years ago and Erich now runs the practice and enjoys his work. He always says that whatever you do in life you should enjoy your work. It is a good thought.'

'Well,' says Mary, 'as my dad would say, you know what thought did?'

'I'm sorry,' says Martina. 'What did thought did, sorry, I mean do?'

'Followed a muck cart,' replies Mary, 'and thought it were a wedding.'

Martina stares at Mary then looks at Annie. 'A muck cart? I don't understand. Why is it a wedding?'

Annie laughs. 'It's one of our father's sayings, it's not important, it doesn't make much sense.'

'And just when I thought that my understanding of your language was improving. I will never fully grasp it, I think.'

'Don't worry yourself, there are folk outside Lancashire where we live,' says Mary, 'who are confused about our sayings and our ways.'

'But I suppose if you are going to enjoy your work,' says Annie, 'it all depends on what your job is.'

Mary finishes her tea and puts the cup down on the table, she looks into the teapot to see if there's the possibility of another cup. When she sees that the pot is practically empty, she sits back. 'I wouldn't mind another cup, but I'm getting worried about that young man, the waiter I mean. I think he'll overdo it and I don't want to be responsible for him keeling over.' Mary seems to be amused. 'Course, talking of keeling over, I'd like to have had more children but it seemed to wear poor Henry out helping to produce two. I became worried about his health, all that huffing and puffing and doing. Still, he's good at fishing apparently.'

The ladies laugh. Martina's pleased that Mary is starting to feel relaxed in her company.

'I'm not sure what *keeling over* means exactly, but I think I understand.' Martina sighs. 'Life goes on and we must look to the future, and hope for a good future.'

'For our children,' adds Annie.

'Yes,' replies Martina. 'As always, for the next generation.'

Annie and Martina continue to talk, and Mary looks across the increasingly busy street. Amongst the hustle and bustle she's sure that she's spotted Emma and Peter. She stands to see if she can get a clearer and uninterrupted view. Mary confirms that it's as she suspected and the couple she's spotted are standing on a corner of the street, deep in conversation. They seem to be standing close together, perhaps too close. 'Well, just look at that, what's going on over there, well I never.'

Martina also stands and nods. 'It is your Emma and my Peter,' she sits down. 'It is natural I think,' she turns to Mary. 'Perhaps you are of the opinion that they should be, what is it called, chaperoned?'

'Chaperoned?' answers Mary. 'Only if they're walking out.'

'Walking out?' questions Martina.

'Mary means courting, romantically attached, leading perhaps to something more permanent, like marriage.'

Martina eats a small piece of cake and touches the sides of her mouth with a napkin. 'I just see two young people enjoying talking to each other, we could be a long way from a marriage.'

'Well,' replies Mary, 'that's how it starts, better not let John catch them or there'll trouble.' She looks around to see if there's a waiter close by. 'I fancy a piece of that cake, it looks very nice.' She then turns to Annie. 'Anyway, Emma's seeing someone, Robert something, isn't it?'

'Oh, Robert Shaw you mean. That finished months ago, Mary.'

Martina looks again at Emma and Peter, her view is now clearer. 'Where is the harm, I think that they make a nice looking couple.'

Annie nods in agreement and speaks quietly, almost to herself, 'Yes they do don't they, they look good together.'

Martina stands up ready to leave. 'Thank you very much for your company. I have enjoyed it. But I must meet my husband, we are going again to where our son is buried.'

'Of course,' says Annie. 'I forget that there are German soldiers buried here, you don't see many graveyards, do you? Where's your son buried?'

'He lies in a cemetery called Langemark, which is to the east of here, perhaps a little to the north as well, it is something of a drive.'

Mary chuckles. 'Just as well you've got that posh car then.'

'Yes we are fortunate, very fortunate, it helps my husband when he has to go to visit a patient at home and especially when his help is needed on an urgent case.'

'I expect he makes a lot of money with his doctoring,' says Mary.

Martina smiles. 'Not as much as he should. His father, who set up the practice, was more of a businessman and he used to tell my husband that he should be firmer and insist that patients pay their bills on time. He is, shall we say, lenient, and it is not in his nature. It is one of the things that I appreciate about him, or should I say, I love about him.'

Annie stands and holds out her hand. 'Well, goodbye.'

Martina takes Annie's hand and holds it for a brief moment. 'Auf wiedersehen. Sorry, I mean goodbye.'

'No,' says Annie, 'as you say, auf wiedersehen, is that right?'

'Perfect,' Martina smiles. She opens her parasol before stepping out onto the street and then slowly walks away.

Mary has been successful in attracting the attention of a waiter. She asks for another pot of tea and after confirming with Annie that two slices of cake are required, sends him on his way. She looks once more in the direction Martina is heading and watches as she disappears from sight. 'Seems you've got a new friend there, Annie.'

Annie smiles at her sister. 'She seems to be rather pleasant.'

'Well, appears to be all right. Not her fault she's German I suppose.'

Chapter Twelve

8 April, 1915 – Etaples, France
The Royal Lancastrian Light Infantry Base Camp

The heavily built and rugged-looking Sergeant Clayton walks through the line of makeshift huts and sheds, most of which have been hastily erected, and some existing structures very obviously repaired. His mission is to find his commanding officer, Colonel Simes, and after asking various soldiers for directions he arrives at a hut where the colonel is waiting. The sergeant is in no doubt about the reason he's been ordered to attend a short briefing session. Two young recruits had gone missing, they'd been caught by the Red Caps, court-martialled and sentenced to death for desertion. Because they're in the sergeant's platoon, it's his responsibility to select and organise a firing squad. It's the worst order that the sergeant will be given and it's an order that he has to obey without question. The sergeant marches into the tent, he stands to attention and salutes. The small-framed and grey haired Colonel Simes, who's seated behind a desk, looks up at him and taps his forehead in recognition of the salute.

'At ease. I think you know what this is all about, Sergeant. It's very unpleasant, but it has to be done.'

'Yes, Sir, the two deserters, that's it isn't it, Sir?'

The colonel looks down at a paper in front of him and puts a thin pair of spectacles on his nose. 'Yes, that's it. Harris and Stephens, both eighteen, bloody fools. Pick your men well, Sergeant, I don't want any shirkers, make sure you get the right men.'

'I will, Sir, we'll draw lots as usual, but if I'm not satisfied, I'll draw again.'

'Good man. It'll be five tomorrow morning, usual form. I'll be there to officially read the order and cut off their regimental insignia. You know the form, not fit to wear the badge and all that. Assemble the entire platoon to witness it.'

The sergeant salutes once more, about turns and marches out of the tent. Once outside he stops and sighs deeply. 'Bugger,' he says under his breath.

Back at the barracks, Sergeant Clayton walks into the hut where his platoon has been billeted. 'No time like the present,' he says to himself. He stands at the door and shouts, 'Right you lot, listen to me, I'm looking for six fine chaps to help me out with a bit of a problem that I need to sort.'

'Bit of a problem,' says a voice from somewhere. 'That what you call it, Sarge?'

'Who's asking the question, a volunteer I think, was that you, Smithy, let's see you, don't be shy.'

The tall and slim, almost thin-looking, corporal stands up. 'Volunteer for what, Sarge?'

'You know what it is, two lads have stepped out of line, need to be made an example of, lesson to others like.' The sergeant prepares the straws, holds a number of them in his left fist, walks down the aisle of the hut and stops at each soldier in turn. The soldiers nervously select a straw, as they pull out the straw from the sergeant's hand they hold their breath until the length is established. He repeats this until he's one short of his required number of men. Finally he stops at the bed where Private Williams is sitting. Five soldiers have drawn short straws and in his hand is the final straw. He takes out the straw and shows it to Private Williams. 'That'll be you, Williams. You'll make up the six, Bert.'

Private Williams swallows hard. 'Blimey, why me?' he says to Corporal Frank Jenkins who's sat next to him. 'When I go back home, people ask if I've shot anybody yet and I tell 'em, not that I know of, now the first bloke I'm going to shoot is one of ours.'

Corporal Jenkins stands up and looks at his reflection in a small mirror that's propped up on a shelf that the previous occupants of the hut have conveniently left behind. He smooths down his dark, greasy hair and checks to see if his moustache needs a trim. 'I wouldn't worry too much, Bert, you might not be killing anybody in the morning.'

'How do you mean, Frank? Sarge said I were in the squad.'

The corporal lights a cigarette. 'You won't all have live ammo and you won't know. Hopefully you'll never know.'

That night, sleep, a restful sleep, is beyond Private Williams' grasp. Try as he might he can't dismiss the thought of the duty that he has to perform in the morning. He turns one way and then the other, lying first on his back then on his side. He wishes it was morning and yet he dreads the coming of the new day. From time to time a soldier gets out of his camp-bed to visit the latrines, cursing the fact that he'd stayed to have the extra beer that has now disturbed his sleep and given him a thumping headache. Slowly, a natural light filters through the shutters on the windows, there's a sound of movement outside and then, suddenly, the main door is pushed open violently and with such force that it smacks loudly against the wall of the hut. The soldier who's opened the door stands aside to allow the large figure of Sergeant Major Gaunt to enter. He marches to the centre of the hut and shouts, 'Right, you lazy, idle, excuses for fighting men, let's be having you on parade, at the double.'

There is no debate, there's no discussion, Sergeant Major Gaunt, known to his men as Sergeant Egghead, has spoken. His nickname is appropriate because of the sergeant major's large round head that's either naturally bald or has been very closely shaved. However, no one has ever seen him shaving his head and the story amongst the soldiers is that when he was very young and had a full head of hair, he caught sight of his reflection in a mirror. He was so frightened by what he saw, that his hair immediately fell out and never grew back again.

He barks his orders and the soldiers respond by quickly

dressing. They step into their trousers and pull them up over the tails of their nightshirts which are instantly transformed into day shirts. A quick visit to the latrines is made, they throw the cold water that's provided in buckets onto their faces; teeth cleaning will come later. Still dressing, they rush out of their barracks accommodation into a large courtyard area. They've been told to leave their rifles in the hut. When they're in the open air they realise how bitterly cold it is. One or two soldiers are late because they've mislaid their belts, boots or caps. Their late attendance on parade has not escaped the attention of the sergeant major who instructs the parade corporal to take the last two soldiers' names and there is little doubt that this will result in them being put on a charge.

Sergeant Clayton marches in and shouts, 'Firing squad, fall out!'

At his command, the six soldiers, including Private Williams, step backwards from the line, they turn to the right and march towards the corner of the courtyard. Sergeant Major Gaunt directs them into a room and orders them to wait for further instructions. A very young-looking lieutenant comes into the room, he gives the men permission to smoke and all but one of them begin to light up. Private Williams feels sick, he's shaking and he quickly draws on his cigarette. It's like a dream and it's as if they're in a different world; a world of horrific fantasy. Sergeant Clayton hands each of the squad a rifle. 'Now, lads,' he says, 'one bullet each. One of you will have a blank cartridge and you'll never know who it is. When you're asked if you've ever shot anyone when you've been in a firing squad, you can say, you might have done.'

This is of little consolation to the six soldiers, although they know that there's no other way of conducting the squad, even a one in six chance is better than a certainty. The soldiers are ordered out of the room, they shoulder their rifles and march towards the front of the platoon. When in position, they form a line and obey the order to stand at ease. They look up to see two wooden posts that have been dropped into holes in the ground and stand at about six foot in height.

The soldiers who have erected the posts make sure that they're secure and are firmly locked in position. It's quiet and when the doors to a makeshift cell block are loudly swung open, the noise takes many of the platoon members by surprise and some step back, much to the annoyance of the sergeant major. 'Stand still you lot!' he yells. 'Keep a line. You're the Royal Lancs not the bloody boy scouts!'

Private Williams doesn't move. He's rigid with apprehension. He's shaking and is starting to worry that his trembling will be noticed. He knows that if his uncontrollable shivers are detected by the sergeant major, this weakness will be broadcast to the rest of the platoon and he'll be ridiculed. From the open door the two young soldiers who have been found guilty of desertion are led out. The first deserter, a tall, thin youth with a pasty, almost grey complexion and clearly in need of a shave, walks with some dignity towards his allotted place of execution. By contrast, the second deserter, who's sobbing loudly, is somewhat shorter and of a stockier build. He has to be helped to walk with the aid of two guards holding each arm. He stumbles and eventually has to be almost carried to the post.

Once in position they're tied to the posts, the shorter man slumps down as his legs finally give way. A guard steps forward to make him more secure so that he remains upright and presents a viable target. This deserter sobs and cries, he shouts out that he's sorry, so sorry. The taller deserter stares forward and seems to be unaware of what is taking place. Colonel Simes marches towards the condemned men, reaches into his pocket and takes out a piece of paper, he puts on his spectacles and reads out aloud, 'You men, having been given the great opportunity to serve your country, have dishonoured the uniform that you wear. You have let down your country, your families and your fellow soldiers. Discipline must be upheld if we are to achieve the victory that will surely be ours.' The colonel takes off his spectacles and carefully folds up the piece of paper before putting both items into his pocket.

A soldier steps forward and hands a small knife to the colonel, who then approaches the taller of the two men and cuts off the regimental insignia from his tunic. He attempts to do the same with the second deserter, although, because he's struggling, the task is made more difficult. The colonel leans towards him. 'Steady now, steady I say, what would your mother think of you, this is your last act on earth, leave it with some dignity.'

These comments by the colonel have little or no effect, the doomed young soldier continues his pleas and shouts out that it's all been a mistake. Having completed the task of removing the insignia, Colonel Simes steps back while the regimental padre steps forward. Before each soldier, he makes the sign of the cross and blesses them. Sergeant Clayton addresses the six members of the firing squad. To the first three he says, 'Now, you aim for a white marker that will be pinned to the chest of that deserter directly in front of you, that's the one on the left. When it's done, that young officer will put a bullet in his head from his revolver, got it?'

The three soldiers nod and indicate that they know what they are expected to do. The sergeant repeats his instructions to the second three members of the squad and tells them that they must take aim at the deserter tied to the post on the right. Unfortunately, the target for Private Williams to aim at is the wretched figure of the protesting deserter who's still sobbing and crying. Two soldiers approach the deserters; one puts a blindfold on each of them and the other soldier pins a white handkerchief onto their chests.

Private Williams stares at his victim and is horrified to see that a small damp patch on the front of his trousers grows rapidly until urine is clearly seen flowing down his trouser leg. All the time the wailing continues. Sergeant Clayton shouts his orders, 'Squad, squad attention, shoulder arms!' He waits for a moment until they have shouldered their arms. 'Take aim!' he hollers. The squad pull back the bolts on their rifles and hold them in the firing position. The sergeant pauses for a moment, waits until the soldiers have taken aim, and then shouts, 'Fire!' The courtyard is filled with the deafening boom of the rifles being fired. Because of the close confinement of the yard, the sound ricochets all around and bounces off the walls. The men slump, the taller of the deserters still moves and the young lieutenant, holding a revolver, walks up to him and shoots him in the side of his head. He repeats this with the second man although the once-struggling deserter appears to be perfectly still and no longer alive.

Sergeant Major Gaunt dismisses the platoon and they fall out to return to their hut. Once inside, Private Williams sits on his bed, props his rifle up against the wall and removes his cap. Corporal Jenkins sits opposite him. 'Well, it's done now, Bert. That were your first, let's hope it's your last.'

Private Williams lights a cigarette, smokes it for a moment and leans back to rest his head on the pillow. 'It's strange isn't it? Did you see that tall bloke, Harris, he didn't seem to be at all concerned about dying, did he?'

'No, he didn't, he seemed to be very calm.'

The private sits up slightly and rests on one elbow. 'Thing is, if he weren't bothered about dying, why did he run away in the first place?'

'Well,' replies the corporal, 'we'll never know the answer to that. He'll always be a deserter, that'll never change, shot at dawn.'

'Well, there's one thing I know.'

'What's that, Bert?'

'I'm not going to run away to get caught and called a coward. There's no way I'll get shot for desertion.'

'You'd be the last bloke to run away, Bert. You're not a coward, I know that. It's not a good thing for you or your family to know that you'd been put up against a wall and shot by our blokes.'

'It's not that, Frank.'

'Well what is it?'

'I don't want to be seen peeing in my pants in front of my mates.'

Chapter Thirteen

1 August, 1932 – Menin Gate, Ypres, Belgium

The evening is as you would expect it to be after such a warm and pleasant sunny day. The sun is starting to set and the wispy, light, almost transparent clouds are reflecting and developing a red, orange and pink range of colours. The temperature is now more agreeable, still warm, but now, pleasurable. It's just before eight o'clock and members of the local fire brigade, who are dressed splendidly in their ceremonial uniforms, march solemnly and purposely towards the Menin War Memorial. Once in position they raise their bugles to their lips and start to play the *Last Post*.

Three soldiers standing to the side of the Gate slowly lower the standards that they are holding. After the buglers have finished there's a moment of silence and meditation, then the chief fire officer shouts out the well-known and practised rendition, speaking in Dutch at first and then in English. Watching from close by is John Williams and his family. After the buglers play the *Reveille* and the brigade raises their flags, the crowd starts to disperse. The members of the fire brigade march away. 'Very moving,' says John as he positions his trilby hat on his head.

'And fitting, John,' adds Henry. 'Very much in keeping.'

Mary starts to walk back towards where she thinks the coach is parked. 'Hard to imagine, every night, they must get tired of doing it.'

'They're very respectful,' says Annie. 'It's tradition, Mary.'

'They honour us, Annie,' adds John, 'showing their respect, saying thank you like.'

The family walk along a pavement and proceed down the road. Emma walks quickly to catch up with her parents. 'What do the Germans do? Does anybody remember their dead boys?' she asks.

'That's an interesting thing to ask,' says Annie. 'Their family, they must remember. I suppose that's it and small ceremonies.'

'Like Dr Lehmann and his family,' says Emma, 'coming here and paying their respects, remembering their son.'

John, who's stepped to the front of the group, raises his hand like a platoon leader bringing his troops to a halt. He looks around to get his bearings, it's important not to take a wrong turn and suffer the embarrassment of having to retrace their steps. John would then have to admit that his sense of direction was at fault. Henry steps up to offer his advice and puts his hand up to his forehead to shield his eyes from the bright red setting sun. As he looks, he spots some familiar figures. 'Look o'er yon, over there John. They're here, I thought they might be.'

John follows Henry's directions and also spots the Lehmann family walking on the other side of the road. He sighs heavily. 'Well I don't know what they think they're doing here. That ceremony, it's got nothing to do with them. There aren't any German names on the Gate and there never will be.'

Peter spots Emma and raises his hand. Emma returns the gesture with a small wave that she hopes is discreet enough so that it won't be noticed by her father. Unfortunately, her wave is seen by John, he turns and speaks abruptly to his daughter, 'Well you can cut that out for a start, young lady, I'm not having it, I won't be let down, do you hear?'

Emma doesn't reply; no reply is needed. John composes himself and then decides to make a decision on which direction to take. He leads the family down another street and to his delight and relief, he spots a building that he recognises. 'I remember that church,' he says and turns to address the family. 'No need to worry, we're on the right track.'

The family continues down the street and arrives at the place where the coach is parked. Paul is reading a newspaper and when he sees his passengers, he puts down the paper, adjusts his tie and with the aid of the rear view mirror, makes sure that his hat's placed in a central position on his head. For a big man he moves effortlessly and with some speed as he jumps down from the cab to assist his passengers. Paul steps forward to open the door to the vehicle. John's leading the way and rather than being the first to be seated, stands by the young driver to make sure that all the family are safely aboard. In this way he feels that he will have carried out his duties with some success and fulfilled his brief. 'Well done, Paul, much appreciated as always, to your station, young man, start her up and we'll be off.'

Paul cranks up the vehicle and climbs into his cab. John satisfies himself that all are aboard and safely seated. As if he's a guard on an express train, he looks one way and then the other to make certain that all is well and that there are no traffic or pedestrian obstructions. He slaps his hand on the side of the coach to signal that it's time to move off.

Once on board John sits in the vacant seat next to Annie. 'I'll be glad to get back to the hotel,' she says. 'It's been a long day, interesting though. Me and Mary had some tea at a nice little café on the main street and we were joined by Mrs Leh...' Annie looks towards her husband, it's clear that his thoughts are somewhere else. 'John, are you listening to me?'

John's looking out of the window. 'I said they'd spoil things,' he mumbles, 'the first time I saw them, I knew what they were up to.'

Annie realises that it would not be the right time to tell John of the conversation that she and Mary had had with Martina Lehmann. 'You mean the Lehmann family.'

'Aye, I do, those Germans, I said they'd make us feel awkward.'

'Oh, you've got to ignore them, John, don't get so worked up all the time.'

'Can't help it, Annie, I wouldn't mind thinking that they followed us here to spite us, just to make a point like.'

'Oh John, I don't think so.'

'Well, it wouldn't surprise me, coming here uninvited.' John moves closer to Annie and speaks quietly. 'While we're about it, what's this with the waving from our Emma, did you see? What's that all about?'

'It's just a friendship thing, John, I'm sure it's nothing serious.'

John turns to stare at Annie, he appears to be shocked and his facial expression then changes to a look of annoyance. 'You knew and you didn't think to tell me. I'm very disappointed Annie, I've got to say it.'

Annie is somewhat exasperated, after thirty-five years of marriage she knows John so well, it's all either right or wrong to her husband, black or white, maybe or perhaps is never considered. 'I've seen them, course I have. Look, John, I knew how you'd react.'

'Well she'd better cut it out and make an end of it. I've told her, she knows now.'

Annie looks sternly at him, 'Don't be too unkind, John.'

'I'm not having it, Annie, I'm not.'

'As you say, John.'

'I mean it, Annie.'

'You always do, John, you always do.'

Chapter Fourteen

2 July, 1914 – Blackburn

John, feeling tired, but pleased with his day's labour, puts his key into the lock of the door of his home in Bromley Street. When he enters, he removes his waterproof coat and puts it on one of the pegs on the hallstand. He runs his hands down the fabric of the coat to ensure that there'll not be any creases in the material that will be visible when he next wears it. This careful attention to detail is the result of many years cutting cloth and creating clothing and garments.

He walks through to the back room, looking forward to having his supper. Although it's July, it's been raining and it's slightly chilly for the time of year. Because of this, John is anticipating a short period of relaxation by sitting next to the small fireplace in the back room and enjoying a pipeful of tobacco. However, as soon as he enters the room he senses that all is not well and not as it should be. Sitting by the table in the corner of the room is a sheepish-looking Herbert. Annie is busy preparing the meal and when she sees her husband she looks at Herbert and speaks in a voice that has a tone of intense irritation and annoyance. 'Well!' she says to her son. 'Will you tell him or shall I?'

'What's all this about, Annie,' says a puzzled John. 'I could tell there were an atmosphere soon as I came in.'

'Well you're not wrong there, John.'

'What is it, Annie, you've got me all worried. What's happened like?'

Annie puts both hands on the table and bows her head. She turns to look at John. 'He's only gone and joined the army. He's going into the Royal Lancs. Can you believe it, without so much as a word to us.'

John sits down and thinks for a moment, he looks at Herbert. 'That were sudden, Bert, no hint of it this morning, how did it happen so quick and what about your job?'

Herbert speaks quietly, 'I were running an errand for Mr Fletcher from work, he told me to get some silk from that shop on the corner of Kings Street, you know the one run by Mrs Leyton?'

Annie's becoming increasingly agitated. 'Get on with it, Bert, I'm not bothered about silk.'

'I were walking by the Town Hall and I bumped into David Unsworth, you know David?'

'Aye,' says John, 'he's Arthur's son, they've got the tobacconist on New Bank Road.'

Annie looks towards the ceiling. 'Oh, give me strength.'

Herbert looks back towards his father. 'He told me that the Royal Lancastrian Regiment were doing some recruiting and they were in the Market Hall. So, I went with him and had a chat, they seemed keen and this sergeant told me to go back to where I worked and if I still wanted to join, to come back and sign on.'

'They didn't ask to see us,' asks John. 'Do they know how old you are?'

'I told 'em I were eighteen.'

Annie throws the dishcloth onto the table. 'Oh this just gets better. You're not eighteen, you're seventeen. John, you'll have to go with him tomorrow and tell them.'

'Tell them what?'

Annie shakes her head again. She can't understand why John hasn't grasped the seriousness of their predicament. 'Tell them he's not old enough and he's not joining till we say he can. Oh, and apologise for wasting their time.'

John thinks for a minute. 'Let's not be too hasty, Annie, there'll be a war, no doubt about it, and they'll need young men. It's a question of duty. They'll take him at seventeen.'

'Oh, I thought you'd take his side of it, you want him killed do you? He's only a boy for heaven's sake.'

'Annie, talk sense, it won't come to that, once the Germans see that we mean business, they'll see what they're up against and ask for peace, he'll be home by Christmas.'

Annie stands in front of John and puts her hands on her hips, presenting a defiant stance. 'So, you know that, do you? You know all about it, where do you get your ideas from, John, from books and people you've met in the pub?' Annie shakes her head and storms out of the back door to take some washing in.

John stands and steadies himself by resting his hand on the mantelpiece. He looks at Herbert. 'What about your tailoring, Bert, your apprenticeship? What did Mr Fletcher say, we had plans you and me, the business, you know?'

'He were all right, he said he'd keep my job open and I could go back when it were all over. I'm sorry I've upset Mam, I didn't mean to.'

'Well, she's worried, all mums worry, it's natural. Still, keep your job open, eh, that's something I suppose.'

'Once Mr Fletcher said it would be all right, I went straight back and had a medical. They had a doctor there, so I went behind a screen, took my shirt off and he looked at me. He walked around me, measured my height, listened to my chest, made me open my mouth and he looked into it. Then he held up a card with some letters on and made me put a hand over one eye, then the other, and told me to call out what I could read. He then said I were fit and were a good height for my age.'

'When will you go?'

'Two weeks on Saturday, we're supposed to meet at the station at two o'clock and they'll give me a pass for the train. We've got to go to Preston to be kitted out, then onto somewhere near Bacup for basic training, I think that's what they said.'

'Right, now look, Bert, you take a bit of a walk, go and tell that girl of yours about your plans and I'll settle your mother down a bit.'

'Oh aye, Liz, I'd forgotten about her, I'll go and see her now, she'll be all right about it.'

Herbert leaves the house and John paces around the room. He considers the tactics he needs to employ to win Annie over. He knows it'll be difficult but not impossible. His thoughts are interrupted by Annie who walks abruptly through the backdoor. She's carrying a basket of washing and slams it down on the table. She picks up a shirt and looks at it. 'As damp as when they went out, no wind.' She looks at John. 'Where is he, where's soldier boy?'

'Now, Annie, don't be like that, he's gone to see Elizabeth, to put her in the picture.'

'Well I don't think we can rely on Liz to talk sense into him, not if we can't. Oh I'm sorry, I mean if I can't, you're obviously on his side.'

John walks out into the yard and looks up at the early evening sky, he looks at a pigeon standing on the privy roof and wonders if it belongs to his brother, George. He sighs heavily and walks slowly back into the house. Annie's folding up the washing and John puts his hand on her shoulder. 'Think on, Annie, he's made his choice, even if we talk him out of it they'll take him one day. He's a credit to us, I'm not ashamed to say that I'm proud of him. I'll be able to hold my head up in the Lion. You know we've been a bit overcrowded since our Emma came along, and our Bert going away will help a bit.

Annie shakes her head. 'Oh well, that's all right then, as long as you feel happier in the pub and we get our front parlour back. That's all that matters to you.'

'Now, Annie, don't get so bothered about it, I'm only trying to make the best of a bad job.'

Annie sits and thinks for a moment. 'It's not as if we haven't lost a child before, but when our Mary died, although she was only five, it were an illness, diphtheria, there was nothing we could do about it, nothing anybody could do. If you like, it were natural. But going off to war to shoot people and get shot at, it's not what we bring children into this world for, it's not right.'

'But it's life, Annie, it's the way it is.'

Two weeks later John, wearing his best suit, stands in front of the hall mirror and selects the hat that he's to wear. He decides on the bowler. 'Hurry up, Bert,' he shouts, 'we said we'd walk into town and we need to give ourselves time, don't want to be rushing.'

Annie walks through from the back room, picks up a clothes-brush from the hall stand and brushes John's back and shoulders. 'Well, you look very smart, John, well turned out, anybody would think that you were off promenading round the Corporation Park on a Sunday afternoon.'

John turns and faces his wife, he holds her by placing his hands on her upper arms. 'I'm making the best of it, Annie, it's going to happen, we're agreed on it. I want him to remember me and feel proud like.'

The couple are disturbed by Herbert coming down the stairs. He walks into the hallway. He's also wearing his best suit. 'Here we are then,' he says. 'I'm ready to go.'

John puts his hand on Herbert's shoulder. 'There, Mother,' he says, 'don't we look a picture?'

Annie smiles. 'Course you do, well you would, being in the tailoring business. I just wish I was putting on my bonnet and we were going for a nice walk in the park.'

'There'll be plenty of walks in the park to come, Annie.'

Annie picks up a small suitcase. 'I didn't know what to pack, don't know what they'll provide for you, so there's some toilet things and a change of underwear. Oh, and I've put a short-sleeved pullover in, just in case. I've put a cheese butty in there and a piece of potato pie but you'll have to eat it cold. Make sure they look after your suit, Bert.'

John opens the front door, and Annie and Herbert follow

him out of the house. John walks down the street and stops, and turns around to see Herbert embracing his mother. Annie straightens Herbert's cap and kisses him on the cheek. She then turns and without looking back goes into the house.

Father and son walk down the street and turn left heading towards the town centre. The closer they get to the centre, the busier it gets. When they pass people they know, John holds the brim of his hat and nods slightly. After they pass the Town Hall they enter the large square where the weekly market is taking place. John stops by a fruit and veg stall, carefully selects a large red apple, pays what he owes to the stallholder and hands it to Herbert. 'Put that in your pocket, son, for later. It'll keep you going till you have your supper.'

As they walk through an area known as the Boulevard, trams and buses are stopping by and leaving their designated pick-up and drop-off points. It's a busy place and a scene of vibrancy and feverish activity. In most cases the coaches and vehicles are packed with passengers, many of them making for the weekly market. Some men are talking together while sitting on the benches along the broad front where the trams stop. Having spent their free time in one of the numerous public houses, they're waiting for their wives who will no doubt return from shopping proclaiming that they have spent very wisely and that there were many bargains to be had.

John and Herbert carefully negotiate their way through the hustle and bustle of the Boulevard. As they approach the railway station they become aware of many other people who are undertaking the same journey. They enter the busy booking hall and amid the commotion of the confined space, they're immediately organised, with the help of soldiers, into some form of queuing system. A corporal walks down the line asking who's joining and when the new recruit is identified he's pulled out of the queue and directed to another row near to the gate that leads to the platforms. Another corporal takes the names of the young men and ticks some boxes on an official-looking document attached to a board that he's holding.

The corporal who's taking the names stops by John and Herbert. 'Name!' he shouts.

'Herbert,' replies Bert.

The corporal sighs. 'Name?'

'Oh sorry, Herbert Williams.'

The corporal scans and checks his list. 'H.E. Williams, is that right?' A sergeant approaches. Herbert recognises him as being the soldier who he talked to when he enquired about joining up.

'Hello,' he says, 'do you remember me? We had a chat about joining.'

The sergeant glares at Herbert; the friendly, warm and smiling soldier now looks very severe and very different. 'A chat? What's your name?'

'Herbert, but you can call me Bert.'

'He's called Williams, Sarge,' says the corporal.

'*Herbert, you can call me Bert*, you're Williams, Private Williams now!' yells the sergeant.

'Right, Sarge,' replies the apprehensive young man.

'I'm Sergeant, not Sarge, I'll tell you when you can call me Sarge. Now get in line with those other buggers by the gate.'

Herbert obeys his first order and leaves John, to line up by the gate. A stoutly built soldier wearing a red sash, that establishes his rank as a sergeant major, marches towards the group. He starts to shout instructions and orders. Although his voice is loud, because of the echoes and the sound of many voices John can't quite hear what the sergeant's saying. Then some soldiers pull open the gates and the recruits are encouraged with some force to go through the opening up to the platforms. For a moment John loses sight of Herbert, then just for a brief instant he sees his son's anxious face as he looks round to catch a sight of his father. Herbert raises his hand and John does the same, then his son has gone from view and disappears in the crowd. 'Bye son, take care of yourself,' he says to himself.

It's a relief to enter the open busy space of the Boulevard after the confined and claustrophobic atmosphere of the booking hall. John takes a deep breath of air and takes out his pipe, fills it, strikes a match and places it over the bowl containing the tobacco. He sucks the air through the stem of the pipe to ignite the tobacco. He thinks for a moment and quietly says, 'We've lost our boy, Annie, when he comes back he'll be a man.'

Chapter Fifteen

2 August, 1932 – Poperinge

John sits alone on his selected and favourite chair in the corner of the reception room. He sips the tea that one of the maids has provided for him and studies a newspaper that's written in the Dutch language. He tries to decipher the information and attempts to pronounce some of the words which he partly recognises. His concentration is hampered by a dull thumping sound that appears to come from the wall at the back of the room. Madame De Vos enters the room carrying a large ceramic jug and proceeds to water some of the plants.

'Look at this, Mr Williams, I watered these only the other day and they are dry already, I cannot keep up with it.'

'Aye,' replies John 'it's warm all right, nice for some though, you need to keep an eye on plants and flowers like. Not that I know much about it, that's my Annie's department, cloth, now that's my thing.'

Again, the dull thumping sound takes his attention. 'Are you having some work done, Madame De Vos?'

'No, why do you ask?'

'Well, somebody's hammering and hitting something from what I can hear.'

Madame De Vos listens and very quickly recognises the sound. 'Ah' she explains, 'that is my son Hugo, he is playing with his football. He kicks it against the wall. I'm sorry, Mr Williams, I tell him not to do this when guests are in the hotel. I shall instruct him to stop immediately.'

'No, Madame De Vos, I'm not complaining, I just wanted to know what it were. Let the lad be, he's enjoying himself.'

'Are you sure about this?'

'Quite sure. I've got four boys, well, had, and I know what they're like, need exercising, they're like puppies.'

John spots Herbert walking through the foyer. 'Bertie,' he shouts, 'young Hugo is playing football in the back garden and he might let you have a kick-about if you ask him.'

John looks at Madame De Vos. 'Would that be all right with you?'

'That is fine by me,' she says and smiles at Herbert. 'Oh, Bertie, would you remind my very enthusiastic son not to kick the football into my flowerbeds, please?'

Herbert nods, smiles and leaves the foyer by the back door. He walks down the steps to the garden, removes his coat and calls to Hugo. Hugo's pleased to see him, he kicks the heavy leather football to his new friend and the game begins. In turn they kick the football against the wall. Herbert uses all his strength to put in an aggressive shot and Hugo sticks out his foot to stop the ball. It spins off his leg and speeds towards the flowerbeds. Fortunately, Peter Lehmann has entered the garden. He immediately spots the danger of possible damage to Madame De Vos's priceless blooms and makes a save that any goalkeeper would be proud of. He picks himself up and kicks the ball back to the boys.

'Thank you,' says Hugo.

'You are very welcome,' Peter replies. 'Would you mind if I join you? I enjoy kicking the football.'

The boys readily agree and Peter removes his jacket. 'I have an idea. I shall stay back and protect the flowers, just in case.'

The boys laugh and quickly become involved in their game again. After a time, Peter and the boys begin to feel the heat of the morning sun and seek some shade by retreating to a bench located under a tree. Once they've started to recover and feel more comfortable, they talk. Herbert asks Peter, 'Do you follow a team when you're at home?'

'Yes I sometimes go to watch Eintracht Frankfurt, have you heard of them?'

'No,' replies Herbert.

'I have,' says Hugo.

'I am not surprised that you have not heard of my team, Herbert, but I know of your team, Blackburn Rovers.'

Herbert's surprised. 'You know about the Rovers?'

'Yes, of course, they won the Football Association Cup three or four years ago.'

Herbert eagerly engages in the conversation and proudly says, 'We beat Huddersfield three-one, I was there, with my dad and Uncle George.'

Peter turns to Hugo. 'And what about you, Hugo, do you have a team?'

'Not really, but I like to play.'

'That is better I think. And when you leave school, what will you do for a career, for a job? A professional footballer, perhaps?'

He shakes his head, his face turns red and he smiles. 'No, not good enough for that. My grandmother would like me to work here at the hotel.'

Peter nods. 'And your mother, she would want this also.'

'Not so much, she says that it is up to me and I don't know yet.'

Herbert's eager to talk of his ambitions. 'I'm doing an engineering apprenticeship and I'm going to join the RAF when I'm old enough.'

'Ah,' says Peter, 'the Royal Air Force, you want to fly?'

'If I can, yes.'

'Well,' says Peter, 'if you want it badly enough, you are halfway there.'

Herbert is throwing the ball in the air and catching it, he chuckles. 'Well, I'd like a car like yours, but I don't think that I am halfway to owning one.'

'Yes,' says Peter, 'it is a…how would you say it, a desirable motorcar.'

'It is a Daimler,' says Hugo. 'That is a nice car.'

'Yes, a Daimler Benz. I must say that I'm not halfway to owning a car like that, it belongs to my father.'

The two boys and Peter watch as Emma walks into the garden. She slowly strolls over to them. When she approaches them, she stops and puts on her cream-coloured straw hat. Peter smiles at her. 'Good morning, Emma, how are you this lovely morning?' Emma is amused by Peter's very over-polite manner, she knows that it's something of a performance.

She nods courteously to him and returns Peter's smile. 'Morning, Peter, you're right of course, it's a lovely day again.'

'Are you well?' he asks.

'Yes, I'm very well, thank you.'

Peter coughs a little and clears his throat, aware that Hugo and Herbert are listening intently to their conversation. 'Are you well enough to take a walk later?'

'Yes, but no,' replies Emma. She glares at her brother and her fixed stare is designed to instruct Herbert to go away and to take Hugo with him. She frowns again, Herbert shrugs and doesn't move. Emma tips her head towards the door to the hotel, Herbert smiles back at her and still doesn't move.

Emma feels uneasy and looks around. She moves closer to Peter and speaks quietly, 'Shall we move to a quieter part of the garden, Peter?'

Herbert stands as if to follow them, Emma turns and raises a finger, she doesn't need to say anything, Herbert sits back down, he pushes his elbow into Hugo's side and both boys snigger.

As Emma and Peter walk slowly to a distance where she feels that they can't be overheard, Emma says, 'Mother had words with me last night. My father is not happy about us seeing each other.'

'I'm sorry, Emma, I have put you in a difficult position.'

'It's not your fault, it's the way he is.'

'I understand.'

Emma looks at him, 'Do you? Do you really understand or are you just being polite?'

Peter looks down at the array of brightly-coloured flowers. After a moment's pause he admits, 'If I'm really honest then no I don't fully understand, I have to say that.' Peter thinks that enough has been said about their situation, after all, little can be done to change things, but he's eager to continue his relationship with Emma and to him it's important. 'I could take a walk back to the park where we met yesterday.'

Emma quickly identifies Peter's plan. 'I could also take a walk to the same park and we might meet.'

'Bump into one another, as you might say, by chance.'

'Yes, it would be coincidence,' says Emma.

'Exactly, a coincidence.'

'Then I look forward to our unplanned meeting.'

Peter studies his wristwatch for a moment. 'In about half an hour, should we say?'

'Half an hour it is,' says Emma as she smiles at Peter. She bids him farewell with a slight wave of her hand and turns to walk to the door to the hotel. Herbert and Hugo continue to play their football game and Herbert grins at his sister as she passes. Emma looks at him and sticks out her tongue and immediately wishes that she hadn't because her brother laughs back at her.

Chapter Sixteen

2 August, 1932 – Poperinge

Later in the morning, Mary and Henry are sat by themselves, enjoying the relaxing and tranquil atmosphere of the reception room. They don't speak, which is unusual for Mary, but she does recognise that it's a moment for quiet contemplation and Henry is looking rested and contented. They slowly sip some tea that has been provided for them. Their peace is interrupted by Madame De Vos who enters the room and begins to do some dusting and rearranging some of the chairs. She doesn't mean to disturb her guests but her over-enthusiastic manner and the way in which she goes about her chores is unwittingly disruptive and distracting. Henry sits up in his chair. 'Madam De Vos, can I ask you something?'

Madame De Vos continues to rigorously rub the cloth over one of the table tops. 'Of course,' she says. 'As long as it is not too personal.' She laughs and sits down opposite the couple.

Henry takes her seriously and clears his throat by making a small cough. 'No, hopefully not. When Mr Williams and I were talking to your mother…'

Madame De Vos corrects him on a detail. 'Mother-in-law.'

'Sorry,' he says, 'that's right, your mother-in-law.'

'What is it, what do you wish to ask, Mr Reynolds?'

'It seems that she, that's your mother-in-law, is not called Madam, she's, how do you say it, mever… mivrou…?'

'Mevrouw,' says Madame De Vos helpfully.

'Aye, that's right, but you're called madam?'

Madame De Vos smiles. 'I see, it is madame and not madam, it is confusing, I can see. Well, I will try to explain, it is because I come from a town in Southern Belgium called Mons. There we speak a form of the French language and that is why I keep the title of madame, it is used where I come from. My mother-in-law was born in Ypres and her language is Dutch or can also be known as Flemish. Mevrouw is the title that a woman uses in this region of Belgium. My mother-in-law's family originally came from the Netherlands and that is also why she wishes to be known as mevrouw. Of course many of my guests are from Britain and they refer to me as madam but I am really Madame De Vos, because of my marriage you see?'

'I see,' says Henry, still obviously confused. 'Not being too personal again like, but the thing is, back at home, madam is what, well you know, is an owner of one of those places with those women. If you're a madame then you're not one of those.'

'You mean a place of ill-repute,' says Madame De Vos as she laughs, 'a brothel, where ladies of the night go about their business.'

'Aye,' says an increasingly embarrassed Henry, 'that's what I mean, that's what I were getting at.'

'You're right and we don't want any confusion, although madam is a term we use for a landlady and the owner of a business. But I can assure you we do not have any ladies of that sort in this hotel. In the war it may have been different.'

Mary becomes interested in what's being discussed and is intrigued to discover something of the family history. 'How did you come to be running the hotel, it's got your name over the door, did you buy it?'

Henry feels that his wife has overstepped the mark and that her question is too intrusive. He's embarrassed, although he would like to know the answer. 'Mary!' he says. 'Don't, it's too personal, it's Madame De Vos's business.'

Madame De Vos puts up her hands and laughs. 'No, it is interesting, you will find it interesting I think.' She sits back and begins to tell her story. 'In 1911 I was Emma Lombaerts and I came to work for the De Vos family here in their hotel. We had family living in the area. In 1912 Mevrouw De Vos's husband died and the same year I became attached, as you might say, to her son who was called Vincent.'

'What was he like?' asks Mary.

'Oh, what was he like?' says Madame De Vos thoughtfully. 'Nice, nice enough for me to marry him, handsome, well-behaved and a good man.'

Henry asks, 'What was it like here in the war?'

'It was too dangerous to stay. We were evacuated and went to stay with relatives in Holland. During the war this house was used by the British Army as a sort of headquarters and officers would sleep here. The Germans would shell Poperinge from time to time and we were surprised that there was only a small amount of damage to the house. We repaired the building, opened it up and here we are.'

If you don't mind me saying,' asks Henry 'it doesn't bother you having these German people staying here?'

'No, why should it?'

'Well, your husband, didn't he die in the war? That's what I were told.'

'No, my Vincent died at the end of January in 1919.'

Henry thinks for a moment. 'Were it as a result of the war, an injury like?'

'No, he didn't fight, it was Spanish Flu; a lot of people died of the flu then.'

'Oh then we heard wrong,' says Mary. 'When was Hugo born?'

'In July 1919.'

'So your husband didn't see his son?' says Mary

'No, and it is still a great sadness to me and he would have been so proud.'

'Well, what about your brother?' asks Henry. 'He were killed in't war, weren't he?'

'Bernard, yes, he was killed at Verdun in 1916. We weren't that close, never saw each other for years. Of course when I heard that he was dead, I wished that I, we, had tried harder to see each other. I do have another brother and a sister living in Liege.'

'So you don't mind Germans then?' says Henry

'People are people, Germans, French, English; it's business.'

Mary is now fully engrossed in the story. 'Still, it must have pleased your mother-in-law for you to run the hotel, rather than it not being run like?'

'She is pleased that I have run the hotel but she will be happier when Hugo is in charge.'

Mary chuckles. 'And Madame is removed from the sign.'

Henry is further embarrassed. 'Mary, no need for that,' he says sternly.

Mary glares back at her husband. She's somewhat taken aback by Henry's abrupt manner because he's had the audacity to correct her and it's a side of him that Mary is unfamiliar with. Madame De Vos smiles. 'No, Mrs Reynolds is right. I like you, Mrs Reynolds, you speak your mind.'

'It's a Lancashire trait,' answers Mary.

'Aye, and being nosy,' adds Henry.

Mary gives him a stern look. 'No, Henry, being curious and interested you mean. Folk from Lancashire are curious; it's Yorkshire folk that are nosy.'

Madame De Vos stands up, laughs and shakes her head. 'Now I'm confused, it sounds very complicated.'

'That's what Mr Williams said about Belgium,' says Henry.

Madame De Vos continues to laugh. 'And Mr Williams is right. Now you must excuse me, there is work to be done, there is always work that needs seeing to.' Madame De Vos leaves the room.

Mary looks at her husband and shakes her head, 'It's business, you heard what she said, can you believe it?'

Henry sits further back in his chair, rubs his chin and breathes out, making a slight, slow whistling sound. 'Well I'm surprised, I can't say I'm not.' He stands up and takes out his pipe.

Mary shakes her head with some purpose and he puts the pipe back into his pocket and looks out of the window. 'You know, Mary, I don't mind it here but I'll be glad to get home, it's all very confusing.'

Mary walks over to him and also looks out of the window. She puts her arm on his shoulder and then slowly rubs his back. 'And you can report back to that committee of yours in the Red Lion.'

He looks at his wife. 'Aye, and have pint of Thwaites' best bitter, I'm really looking forward to that, Mary.'

John and Annie sit in the garden at the back of the hotel watching Herbert and Hugo as they play football. 'We've been very fortunate on this visit, Annie, with the weather. A bit too warm at times but we can't complain.'

Annie agrees and stands up, slowly walks around the flowerbeds and views the well-designed and skilfully cultivated floral displays. She follows a path through some bushes and past a line of small trees. She waves to John to tell him to join her and he reluctantly agrees. 'Are you going to talk about plants and that, Annie, you know I can take it or leave it, it's more of interest to you.'

'I just thought that we should have a chat, John, and it's not about flowers.'

'What about then?'

'Now don't get all upset and in a state before I start.'

'I don't like the sound of this, Annie, I think I know where this is leading.'

'Right,' she says, 'it's about this business with our Emma and Peter Lehmann…'

'I don't want to talk about it, Annie.'

'I don't want you to talk about it, I want you to listen,' she says firmly. 'We've got to deal with it.'

John doesn't respond, puts his hands into his trouser pockets and stares at the ground. 'I'm not saying that anything might come of it,' she says. 'In fact, like you, I hope it won't, but it might.'

Annie guides her husband over to a small bench located under a tree. He sits down and continues to look at the ground, purposely avoiding any eye contact. 'In the end,' she says, 'would it be so terrible? After all, he's good-looking, polite, well-educated and has good prospects.'

'And he's a German,' mumbles John.

'Yes, he's a German, is it so bad?'

John's shocked and he stares at her. 'Well, you've changed your tune, Annie, I didn't think you'd any time for Germans but you've been fraternising with 'em behind my back, talking to the enemy.'

'Oh, I'm sorry, John, I didn't know that we were still at war with Germany. I seem to remember that the Germans surrendered in 1918, but I must have got that wrong.'

John stands up. He's becoming more and more angry. 'It were 1919 actually, it were the armistice in eighteen. Anyway, 1919 or 1918, they'll always be the enemy, they'll never change and given half a chance they'll be back at it again.'

Annie stands to face him. 'Oh, I thought that when Mevrouw De Vos suggested that, you dismissed it as being rubbish, they wouldn't dare you said.'

John thinks for a moment, realises he's contradicted himself, and having gathered his thoughts he replies, 'I said that to calm her down because she were in a state and I didn't want to see her making herself all poorly. If I'm honest, Annie, I still don't really think that there'll be another war.'

'Well, what on earth are we arguing about, John?'

'I don't want our Emma to betray our Bert's memory. If it happens and she goes to live in Germany then she'll have let us and our Bert down, no doubt about it.'

Annie sighs and looks up to the sky. The sun's rays filter through the flickering leaves and she feels the warmth on her face. 'Well, John,' she says, 'you might just have to decide between our Emma and our Bert.' Annie turns and slowly walks back towards the hotel.

Chapter Seventeen

12 January, 1918 – Blackburn

Henry carefully carries three tankards containing pints of ale towards the table by a window in the Red Lion public house. He cautiously manoeuvres and navigates his way through the packed public bar. Henry is charged with ensuring that any spillage is kept to an absolute minimum and he knows that upon delivery, the three containers will be thoroughly examined. The atmosphere is heavy with smoke because the majority of patrons are either enjoying a pipe or smoking cigarettes. The numerous discussions that are taking place compete with one another, resulting in a steady increase in volume levels as the conversationalists struggle to be heard. Henry successfully completes his task and places the ale on the table. He hands one tankard to John, another to John's older brother George, and sits in the vacant chair that his two companions have saved for him. Drinking with the three men are James Turner and Frank Clayton, friends and companions of many years standing and members of the unofficial Red Lion debating society.

'Well done, Henry,' remarks John, 'your drayman skills came to the fore with that undertaking; ale safely delivered and little in the way of wastage.'

Henry looks back towards the bar and leans forward to speak to John and George to ensure his conversation is heard but not overheard. 'Can you see that bloke over at the bar talking to Jim?'

John looks over and sees a man who he judges to be in his

early thirties. He's talking to Jim Meadows, the landlord of the Lion. Jim starts to look around. It's clear that the unidentified man is seeking somebody and the landlord appears to be assisting him in his search. 'Aye,' says John, 'he looks as if he's looking for someone.'

'It's you, John,' replies Henry. 'He's looking for you'.

'Me? How do you know that?'

'I heard. I heard him ask for John Williams.'

'Might be another John Williams,' says George. 'Common enough name. There's three that I know of, two of them come in here from time to time, although I think one of them might be dead now.'

'No,' answers Henry, 'he knew your address, John. Bromley Street he said, he'd been there and Annie must have sent him here like.'

George, who's unmistakably John's brother being similar in features, build and manner, looks confused and asks Henry, 'Why didn't you tell him and point him in John's direction?'

'I didn't like to, 'answers Henry, 'he might have been one of those.'

'One of those?' asks John. 'One of those what?'

'Well, you know, wages and money investigators,' replies Henry, 'you know, with all the stuff John does on the side like.'

'You mean a taxman,' says James.

'No, no,' says John, 'I pay my way, what I owe, no concerns there.'

'Well I did wonder at times,' says Henry.

'Now look, Henry,' says John, 'I've never been on the fiddle and…'

John's attention is distracted when Jim approaches him. 'Aye up, Jim, what is it?' asks John. 'Who have you been talking to?'

'There's this bloke at the bar asking for you and I said I'd look for you.'

'Well you know where we always sit, Jim,' says John. 'All this cloak and dagger stuff, send him over, let's see what this is all about shall we?'

'Right,' replies Jim. 'didn't know if you wanted to be disturbed, you know, Sunday day of rest and all, he might be selling something.'

'Or investigating something,' adds Henry.

Jim beckons over to the stranger and having picked his way through the crowd he arrives at John's table. He stands before the group of men and offers John his hand. While staying seated, John shakes the stranger's hand. 'Mr Williams,' says the visitor.

John looks the stranger up and down. He's suspicious and cautious. 'Aye,' he says, 'that's me, and you are?'

'Michael Davies. I served with your son, Bert.'

John's expression changes from being guarded to a welcoming smile. 'Of course, you must be Sergeant Davies, Bert mentioned you, so that's it,' John looks around and asks Henry to pull up a chair for his visitor. 'Now, please sit down, let me get you a drink.' He looks at Henry. 'Will you oblige us and get the sergeant a drink of something he'd like please?'

Henry stands, places a chair next to the table and asks Sergeant Davies what he'd like to drink. 'I'll have half a bitter please,' says the sergeant. 'Thwaites, isn't it?'

'A half?' says John. 'That won't do at all, we don't do halfs here. Get the man a pint, Henry, he looks like a chap who can see off a pint if I know anything about it. Once he's tasted Jim's ale, he'll regret not having a pint.'

Sergeant Davies starts to argue and then thinks better of it. He sits opposite John and waits for his drink to be delivered to him. Henry anxiously looks for a possible route to the bar, braces himself and sets off to complete his mission.

'Now,' says John, 'tell me about how it were with our Bert, if you'd be so kind, I take it that's why you're here, I'm sorry about all this cloak and dagger stuff but you're not in uniform, so Henry did wonder, he's got quite an imagination my brother-in-law.'

'That's right, Mr Williams, I would have preferred to wear my uniform, I get some of those funny looks with people thinking that I'm in a reserved occupation or, at worst, a conschy, and I don't feel that comfortable. I'm waiting to go to the depot to pick up some new kit and I'll do that next week. I've come to tell you as much as I can about your son, Mr Williams; we both agreed to visit the families if we survived and here I am.'

'Are you on leave, Sergeant?' asks George.

'I were wounded the same day that Bert was injured, shrapnel in the thigh, that's what I had. I were convalescing at a hospital in Somerset and when I were discharged, I took the opportunity to come home to Accrington and then to visit you.'

'You'll be going back then,' asks John. 'Are you all right now? I noticed a bit of a limp.'

'When I'm over it and fit enough I'll go back. They say it'll always be a problem, later on things will get worse with age, it's always the same.'

Henry returns with the ale and the sergeant takes a long drink, smacks his lips and puts the tankard on the table. A smug-looking John looks at the reduced level of beer in the glass. 'There you are, a half pint wouldn't have suited a chap like you, you can always rely on Thwaites. Not so sure about other ales around these parts, not as easy on the palate in my opinion.'

Sergeant Davies gives a detailed account of the final hours before the battle and up to when Bert was fatally injured. 'He were taken to the casualty station at Dozinghem, I didn't even know whether he'd survived, a stretcher bearer had told me that they found him in a shell-hole and he were barely alive. I were told that he lived for two days and all that they could do for him was give him morphine to help with the pain.'

'So he didn't suffer too much then?' asks John.

'I'm sure he didn't, Mr Williams, he were barely conscious and they managed his pain well enough, that's what I were told and I believe it.'

'You wouldn't just say that, would you, to make me feel better like?'

'No, I wouldn't do that, I'm here to tell you as it was.' He takes another long drink of his beer. 'One thing I need to tell you. I were told that with his head injury and the loss of blood, if he'd survived, well, he wouldn't have been the same Bert that you remember, not by a long way.'

John sighs deeply. 'I needed to hear that, Sergeant, I'd always wondered, well you would wouldn't you?'

The rest of the conversation referred to happier times when the two companions were on leave in France. Sergeant Davies recalls and tells of enjoyable and amusing tales involving drinking sessions and relationships with local girls.

John leans closer to Sergeant Davies. 'He were popular with the ladies our Bert. He were seeing a young lady here, Elizabeth were her name, but I always wondered if he…were, or did, you know, I'd like to think he did.'

The sergeant smiles back at him. 'No problems in that direction, Mr Williams, rest assured.'

George looks at the well-drained empty tankards. 'Just look at that sorry sight and it's my responsibility on this occasion I think, give me a hand will you Henry?' He stands and gestures to James and Frank to accompany them. As they walk towards the bar George says, 'Thought we'd give them a bit of time on their own, in case, well, the sergeant wants to be a bit more open like, we'll linger o'er yon for a bit.'

John watches the men depart and leans over towards the sergeant. 'Now we're on our own there's a few things I'd like to know, things our Bert didn't or wouldn't talk about.'

The sergeant sighs deeply. 'Earlier I told you that I'd be going back. I need to, not because they'll make me, but because I want to.'

'Well that's the type of chap you are,' says John, 'it's to your credit.'

Sergeant Davies stares directly at John. 'Do you know how many we lost at Passchendaele, how many casualties there were?'

'I know it were a lot, thousands I reckon.'

'Well, they're still counting but it's going to be two or three hundred thousand, killed and wounded.'

'My God, that many?'

'We've got to win this war, beat 'em and finish them off, otherwise, what will it all have been for, losing boys like your Bert. I can't even think of losing. I'm not bragging but it's experience that'll count now. Blokes like me appreciate what it's all about, been there, had a go, know the tricks and how to cope.'

'I suppose you're right, Sergeant,' utters John, 'when you put it that way, but we won't lose will we?'

'I hope not, Mr Williams, I really hope not, to have gone through this and not win, it doesn't bear thinking about, but it does bother me at times.' He looks at John and feels he might have been a little negative. 'Mind you, now the Americans, the Doughboys, are in with us, it should help a lot.'

The gloom seems to lift from John, he sits more upright and lifts up his shoulders. 'Aye, I thought that, make a real difference like.'

'When I heard that the Russians had packed it in, I were really concerned, we knew it might happen and we'd heard all these stories about, well, almost a million blokes being transferred from the east. These blokes will be battle-hardened and ready. There's no doubt it'll give them an edge and they'll start making more attacks and gain ground. When the Doughboys came in, their first blokes arrived in June. They were raw, knew sod all, like us in fourteen. Course they thought they knew it all, made some daft mistakes at first, but they learned and they learned quick. This year they'll really start to make a big difference, they'll pour in men, supplies, arms and equipment, never-ending. Thing is, it's not just about at the front, things aren't that good here with rationing and shortages and the like, but in Germany it's really bad, they're starving.'

'Serves, 'em right.' says John. 'How do you know about all this in Germany?'

'Prisoners, blokes we captured, they were in a poor state, most of them were glad it were over for them. Couldn't believe the supplies that we had and they told us about how things were back in Germany. Last winter it was so bad that when a severe frost killed the potato crops, a lot of the people had to survive on eating turnips. They called it the Turnip Winter. These prisoners we had even liked our tea and I thought that things must be really dire for them. Anyway that's their lookout, but for the sake of all our chaps I hope it finishes soon, but you know, Mr Williams, we never thought we'd lose as many as we have. There's not a lot of the original expeditionary force that went out in fourteen left, I were one and so were your Bert.'

A short moment's pause follows while John thinks of what the sergeant has told him. 'All those sons,' he says. Then after another short period of silence John asks, 'You knew a bit about our Bert's end and his injuries, how were it that you were able to find out?'

The two men are interrupted by Henry who puts two full tankards of ale on the table. John looks around, 'Where is everyone?'

'O'er yon, having a talk by the bar, we thought it were the right thing to do, then I thought you'd be dying of thirst.'

John nods in approval, picks up his tankard and when the sergeant does the same, they push their glasses together. 'Here's to you, Sergeant, thank you for coming to see us. Now, you were going to tell me more about Bert. Were you in the same hospital at the same time like?'

'It were a dark and miserable morning but at least by the time we went over the top the rain had stopped. In all the time that I'd served at the front, I'd never seen so much mud, not even at the Somme. I made sure all the lads had gone, then I went. A few shell-holes in and I saw Bert and I thought that he were a goner, there was nothing I could do for him, I looked around but couldn't see any stretcher bearers, so I went on.'

'Well you had to didn't you?'

'Aye, no choice.' The sergeant takes a drink of his ale. 'I didn't get much further before I were hit, a bloody sharp, agonising, burning pain at the top of my leg. I fell into a pit and lay still for a minute, that's me buggered I thought, if I'm lucky it's a Blighty one, bit of time at home. I put my hand onto my thigh and felt a damn big hole full of blood. Then I thought, bugger Blighty I might go on and lose the blooming leg and I'll be a real cripple with a wound this high up. A bloke slid into the hole by me, put a hand on my shoulder and I looked him in't face. I saw from his collar that he were a padre or something like and he were holding a small book. That's a bible I thought and I said, *give us a chance reverend, I'm not done yet.*'

'Last rites like,' says John.

'Aye, it were hell out there, the rat-a-tat of the machine guns, grenades and mortars going off all over the place, bodies, blood everywhere and this padre's going round to see if we're all right. It were nearly enough for me to turn religious. Then a medical orderly slipped in on the other side of me, said that I'd run out of blood at this rate and he put a strap around the leg above the wound and pulled it tight, that stopped the bleeding, it saved my life I think. Well, I looked at the padre and then at the orderly and said to myself, *I'm well looked after here, one to help me into the next world and another bloke to try to keep me in this one.* I thought I'd died, I were confused and not with it. Anyway, I came more to my senses and told the orderly to see to Bert. He went off, the padre put a Woodbine in my mouth, lit it and said, *bless you.* Then I must have passed out because I don't remember anything else.'

'They must have taken you to hospital?'

'Casualty station at Dozinghem, same place they took Bert, I woke up in bed a day later. I pulled back the covers to check that the leg was still there. Two doctors came to see me and said if it were all right by me, they thought they'd take the leg off. I said that I'd like to leave this world with the same number of things that I were born with. They told me they'd take out any shrapnel they could find, stop the bleeding as best that they could, stitch it up and see how it goes.'

'And hope for the best like!'

'I said that were good enough for me. I still didn't trust them mind but I needn't have worried, they did right by me. A lot of blokes were dying because there weren't enough staff and drugs. I were concerned that Bert had been neglected and might have been saved. What I said earlier was true, nothing could have been done for him, I know that because I talked to the doctors, nurses and the rest, I made it my business.'

'I'm thankful for that, it puts my mind at rest.'

'All I can say, Mr Williams, is that he passed away in a better place than many of his mates.'

'I've heard all these stories about the mud and the wet, must have been bloody awful.'

'It were bad, but for me the worst of it was the cold. Last January the ground were frozen solid, it were so bad that we couldn't dig any graves. At least the bodies were preserved and weren't rotting like.' Sergeant Davies suddenly remembers who he's speaking to and feels that he's being very insensitive. 'Oh, I'm sorry, Mr Williams, you don't want to hear this. I'm getting a bit carried away.'

'No, Sergeant, I want to know what it were really like, I need to know. You see, our Bert changed a lot. We tried not to think about it but every time he came home he were just a bit different, more withdrawn, not so cheerful and not himself.'

'When shells hit the soft mud they went in deep and we got splattered. But when the ground was hard the bits of the shell flew right over our trenches. I even heard of a bloke getting killed nearly a quarter of a mile away from the blast.'

'Bloody hell.'

'You said Bert changed, Mr Williams, and we all changed. At the front we were always the same. We put on a bit of a face, more joking about, but inside it were different.'

'I always thought that if he came through it and came home, after a bit we'd have our old Bert back same as before he went.'

'You might be right, Mr Williams, but I know that as long

as I live what I've seen and what I've felt will never leave me.'

John and the sergeant are joined by the other men and the drinking continues. All subjects are covered, from union rights to the suffragette movement, which is a hot topic because women were now employed in work areas where, historically, men had dominated. The only awkward moment is when discussing football; the sergeant admits to favouring Burnley Football Club over the Rovers. The theme of the conversation returns to the war and Sergeant Davies provides a detailed account of past manoeuvres and campaigns. Henry's eager to ask the sergeant, 'Why do you call the Germans the Bosche, I've always wondered?'

John steps in to provide an answer. 'If I may interject, Sergeant Davies.' He draws on his pipe. 'Now, Henry, that's quite a puzzle. The thing is, it were the French who came up with it, *tete de bosche,* it means a stubborn or an obstinate person.' The debating society is clearly impressed and John sits back and looks very smug. He turns to Sergeant Davies and smiles. 'That's it, isn't it, Sergeant?'

Sergeant Davies shakes his head. 'Well, if you say so, Mr Williams, I'd never thought of it before, most of the time we called them the Hun. I knew it were the French who mainly used Bosche. Mind you, Bert always said that you were a clever chap, and that you read a lot.'

'Thing is, I didn't have much in the way of formal schooling but there's nothing to stop a chap picking up a book or a newspaper and adding to what he knows,' replies John. He finishes his pint and looks at his companions' empty tankards and as if to announce that the session is now closed, deliberately brings his own tankard rather heavily down onto the table. 'Now, Sergeant,' he says, 'you can do me the honour of coming back to my house and having a bite to eat with us. It's pork today and my Annie cooks a nice bit of meat, she knows how to handle a roast. The meat is of very good quality, we get it from a cousin of ours who's got a farm out Samlesbury way.'

Sergeant Davies begins to offer his excuses, feeling that he's turned up uninvited and it would be an imposition. 'I'm not sure that your wife will be too pleased to have an extra mouth to feed.'

John looks directly at the sergeant with a serious expression on his face. 'Now look, Michael, if you don't mind me calling you by your Christian name?'

'Please do,' replies Michael.

'Are you a married man?'

'I were,' replies Michael. 'She went off with someone a number of years ago. She weren't that keen on army life. But she weren't much of a wife to me in any case.'

'Well, it's like this, you see. If I go back and my Annie asks me, *where's that young man got to*? Well, I say, *he came over here, all the way from Accrington and I didn't ask him to have his dinner with us*, well I don't know how she'd be. I know she'd make the rest of my Sunday afternoon most unpleasant. We have to be a bit careful with Annie at the moment, we've just heard that she's in the family way, she's expecting.'

'Congratulations, Mr Williams, that's good news I suppose.'

'Oh, best news ever, Michael, thing is if it's a boy we're going to call him Herbert Edward after his brother, we're agreed on it and it's the right thing to do. Now leaving that aside we don't want to keep the lady of the house waiting.'

The sergeant accepts John's invitation and the men walk to the doorway of the now half-empty public bar. John holds Michael by his arm. 'Don't worry about reduced rations, as soon as you told my wife who you were and why you've come here, she'd have got out some extra spuds and vegetables and there's always enough meat. You've no say in it, that's the way it is and we'll have you on that last tram home.'

'We're here, Mother,' says John as the two men enter the house. They take off their coats, hang them up and put their caps on the hooks above the mirror of the hallstand. They walk through to the back room. 'Here we are, Annie. I said you'd be none too pleased if I came back without this young man. I know you've met, it's Sergeant Davies, but we can call him Michael.'

Annie wipes her hands on her apron and shakes Michael's hand. 'I'm glad he persuaded you to come back, he knows I wouldn't have been best pleased if he'd let you go off without a bite to eat.'

'I've been well-trained, Michael, and I know the right thing to do. Now sit in the comfy chair in the corner and I'll get us a couple of bottles of brown ale.'

Before Michael can sit down a boy comes from the kitchen into the room. He looks like John although he has a head of hair that's strikingly red, almost ginger in colour. John puts his hand on his son's shoulder. 'This is our eldest boy James. He's a good lad but I'm not sure where he gets his hair colour from. Mind you, he's got my ears you'll have to agree. He's twelve years of age and we call him Jim.'

Michael shakes James's hand and then sees that standing behind the boy is a small girl. 'Hello and who are you?'

John holds the girl's hand and leads her to stand in front of her brother, she has dark hair, is slight in build and very pretty. 'This is our Emma,' says John. 'She's six now.'

'Seven!' shouts Annie, from the kitchen.

Michael smiles at her, shakes her hand and, in response to John's instructions, sits in the chair. John pours out two beers, sits on a hard table chair next to Michael, hands him the beer and raises his own glass. 'Here's to you, Michael. Thank you for coming to see us, much appreciated.' He takes a drink, looks at his glass and smacks his lips. 'That'll do for now, it'll pass for beer. Can I get you something, Annie? We've still got some port in the front parlour, it were left over from Christmas.'

Annie walks through from the kitchen. 'Do you know, I don't make a habit of it but I just might join you.'

John stands up and Annie chuckles, 'Sit down, John, I know you've had a tiring time at the Red Lion, you take it easy, after all, all that talking really takes it out of you, it must be exhausting.'

The two men laugh. John looks through to the small kitchen and then through the window to view the backyard. 'Where's our Harry, where's Harold got to?'

Annie, carrying a bottle of port, comes back into the room. 'You know our Harry, law unto himself that one, does as he pleases. I told him, quarter to three at the latest. Anyway, I'm dishing up in five minutes whether he's here or not.'

The hungry diners sit around the table. John carves the meat while Annie puts out the vegetables. 'There you are, Michael, and there's a nice bit of crackling for you.'

Michael looks at his plate and smiles. 'This looks very tasty, Mrs Williams, very good of you.'

'Please call me Annie.'

'As I said, Michael, Annie knows how to cope with meat and deals with it in a very skilful manner.'

Annie sits. She asks for silence for a moment, bows her head, holds her hands together as a sign of prayer and says grace. John, the children and Michael follow her lead and at the end of her prayer they all quietly say amen. As they're eating they're interrupted by the appearance of Harold. He's very different in looks to his brother and although he's a year younger than James, he's taller, slimmer and has dark brown hair. Harold has been playing with his friends and shows signs of being involved in activities that have been robust, energetic and very physical. The result is that his face and legs are quite dirty and he looks somewhat dishevelled. 'There you are, Harry, 'says Annie. 'You told me that you would be indoors with your friend Jack, but I can see that you've been on that waste ground near Buncer Lane, look at the state of you. Now, get washed up and come and meet our guest, your food's on the stove, probably getting all dried up.'

Having made himself as presentable as he can, Harold returns to the table and puts his plate down. 'Harry,' says John, 'this is Sergeant Davies. He served with your brother in the Royal Lancs. Michael nods at him and smiles. Harold returns the gesture of acknowledgement.

After the main course has finished, Annie produces a large apple pie and a jug of cream. As Michael scrapes the bowl and puts the last of the pie into his mouth he sits back and taps his stomach. 'Eh, that were splendid, Annie, thank you very much, it were very nice, now there's some dishes that need my attention.'

Annie stands up and starts to collect some of the crockery together. 'You're a guest, Michael, and I'll not hear of it.'

Michael stands up and takes off his jacket and starts to roll up his sleeves. He points to his upper arm. 'I usually have three stripes on this arm, and I don't want to pull rank, but I'm going to insist. I wouldn't like to think that if your Bert knew that I'd visited you and I'd not carried out my duties as expected, well it wouldn't be right.'

Annie looks towards John for support, but she can see that the lunchtime pints and the last bottle of ale have taken their toll. He's settled into the comfy chair in the corner and his eyelids are clearly struggling to stay open. 'Insist is it, Sergeant? Then I'll wash and you wipe. I remember our Bert saying that you were a fair man but when it came to orders they're to be obeyed at all costs.'

Michael takes the tea towel from her and laughs. 'Well that's the army for you, Annie, you know where you stand.'

Chapter Eighteen

2 August, 1932 – Zillebeke, Belgium

Paul brings the coach to a halt, takes out a map and studies it very carefully. It's now clear to him that he took the wrong turn back at the crossroads a short distance ago. John steps forward to offer his advice and provide what he considers to be his natural ability to understand and interpret directions. Both men study the detail of the plan very carefully, then they pause, John scans the region and looks one way then the other. He points to certain identifiable landmarks and refers back to the map. 'That church spire is in Zillebeke and if that's right, then Bellewaerde must be over there.' John turns and points in a direction away from the church spire.

Paul lifts his hat and scratches his forehead, he's a little embarrassed that he seems to be lost, he is after all in his own country. 'Where can it be? What is that church over there in the distance, Mr Williams?'

'Oh no,' says John, 'wrong direction altogether and too far away, that'll be Zonnebeke o'er yon.' He points purposely at the map and then looks towards the sky and shields his eyes. 'Now, the sun's over there so we must be looking north and if Ypres is in that direction then we need to go this way.' He runs his finger along a road on the map, a slight breeze lifts the corner of the plan and Paul holds it down to make sure that the map is flat. 'The main battlefield can be found if we take this road and then turn left at this junction.'

Paul nods in agreement although he's not totally convinced,

walks round the front of the coach and climbs into the cab. John steps up into the passenger compartment and as he folds up his map he reports, 'Crisis over, we're all sorted now. Do you know, I'm feeling a bit hungry, as soon as we get there we can get the picnic out, I fancy a bit of pie myself.'

The coach moves off down the bumpy and uneven road. It passes by lush green fields of grazing land and some that are filled with crops nearing maturity and ready for harvesting. Eventually, the coach stops in a small parking space by a gate. John steps down and confidently strides towards an information board that's attached to a fence. John studies the plan and turns to speak to the passengers on the coach. 'Here we are, ladies and gentlemen, a short walk and we'll be there.'

The family steps down from the coach. 'We'll be there,' says Mary, 'where, where will we be? Looks like we're in the middle of nowhere.'

They walk through the gate and follow a path by a small stream. Henry carries a picnic basket and John, holding a rug, leads the party forward. The ladies are wearing light-coloured, floral-patterned, summer frocks with matching wide-brimmed hats. The men are dressed in striped sports jackets and certainly look the part because they're wearing Panama-style hats. Herbert is in shirtsleeves and is wearing a flat barrow-boy type cap. John leads them through another gate and they stand and look at the landscape before them. 'Here we are, this is some of it,' says John.

'I'm still not sure what we're supposed to be looking at,' says Mary. 'It all looks the same to me.'

John looks at her, some guidance is needed here. 'Can you see, Mary, the peculiar lay of the land? Very unusual, I think you'll agree.'

Mary looks again. 'What are these bumps and dips and things?'

'Shell-holes, Mary,' says Henry. 'It's quite clear when you see it and think of it.'

Mary looks again. 'I suppose you can really, didn't they make a mess of it, still looks a bit odd.'

Paul struggles to get through the gate. Madame De Vos has been good enough to lend the family two fold-up garden chairs and the driver has been given the task of carrying them. When he reaches the spot where the family is setting up a temporary camp he sets about the difficult task of unfolding the chairs and making sure that they are safe to sit on. Henry lends a hand and together they make what should be a simple task seem to be very complicated. 'Look at that, Annie,' says Mary, 'talk about the blind leading the blind.'

Annie laughs. 'Well, we'll let Henry sit on one first, just in case.'

John smokes his pipe. He's standing and visually surveying the landscape. He raises his hat slightly and holds it forward to provide a shade to shield his eyes. Having completed the highly technical task of erecting the chairs, Henry and Paul join him. 'O'er yonder is Chateau Woods,' says John, 'and to the left of there must be Bellewaerde. The Second Royal Lancs must have passed through here, they were with the Twenty-Fourth Brigade and attacked with the Second Northants, the Second East Lancs, the First Worcestershire Regiment and the First Sherwood Foresters.'

'How is it that you know this?' asks Paul. 'I do not know it and I live here.'

'Research,' says Henry. 'He's one for research is our John.'

'It's all in the reading of it,' adds John. 'It's all about following lines of investigation.'

'Oh, he does a lot of reading,' says Annie. 'He's very taken with it.'

John looks at Paul and smiles. 'I've made it my business to find out what went on here, talked to lads who were here and studied at the library, wrote to people, usual way, now shall I continue?'

Paul nods. 'Please do continue, this is interesting I think.'

'Now,' says John, 'covered by a lot of mortar fire, the Northants' boys managed to take Bellewaerde. Beyond there, they struggled through Chateau Wood, just about keeping up with the creeping barrage. The Worcesters and Northants advanced and captured what's called Jacob Trench.' John points towards the immediate horizon. 'That's where it is and beyond there is where the Germans were really dug in at Bellewaerde Ridge. Thing is, that when the Sherwood Foresters passed through their lines, they came under very heavy fire.' John looks round to get his bearings and points to another place to his left. 'Eventually, the brigade had to pull back to the shelter of Westhoek Ridge which is o'er yon.'

'What happened then, John?' asks Henry.

'Well,' says John, 'they carried on with the attack, but it were over really.'

John looks at Paul. 'Course, you're used to all this, aren't you young man?'

Paul nods. 'This is very true, Mr Williams, I have grown up in, how do you say…in the shadow of it? All around you can see where the men are buried and of course, there are always many visitors. But I have not been to this field before, there must be many men under this ground.'

John looks at Henry. 'He's right you know, there were a lot they never found.' John lights his pipe again. 'You know Bob Morrison who lives on Ainsworth Street?'

'Aye,' says Henry, 'used to play for the cricket club at Witton, good batsman.'

'His boy, George, I think he were called,' says John, 'he were with the Royal Lancs, killed here about the same time as our Bert, they never found him, no grave as such.' He looks down at the ground. 'He could be under here, where we're standing.'

'I know that farmers here still find soldiers in the ground,' say Paul. 'when they are digging and ploughing.'

John stares at Paul for a moment,' in't war I made a lot of army uniforms, that were my job and standing here now I'm wondering if my cloth or what's left of it is under our feet.'

'Well that's a thought John,' says Henry.

'Aye, that's right I don't know whether to be proud or sad. Bit of both I think.'

While John has been giving his talk, Annie and Mary have been arranging the picnic area; they lay out the blanket and position the chairs. Annie opens the basket and hands her sister a sandwich then she pours some apple-flavoured water into a cup and passes it to Emma. As each of the family members approaches Annie, she responds to their request for food and drink by providing the sustenance that they desire. As the afternoon sun makes its way across the bright blue sky the family relaxes and enjoys the peace and quiet of the day. Somewhere, they can hear the slow drone of an aircraft engine and then the sound of a motorcar is heard as it travels down the road that's close to where they're camped. Apart from these infrequent audible intrusions, it's very quiet and peaceful. The occasional sound of birds singing adds to the serene and tranquil scene.

'Hard to believe,' says Annie, 'that there were all that fighting here. It's so calm now.'

John takes a sip from his cup. 'Nice spot, like you say, Annie, you'd never know what went on, although the scarred landscape gives it away.'

Annie and Mary sit on the chairs while John and Henry choose to recline on the light grey blanket. Emma, Herbert and Paul sit on a small grass bank to the side. Mary looks anxiously first one way and then the other. 'Well it's a nice spot, but are we allowed to be here? You know what some of these farmers are like, they can get very aggressive, I wouldn't like to have an awkward situation.'

Annie laughs. 'Do you remember when we went for that picnic at Pleasington and found a nice spot by the river?'

'I do,' says Mary. 'We'd just got nicely settled and then that farmer came up, shouting and doing and waving his gun, he were in state, he were.'

'Do you remember what Dad said?' says Emma, as she laughs.

John laughs and Annie says, 'I do. I were for making off and apologising, but you, John, what were it you said?'

John seizes the opportunity to report on his account of what took place. 'If you recall, I stood up and I said, *now my man, do you have authority to be waving that gun around like that in such a manner?*'

'I remember,' says Henry, 'he were a bit taken aback, weren't he?'

'He were,' says John. 'He said it were his land and we were trespassing. I said that as far as I knew, he were a tenant of Lord Hornsby and that we were on the Woodfold Estate. Then I said that as I would be measuring up his Lordship's head butler, Mr Baker, for a fine new suit next week, I'd mention to him that our wives were very upset about such aggressive and nasty behaviour. Do you remember, Annie? I also said that you were of a very nervous disposition and if it damaged your health, I'd want that to be reported to his Lordship. I'd make a real complaint.'

'That put him right,' says Mary, 'silly man.'

'Mind you, Mary,' says Annie, 'I don't hold with telling tales, but it were funny, it were hard to keep a straight face. I made out that I were about to faint.'

'That's right,' says Mary. 'I fanned you with John's newspaper, and I glared at that farmer and said, *see what you've done now, this woman's a mother.*'

'Well, that did it, he went off mumbling something about shutting the gate,' says Henry. 'Didn't he come back and give us some milk?'

'He did,' says Annie, 'and very nice it were, very creamy and fresh, course that's what you'd expect on a farm. You must have got him worried, John, because he kept looking at me and asking if I were all right.'

'Milk were nice,' says John, 'but I wished it were ale.' He

turns to Mary, 'Don't have any concerns, we're allowed to be here, the sign on the gate gives us permission, as long as we shut gates and don't make a mess. You see, all around here, there's chaps still buried in these fields, they're like cemeteries these meadows and we're paying our respects.'

As they continue with their picnic, they remember family gatherings, picnics in the woods, walks through the park, and watching the children play on the hills outside the town. 'Where were it,' says Annie, 'that our Bert fell into that river and we had a job to fish him out?'

'Aye,' says John, 'that were Alum Scar Woods, it were on that bridge. You were there, Mary, do you remember?'

'I remember it being a long walk along Billinge End Road, went on for miles,' replies Mary.

'He must have been about eight or nine, weren't he?'

'I told our Bert not to climb on the wall because I could see that he wanted to,' says Annie, 'but he wouldn't be told and when we were looking over the other way he climbed up. I looked round and there he were, bold as brass standing on't top of the wall, all defiant like.'

'I shouted,' says John, *'what do you think you're doing?'*

'You did,' says Mary, 'and that did it, it startled him and he fell off, right in. Our George's boy, Billy, who were only a year older, wanted to jump in after him. He said he were going to save his life, I told him not to be so daft.'

'That's it,' laughs John. 'When we looked over, he were stood up to his waist in't water. I said *are you all right son*, and he told me he were cold.'

'Anyway, we got him out and he were really shivering,' says Annie. 'It weren't a chilly day though water must have been really cold. He had to put up with it till we got to our cousin Tom's farm on the other side of the woods.'

'Now, that were a nice spread that Tom's wife, Clara, put on,' recalls John. 'I enjoyed that.'

'Their boy,' says Mary, 'he were killed in the war.'

'Aye he were,' says John. 'Richard, he were in the Flying Corps, pilot he were and he were killed in June 1918, they never found him. They thought that his plane had crashed behind enemy lines and it were burnt so bad that there were nothing of him left.'

Annie sighs and gazes out across the field. 'Strange isn't it, we can remember really pleasant and nice days out, when the sun always seemed to be shining on warm summer days. I can think of when we laughed and had such good times, a world away from any troubles. Family times, important times, times of joy and happiness and yet…'

'We always come back to here,' says John, 'don't we, Annie?'

'We can never leave it John, it's always with us.'

John has been lying down on the blanket on his side. He sits up and gazes across the field. 'You know, Annie, a lot of folk might think it's strange us having a picnic here, relaxing and having a nice family occasion on this land where our lad were wounded.'

'Well, people can think what they like,' says Annie. 'I'm comfortable with it, aren't you?'

'Oh yes, more than comfortable, I feel very close to him here. It's almost as if he were looking down on us and it's a way of introducing him to Bertie and showing him how our Emma's making out.'

The family is silent for a moment but their quiet contemplation is rudely disturbed by the approach of an elderly man. He has a full white beard, is wearing a flat cap, old white shirt, a rather tatty waistcoat and a pair of ragged trousers. He shouts at them; his language is Dutch so they have no idea what he's saying.

'There you are,' says Mary. 'I knew it, they're all the same, think they own the world.'

'Well,' says John, 'he's either a tramp or an old working farmer. I'll point him in the direction of that sign and show him that we're allowed here.'

When the old man gets close to them John speaks with some authority, 'Now look here, old man, we've every right to visit.'

'British!' shouts the old man. 'British?'

'Aye,' replies John, 'from England.'

The old man smiles, looks out across the fields and then looks directly at John. He opens his mouth as wide as he can and makes a strange loud noise. It now becomes obvious that he's attempting to create the sound of an explosion. Then he holds his hands in front of him and points his fingers. 'Rat-a-tat-tat!' he hollers.

John laughs. 'He's telling us that there were a battle here. We know that, old chap, our son were here, wounded in 1917.'

'1917,' says the old man, 'big war, big battle, big fight, Passchendaele.'

'We need to keep an eye on this one, he seems to be a bit queer and demented,' says Mary.

The old man points to the ground. 'British boys.'

The old man speaks in Dutch and when Paul replies to him, he realises that he has a translator to help him. He speaks to Paul in Dutch and points to the family to indicate that he wishes to make his conversation known.

Paul steps forward to hear what he's saying. 'He tells us that British boys are still here in the ground and sometimes he finds them. He also says that many soldiers were killed here on both sides, but the Germans do not matter to him. He is sorry for the British boys but not the Germans.'

The old man smiles and says something else. 'He says that you are his Allies,' continues Paul. 'He's pleased to see you here. You are most and very welcome. He also asks if he can get anything for you.'

John chuckles, 'Tell him a pint of Thwaites' ale would be very nice at this moment.'

Paul looks a little confused and starts to translate but John stops him. 'No Paul, just a joke, a bit of fun, thank him and tell him we've got everything we need, thank him for his offer.'

The old man waves goodbye and walks away. 'Be funny if he came back with a pint of ale,' says Henry.

'Aye,' says John, 'and if it were a pint of Thwaites, I'd start to become a believer and turn all religious like.'

Chapter Nineteen

24 December, 1916 – The Somme, France
4th Battalion, Royal Lancastrian Light Infantry

It's cold, really cold, the snow has been falling for almost two hours and by ten o'clock in the evening, most of the soldiers in the trench are feeling miserable and somewhat sorry for themselves. Their thoughts are with their families, they can easily picture the scene; the warm fire, the decorated table, still displaying food comprising of bread and butter with jam, mince pies and cakes. There are also jugs of beer and soft drinks for the younger children. Each soldier has his own individual memories; some reflect reality while others fabricate a scene that's made up of idealistic images. However, one thing that they have in common is the shared thought that on Christmas Eve 1916, the last place they want to be is in a wet, dark and cold trench on the Somme. It's a place that they're forced to call home. One soldier starts to play on his mouth organ and the tune *Silent Night* is heard. To some it's a comfort but to others it's a painful reminder that they miss their parents, children, wives and sweethearts.

A soldier carries a large tin flask that contains hot, warming tea and although it's of poor quality, it is nevertheless still very much appreciated. The soldiers form a short queue and once they have received their tea, sit back down and before drinking the steaming liquid, they hold their mugs with both hands for warmth. For a moment, Lance Corporal Williams smells the steam and then he drinks. His thoughts are very much with his mother and he remembers Christmas mornings and the joy of receiving his presents. When he was too old to believe in Father

Christmas he kept up the pretence for the sake of his younger brothers and his sister.

Sergeant Mitchell approaches, as always he has a small cigar lodged in the corner of his mouth, which he rarely removes, sometimes it's lit, but most of the time it isn't. Like all the other men, he's wearing his khaki-coloured greatcoat, but is also dressed in a sheepskin-lined, leather tunic for extra warmth. As he passes each soldier he has a quick word with them to make sure that they're bearing up and to wish them a happy Christmas. He knows that the festive celebration will only mean extra rations of bully beef, more biscuits and if they're lucky, a swig of rum. He does his best to raise the soldiers' spirits. This is very much the nature of the man and although he's slim, almost to the point of being too thin, and has sharp, pointed facial features, his manner is always jocular, which is in contrast to his rather severe appearance. 'Merry Christmas men,' says the sergeant. 'I've a little job for somebody to do.'

The soldiers mumble a return of the compliments of the season even though they don't feel that festive. They also know that when Sergeant Mitchell talks of a *little job,* the reality is very different. It will in all probability mean that a raiding party will have to go over no-man's-land to take prisoners for questioning or to report on the layout of the enemy fortifications. Whatever it is, it will be dangerous.

'Now, where are our volunteers?' the sergeant asks as he looks directly at Lance Corporal Williams. 'Can I see the brave lads who want to do their duty for King and Country? Do we have those sorts of chaps here? I think we do.'

Lance Corporal Williams laughs. 'I'll do it, Sarge,' he says, and looks at Corporal Cook who reluctantly nods his head in acceptance of his nomination. Another soldier, Private Wilkins, steps forward to offer his services. 'That's three,' says the lance corporal. 'We need one more.'

'Yes, one to carry the stick, all taken care of,' replies the sergeant. 'That large fellow, Private Cuthbert, will carry the club.

He's a big chap and he'll knock their blocks off without too much trouble.'

Corporal Cook gives the sergeant a questioning look. 'We're taking a stick-man, Sarge? Why not just send two or three big blokes over, clobber a couple of the bastards and drag 'em back, like we've done before?'

'Change of tactics, Cooky,' replies Sergeant Mitchell. 'Want to try something a bit different. Want to be sure we don't come back empty-handed.'

'We?' says Corporal Cook. 'Thinking of coming with us, Sarge?'

Sergeant Mitchell chuckles, takes out his cigar and looks at it. 'Like to of course but I'm a bit too old for that, you'd have to carry me back. Now you know the drill, in your own time, find out what's going on over there and get a couple of prisoners, if possible more. Don't forget to take the wire cutters, we know they've been putting in new wire over the last few days. As soon as you're back, report to Captain Hillier.'

The sergeant wishes them well and disappears down the trench. Corporal Cook sits on the small bench and leans back. He takes out two cigarettes, lights them both and hands one to the lance corporal. 'Thanks a lot, Bert, just when I were starting to enjoy a bit of boredom.' He takes off his helmet to reveal a small amount of light brown, almost blond, hair. He looks younger than his twenty-five years and his regular features confirm him as being reasonably good-looking.

'I'll lead and you, Bert, take up the rear. My job will be to use the cutters, I'll put some grenades in a haversack and lob a couple in the first trench for starters. Me and Cuthbert will get in first, I'll carry the revolver and you two will cover us, you'll use your rifles with bayonets fixed, we'll be quick and no hanging about.'

Lance Corporal Williams walks a little way down the trench informing the soldiers of the plan. He tells them that when they hear machine guns, they're to get up to the ramparts to provide covering fire. The soldiers understand what they have to do and are pleased that they're not going with the raiding party. Private Cuthbert, who's carrying a large wooden club, joins the three members of the party. He's a menacing and imposing figure, being very tall and stoutly built.

Corporal Cook repeats his plan and the four prepare to start their mission. He hands Private Cuthbert a flare gun to illuminate the German trench before they enter it. Although the snowfall has been heavy it has failed to settle due to the ground being very wet and no-man's-land is a very dark place. They remove their greatcoats, take off their gloves to smear mud onto their faces, slowly they climb the ladders and roll onto the muddy earth at the top of the trench. Taking on a crouched and stooped stance, they slowly move forward, although it is only a few hundred yards, it seems more like a mile. When eventually they reach the first line of barbed wire, Corporal Cook starts to cut as quietly as he can. All the time they listen for an indication that their activities have been discovered. So far so good and as the last line of wire is dealt with, they're at last close to the top of the German trenches. They can hear the German soldiers talking.

Corporal Cook drops the wire cutters, and takes out two grenades from the haversack. He removes the pins from both the bombs and holds down the levers. He hurls them into the trench and before they explode he quickly removes his revolver from the holster in readiness for the attack. Two loud explosions break the silence and the corporal jumps into the trench. Private Cuthbert fires the flare and follows Corporal Cook into the chaos of the dugout. Lance Corporal Williams and Private Wilkins jump over the ramparts and aim their rifles into the trench. They're on standby and are ready to provide covering fire if needed.

The German trench, now unnaturally and starkly illuminated, is a scene of turmoil and confusion. The grenades have killed a number of the occupying troops and those left standing are wounded and stupefied. When they see that Corporal Cook is pointing his revolver at them, they raise their hands and cry out, '*Kapitulation*,' and in English, 'give up, give up, bitte.' One soldier thinks better of it and holding a bayonet in front of him, he screams in defiance and charges towards the corporal. His progress is cut short when Private Cuthbert swings his club, knocks the soldier's helmet off and renders him unconscious.

Another soldier approaches them, then he stops for a moment and his hesitation proves to be costly as the club is swung again and makes a forceful and a violent impact with his head. He drops to his knees and before he falls over he's scooped up by the burly private, who throws him over his shoulder. Private Cuthbert knows that because of the German's hesitation and the caution that he displayed, he'll be easier to interrogate compared to his first victim. The corporal indicates to two of the submissive soldiers that they are to leave with them and they obediently follow the orders of their captors.

Corporal Cook shouts out, 'Let's bloody well get out of here before all the fucking bastards wise up!' He throws another grenade into the trench. Once out of the trench speed is the important factor because the element of surprise has been lost and they are now discovered. The rat-a-tat sound of machine gun fire is heard as the German sentries fire blindly into the blackness of the night. Then the raiding party is lit up for all to see and although they feel totally exposed, they can at least see their prepared route through the wire. Proceeding with caution and yet moving as quickly as they are able to, they successfully pass through.

The British soldiers return fire with their rifles and create effective covering fire by using their Lewis machine guns. They provide an unrelenting and consistent barrage of indiscriminate and murderous fire to cover the return to safety of their comrades. Then, tragically, Private Wilkins steps to one side of the route and becomes entangled on wire, and as he attempts to free himself he's cut down by machine gun fire. Such is the ferocity of the burst of fire that his comrades know that there is no point in attempting to rescue and recover the fallen soldier. When the three remaining members of the party, with their prisoners, reach their home base they gratefully fall into the security of the trench.

As they lean back against the wall of the trench, Lance Corporal Williams is breathing heavily and trying to restore some semblance of physical normality. 'You couldn't resist it, could you, Cooky?'

Corporal Cook lets out a long breath of air. 'Resist what, Bert?'

'Chucking in that last grenade.'

'Well, I thought while we were here, let's get rid of a few more of the swine, a dozen of them gone and about a million of the buggers still to be sorted out.'

The three men with their captors are clearly exhausted, they sink down to sit on the duck-boards at the bottom of the trench and lean against some sand bags, they breathe heavily and gasp for air. Eventually, they start to recover and Lance Corporal Williams looks towards one of their captives. He's a young, slim soldier of about sixteen or seventeen years of age, he's sitting in a crouched position and is shaking and sobbing. The lance corporal wipes the mud off his hand, and reaching into his top pocket he finds his packet of Woodbine cigarettes and takes two out. He strikes a match, lights them both and holds one of the cigarettes in front of the distressed young cadet who nods to indicate that the offering would be gratefully received. He gives the cigarette to the young soldier who draws in the smoke and leans back to enjoy the taste, and for a brief moment tries to forget what has taken place. As a prisoner of war he's alive but it will be some time before he'll see his family, friends and comrades again. He hopes that the propaganda that he's heard is untrue and that he'll be treated well rather than shot as he has been told. Lance Corporal Williams smiles at him, without language, he could be from anywhere, in a khaki uniform instead of the German grey, he could be a British Tommy.

After a time, Sergeant Mitchell returns with two armed guards. Corporal Cook stands up. 'Sorry, Sarge, we were just resting a bit before bringing them on.'

'No problem, Corporal,' says the sergeant, 'thought I'd save you the trouble. Lost one, didn't you?'

'Yes, Sarge,' answers the corporal, 'Wilkins, caught in the wire.' He thinks for a moment. 'If you need somebody to escort these blokes to Paris or somewhere like that, we could help out.'

The sergeant laughs. 'Nice try, Corporal, but I think we'll manage.' He orders the prisoners to stand and the two guards march them off, including the one soldier who was hit by Private Cuthbert's club and although still groggy, is able to comply with Sergeant Mitchell's orders. Before the young soldier reaches the corner of the trench he turns briefly and looks at the lance corporal and raises his hand to thank him and say farewell. Lance Corporal Williams returns the gesture and watches as the prisoner disappears from view and enters an unfamiliar and an uncertain world of captivity. He then thinks of the comrade that they were forced to leave on the wire and wonders if the information that they get from the three prisoners will prove to be worth the life that has been lost. Still, orders are orders.

'We deserve a bloody medal for doing that,' says Corporal Cook.

'Merry Christmas, Cooky,' says Lance Corporal Williams.

Chapter Twenty

22 May, 1930 – Mellor, Lancashire

George Williams pays the barman at the Milltraders Arms for the round of drinks that he's just purchased. He's joined by his brother John and brother-in-law Henry, who help him to transport the sizeable order of drinks to a large table in the centre of the room where the Williams family is seated. The family is dressed suitably for the occasion of John and Annie's eldest son's wedding. The warm spring day has allowed the ladies to dress as they would have wished and they're clothed in smart, pastel-coloured outfits with matching decorative hats. The men are decked out in their best suits and are sporting white carnation buttonholes. George manages the distribution of the drinks and inevitably, some of the requests have been lost in translation. 'Now, Annie,' he says, 'that's your port and lemon, that's right isn't it?' Annie smiles and nods to confirm that her drink is what she asked for. 'Now, Mary, that's your rum and black as you wanted.'

'I asked for a gin with tonic water,' replies Mary as she shakes her head.

'Well who asked for a rum and black then?' says John. 'Somebody did.'

'I asked for a rum, without blackcurrant,' says Harold Williams.

'Don't you like blackcurrant?' says John.

'Not in rum, Dad.'

'I'll drink it,' says Herbert. 'I like blackcurrant.'

John sighs and shakes his head. 'You can't drink that, it's got rum in it. You're only eleven, Bertie.'

'Twelve,' protests Herbert.

'That's your ginger beer,' says George.

'Didn't they have Dandelion and Burdock?' asks Harold. 'That's what Bertie wanted.'

'I would have liked to have had Dandelion and Burdock,' adds Herbert.

John's becoming a bit exasperated. 'Well, what we want and what we get can be two different things, just have a go at that rum and black Harry, you might get to like it.'

The discussion about who asked for what and what they have ended up with continues and it's confirmed that the order was one drink short. Henry is sent back to the bar to purchase a gin and tonic for Mary. When he returns, John raises his glass of beer and announces, 'To the Bride and Groom,' and the family repeats the toast.

Mary looks around the room. 'Well, when we've eaten the buffet in the back room, we'll have a proper toast I take it, with the right sort of drinks. You can't have a toast with beer, it doesn't look right and it's very common.'

John laughs. 'Thing is, Mary, if everybody drank ale like us, there wouldn't be any mix-ups with a complicated order.'

'So you think we should all drink beer do you, John?' replies Mary.

John laughs. He enjoys his skirmishes with his sister-in-law and responds by saying, 'Well, it would make life easier when there's a lot of us, all this fiddling about with rum and gin and stuff.'

'Well,' retorts Mary, 'we don't want to put you out.'

Annie interrupts, 'Now that's enough you two. The answer to your question, Mary, about drinks with the food, is that wine will be provided. Red and white apparently.'

'Oh,' says Mary, 'very French, they can't be short of a bob or two, our Jimmy's new in-laws. Talking of Jim, where is he? I haven't seen him since the service.'

'They're in the back garden having some pictures taken,' replies Henry.

'Are we not being asked to be in the pictures?' says John.

John's question is answered when Mr Bartrop, the photographer, enters the bar area and approaches the family. He's a tall, slim-built man, with a very pale skin tone and with greasy-looking hair that appears to be unnaturally dark and almost black in colour.

'Now,' says John, 'what's the procedure, Mr Bartrop? What do you want of us?'

'First of all, Mr Williams,' answers Mr Bartrop, 'I must apologise for the slight delay.'

'Well we had those pictures taken at the church,' says Annie. 'What's wrong with them, Mr Bartrop?'

'You see, Mrs Williams,' replies Mr Bartrop, 'when the bride's father saw the garden, he thought it would be a nice setting for some more pictures and I have to agree. I've had a bit of a problem with the plates, that's the photographic plates, I thought that they'd been prematurely exposed. I sent my lad, Granville, back to the shop to get some more and I now have replacements. You can't take any chances at weddings, some people have come all the way from Wigan you know.'

'We trust you, Mr Bartrop,' says John, 'to do a very professional job, now what are we to do now?'

'As I said, you can't take any chances, that's why I'm using the old faithful, my trusty Ensign Empress, it's a half plate with f/8 diaphragm aperture lens and a Thornton Pickard roller blind shutter; it might be nearly twenty years old but it's never let me down.'

John looks a bit bemused. 'Is that right? You've nothing a bit more modern then?'

'Oh yes, Mr Williams, I've just purchased a Nagel, Librette 16, it's a 120 roll film camera. I'll use both and it'll be nice to compare the results.'

John starts to get a little impatient and takes out his pocket watch to demonstrate that time's moving on. 'This is fascinating, Mr Bartrop, but I think that we need to get ourselves organised. What are we to do?'

'Of course, it's the mother and the father of the groom,' says Mr Bartrop as he stretches out one of his long arms in the direction of the door to the garden to indicate where they're to go. 'It'll be the same procedure as before, if you would be kind enough to come with me.'

Henry stands and says that he's been sitting long enough and walks around the bar. He sees Tom Watson, Mary's cousin, and engages him in conversation. 'Nice do, Tom, no expense spared by the looks of it.'

Tom's a farmer and very much a part of the rural farming community, the language he uses is in an old Lancashire dialect. Now in his fifties, the hard life that he's led in working outdoors in all weathers and at all times of the day is starting to take its toll. Stocky and muscular in build due to the heavy nature of his work, his face is heavily lined due to the damaging effects of sunshine and harsh winter weather. 'Aye, wait till thee sees bait, I mean food, bin some brass spent, have a look, thou'll be impressed.'

The two men are joined by Mary. 'I'm feeling a bit peckish, I wish they'd hurry up and get us seated,' she says, then remembers her manners. 'How are you Tom, what's your year been like, how are your cows?'

'Not bad Mary, lost Whisky early on, she were owd, thee knows.'

'That's right,' says Henry, 'I remember, you call them after drinks; Brandy, Gin, Beer and the like.'

'We've done alcohol, now wur on't soft variety, Burdock and the like.'

'I don't know how you remember what they're called,' says Mary. 'Our George couldn't recall what we'd ordered when he's just bought a round of drinks.'

'Must be getting hard for you, Tom, working on't farm, no

offence like but with your age and all, you must miss the help of your Richard.'

'Aye, we miss him, but not for help, he weren't for farming, he were too clever thee knows, good at adding up.'

'Pilot weren't he?' says Henry.

'Always good at heights, our lad. When we had tile loose on't barn, he were up there and fixed it, good yed fur it, no fear. But he were cack-handed thee knows. I told him, controls would be on't wrong side.'

'He were a good lad, your Richard, very good-natured' says Mary. 'When I heard that he'd joined the Flying Corp, I thought he'd be all right.'

'I thought that an-all,' replies Tom, 'turned out, lowest life expectancy in't air.'

Henry looks over and can see Herbert talking to some of his cousins. 'Our Bertie's keen to be a flyer one day, he's got books on it.' He then rubs his stomach. 'Like you, Mary, I'm a bit hungry now, me tummy's rumbling.'

'That'll be that beer,' says Mary, 'no good on an empty stomach, I'm always saying.' She looks at Tom. 'He drinks it too quick and I think he's afraid that they'll sell out.'

Tom laughs. 'Be right, when thee's etten.'

In the garden, James Williams and his bride Heather Douglas are standing in position on the spot that the photographer has selected in order to make maximum use of the available light. The small trees and rhododendron bushes provide a more than suitable backdrop. Heather's dressed in a traditional long white dress with lace sleeves and a fine silk collar. Her veil has been lifted up over a floral crown of white carnations which matches her bouquet. She's a small woman, with a pretty round face and has dark, short, bobbed hair which has been set in a modern finger-wave style. James is wearing a smart, dark, three-piece suit, and his short, slightly curly, red hair enhances the handsome features of his face. Being slightly on the stocky side, he takes after his father in build and physique and at the age of twenty-four, his frame is solid and sturdy.

On either side of the newlywed couple stands Walter and Rosemary Douglas, the proud parents of Heather. Both are elegantly dressed. Rosemary is very obviously the mother of Heather in appearance and build. For the occasion, she has had her dark hair cut and styled to match her daughter's contemporary look. Walter's face is easily recognisable because his main distinguishing feature is a long, dark, goatee beard. He's bald and the only hair that he has finishes just above his ears. With them are the three bridesmaids looking a real picture; they're clothed in long cream and white dresses, and are wearing floral coronets. Two of the girls are Heather's younger sisters and the chief bridesmaid is Emma Williams.

John leans closer to Annie and out of the corner of his mouth quietly says, 'No wonder old Bartrop wants to take more pictures, he can charge extra and it'll be a good payday for him.'

Mr Bartrop has two cameras mounted on tripods and placed in position. One is his trusty half plate apparatus and the other, the more modern roll film camera. Once Annie and John are in position, standing to the side of their son, the photographer goes to work. He asks them all to stand perfectly still and he puts his head once more under the black cloth to check the image on the glass-viewing screen of the half plate camera. After placing the plate cassette in position, he calls out, 'Smile please, if you wouldn't mind.' Once satisfied that all is as it should be, he releases the shutter. He then uses the roll film camera and after taking a number of pictures, walks quickly back into the bar to encourage the other guests to have their pictures taken. At the end of the session the much-relieved photographer breathes a big sigh of relief and thanks all the family and guests for their co-operation.

A young waiter, dressed in dark trousers, a white shirt and wearing a black apron, enters the garden. He announces that the buffet food is ready and asks the guests to follow him into the large back room. The guests are more than happy to comply with the waiter's request and need little in the way of further persuasion and encouragement. They enthusiastically and eagerly help themselves to the fine spread of food which has been presented to them. Hot meats, consisting of beef, lamb and pork, are skilfully carved by a more mature man dressed in a chef's outfit. The round dining tables are covered with fine linen tablecloths, and cream-coloured ceramic vases holding white carnations make fitting centrepieces. Place-cards displaying the names of the guests have been positioned on each table to inform them where they're to sit. Nothing has been left to chance.

'Here we are, Annie,' says John, 'this is us. On the top table as expected.'

Annie sits down and looks around. 'Well, just look at this, John, they've done our Jim proud, it's a lovely spread and look at that, wine as well.'

John sits by his wife. 'Must be a lot of brass in scrap, that's his trade you know, he's got several yards around these parts.'

The reception continues, and as the food is eaten and the wine consumed the guests become more and more relaxed. Walter Douglas makes his speech; he talks confidently and the small number of jokes which he has included have clearly been well-practiced and rehearsed. James's words are polite and well-considered, the speech is short but to the point. Then it's the turn of James's best man, Harold, to add to the proceedings and complete the trio of speeches.

'Oh, here we go,' says John quietly to Annie. 'What's he going to say, have you seen his speech?'

'No I haven't, John, he wouldn't discuss it, you know what he's like, stubborn and thinks he knows it all.'

'I did tell him,' says John. 'Just think on, I said, not everybody's got your sense of humour, just be careful.'

Harold looks the part; taller and slimmer than his brother, he's a handsome young man with dark hair and is wearing a dark grey, three-piece suit. He taps a wine glass with a spoon and waits until the hum of conversation dies down. 'Ladies and gentlemen, boys and girls, friends and family,' he says and then he pauses for a moment, looks around the room and continues. 'If there's anyone here who doesn't fit into any of those descriptions, then I suggest that you are at the wrong event. However, if you are here by error, I will forgive you if you buy me a drink in the bar afterwards.'

There's a ripple of laughter around the room and Harold's speech continues in this vein. He tells tales of when he and his brother were small boys, the tricks they played on their friends and the days when they would climb over the wall of the vicarage to get some apples. Stories of adolescence and immaturity are revealed and embarrassing episodes, relating to some first encounters of liaisons with the opposite sex, are disclosed. 'Kathleen Duxbury, she were a rare beauty, she demanded a penny for every kiss. She was so taken with our Jim that he were given special discount rates, two kisses for a penny. As my dad would say, *cheap at half the price*. What our Jim didn't know was that Kathleen gave me a special offer of three kisses for a penny.' He looks at his brother and raises his glass. James shakes his head, laughs and also raises his glass.

Harold brings the formal speech to a close and finishes by toasting the bridesmaids. It has been a humorous and very entertaining speech and knowing Harold, as most of the audience do, they are not disappointed by his performance. Finally, Harold raises his glass and looks directly at his parents and then looks around the room. He has a serious look on his face, 'One final toast,' he pauses for a moment and announces in a loud voice, 'to absent friends.'

Everybody in the room knows who and what he's referring to because there many guests who as a result of the war have lost sons, brothers, uncles and fathers. As well as the men, a small number of deceased female family members are also remembered. The guests all stand and as one they repeat, 'To absent friends.'

John looks over to his son, they make eye contact, Harold smiles at his father and John winks at him. 'Well said, son' he says quietly, 'a nice thought.'

Chapter Twenty-One

3 August, 1932 – Poperinge

John, Annie, Mary and Henry are preparing to leave the hotel to take an early afternoon stroll. They don't really have a plan of where to go or what to do. When they arrive at wherever it will be, they hope to have made some new discoveries and will have had the opportunity to explore areas of the town that they are unfamiliar with. Unusually, John hasn't put his mind to planning a route and when his three companions look to him for guidance, he responds by saying, 'Let's see where our fancy takes us and take it as it comes, it'll be a bit of a mystery tour.'

This is so out of character that Mary says to Annie, 'I think your John's had a bit too much sun, don't you?'

'Give the man credit, Mary,' says Henry, 'he's been on duty ever since we left Bromley Street. If it were up to us we'd still be scratching our heads and looking at the timetable at the station, trying to fathom it out.'

'No,' says John, 'Mary's right, but we might be pleasantly surprised when we find where we end up. This is my time to take a step back.'

Madame De Vos interrupts them when she pushes her mother-in-law, who's seated in her wheelchair, into the foyer from the veranda. Mevrouw De Vos is clutching a newspaper, she's clearly agitated. 'See, Mr Williams, look,' she points excitedly and frantically at the paper.

'What is it now, Mevrouw De Vos?' asks a rather puzzled

John. 'You're in a bit of a state again. It won't do, you know, you need to look after yourself better.'

Madame De Vos intervenes, 'Oh, I'm sorry, Mr Williams, it is this business in Germany, she thinks it is getting worse, she is convinced of it.'

'What business?' asks Annie.

Madame De Vos persuades her mother-in-law to release her tight grip on the paper and holds it up for John and his family to view. 'The newspapers here are concerned about the political situation in Germany,' she says. 'She is now convinced that we should be warned and need to be prepared.'

'Well, what you've got in your hands means nothing to us,' says Mary, 'we can't read it. No wonder they call it double Dutch.'

John steps forward, feeling that there's a need to take control of the situation. 'Now, look,' he says with some authority, 'before we left home we knew that there had been some elections in Germany, but this Hitler chap, he lost, end of story.'

Mevrouw De Vos begins to rant in a very aggressive way, she clutches her daughter-in-law's arm and shakes it with an energy that fully contradicts her frailty and her age. As she speaks in Dutch, Madame De Vos attempts to relay a true account of what she's saying. 'My mother-in-law says that Hitler's Nazi party won thirty-seven per cent of the Reichstag seats and this is a very dangerous sign of things to come.'

John smiles and shakes his head. 'No, no, the thing is he didn't win, that's the point. It's democracy, it works, and it's what we fought for.'

Madame De Vos translates to her mother-in-law what John has said. Mevrouw De Vos shakes her head again and talks quickly while pointing at John, again Madame De Vos translates, 'She says, what about the next elections? Hindenburg won this time, but he will not be around for long, he is old.'

'Well,' adds Madame De Vos, 'she has got a point. Once Hindenburg's gone, there won't be anybody to stop him.'

'I've not got much time for the Germans as you know, Madame De Vos, but I know they're not all daft.'

'Daft?' asks Madame De Vos. 'What is this, daft?'

'Daft, simple-minded, feeble in't brain like,' answers John. 'Well, as I were saying, they'll have come to their senses by then, you've my assurance, I'm right on this.'

Madame De Vos tells the elderly lady of John's assessment of the situation but this time the response comes directly from Madame De Vos. 'Well, Mr Williams, I hope that this will be the case, but it must be remembered that Adolf Hitler has talked about the surrender of the German army as a betrayal. He was a soldier in the war and is very angry I think.'

John responds, 'We get this at home. These politicians, they talk about doing this, that and the other and they say it just to get in. When they do, it all changes, they don't do half of what they say. It's electioneering, Madame De Vos, tell your mother-in-law they're all the same, our lot are just as bad. Once they're in and they get comfortable, they don't want to take any chances.'

Madame De Vos smiles. 'I try, she doesn't believe it and I'm not so sure now that she is as wrong as I would like to think.'

Mary walks to the front door. 'Well, I suggest we take our walk before the German army arrives.'

'Trust our Mary,' says Henry. 'She's got a knack of trivialising important matters.'

'Well on this occasion our Mary's just about got it right,' replies John.

The family leaves the hotel and walks down the street. Although the weather's still very warm, a slight breeze offers a small amount of welcome relief. As they walk, Annie opens her parasol and puts her hand through John's arm. 'They do seem to be worried, don't they? You're not concerned about what they're saying, about this war business, are you?'

'No concern whatsoever. Our boy fought in the Great War, and it weren't that it were just a big fight, it were the war to end all wars.'

'Well,' replies Annie, 'I must admit, I'm a bit confused. When we had that talk in the garden at the hotel, you seemed to have some doubts.'

'A moment of weakness on my part, Annie. Don't read too much into it. I've said what I think and I'll stick to it.'

'So, just to get this right, you're not worried about there being another war?'

John stops and looks into Annie's face. His face presents a confident and yet serious expression. 'No, not at all, Annie, we've talked about this in the Lion, we've discussed it in some detail and looked at all the facts, as you have to.'

'And what conclusion did you come to?'

'We dismissed it without another thought, Annie.'

Annie smiles and as they walk she rests her head onto his shoulder. 'Well, you do put the world to rights in the Red Lion, don't you, John?'

John stops and looks at Annie. 'Do you know, Annie, if Ramsay MacDonald and his ministers wanted to get some good ideas and benefit from some common sense and rational thinking, they'd do a lot worse than call in at our pub.'

Annie laughs. 'Well they're not going to do that are they, John?'

'It's their loss, Annie, it would be their loss entirely.'

The couple laugh and continue their walk.

Chapter Twenty-Two

6 August, 1917 – German Field Hospital, north of Verdun, France

Medical Officer Erich Lehmann's thoughts are with his son as he attends to a critically-wounded private soldier. In the two years that he's been in the service of the Medical Unit, he's dreaded uncovering a sheet that conceals Kurt's body, or finding him in such a condition that little can be done. He works quickly on the young soldier but he knows that it's a lost cause. The enormous loss of blood is too much for the young man's shattered body to cope with and try as he might to stem the flow, other arteries open and rupture.

Eventually, he must make a decision to continue or apply his skills on a casualty where there's the possibility of saving a life. However, the dreadful choice that he has to make is taken from him. The nurse who's stroking the soldier's forehead touches Erich on the arm. He looks at her and she shakes her head. Another family will be given the news that they have been dreading to receive. He throws down the instruments that he's been using, removes his surgical mask and walks slowly towards the door of the old stone building that has been converted for hospital use.

Erich steps outside and from an inside pocket takes out a packet of cigarettes. He removes one and taps his pockets in the search for a match. From his left side, a lighted match is made available; it's held by an officer who's wearing a bandage around his head which covers one of his eyes. Erich gratefully accepts the light and once his cigarette is lit he leans back against the stone wall and inhales the smoke. Although he's not a heavy smoker and indulges only when he really feels the need of a nicotine boost, he knows enough to be sure that smoking is not as pleasurable or as satisfying as it used to be. The war has certainly changed the cigarette, undoubtedly tobacco is still present, although little of it remains and it has been replaced and supplemented by other types of plants.

The officer who's supplied the light attempts to engage Erich in conversation. Erich prefers to be silent, to be alone with his thoughts, and he raises his hand to inform the officer of his wishes. He then walks slowly away and finding a more secluded spot, he leans back against the wall again and continues to smoke his cigarette. His meditation is disturbed by a number of casualty trucks that noisily enter the compound and park in line outside the entrance to the hospital.

The drivers and their assistants are helped by nurses and porters in lifting the stretchers down from the backs of the trucks. In a well-ordered procession, they quickly carry the injured soldiers through the doorway and away from sight. *How many more*, thinks Erich as he allows his cigarette to fall on the ground and he extinguishes what remains of the burning stub by stamping on it. Knowing that his skills will be required he walks back towards the side entrance to the hospital ward. What greets him is a scene of frantic activity; urgent and hasty assessments are being made, the casualties being placed into various and critical groups depending on the extent of their wounds.

A senior surgeon walks down the line and stops by each stretcher. 'Dead!' he shouts. 'Take him out.' Then onto the next and in a loud voice says, 'Not worth it, leave him.' Eventually he identifies a casualty that will benefit from some attention, points to a door that leads to a makeshift operating theatre and shouts, 'Through there, quick as you can!' The voices of medical staff shouting out instructions are almost drowned out by the dreadful screams of great suffering and cries of anguish and pain.

Erich puts on a surgical mask, steps forward to begin his

work and quickly finds himself having to stem the flow of blood from a deep shrapnel wound in the leg of one of the injured soldiers. He knows immediately that his patient will lose the limb. He calls for a porter to hold him down and for a nurse to administer an injection of morphine. Erich is all too aware that the rationed amount of pain relief will help. However, it will not totally allow his patient to be completely free from the excruciating pain that will result from the process of amputation. During his two and a half years of service, Erich has perfected his surgical skills and is able to carry out the procedure quickly and effectively. Speed is to be the important factor and however wretched the young soldier's condition, he's in very capable hands.

As the day progresses, the urgency of the treatment of the patients subsides. The dead are taken away to be prepared for burial and the patients who are considered to be beyond reasonable help are given some pain relief, if they are still conscious. These *lost causes* are removed from the main hospital area and relocated to a large tent close by. Erich is now feeling exhausted and he slumps into a canvas chair. He looks up to see a familiar figure approaching him. It's Colonel Friendrich, Kurt's commanding officer.

Erich had always thought that the colonel looked as if he was too old to serve. Although in his early forties, his stark white hair and heavily lined face make him look many years older. Erich's not too concerned to see him at first because the colonel has visited the hospital many times to see as many of his wounded men as he can. He's always been concerned about the welfare of his troops because it's the way he is. Kurt had always said that the responsibility of command was a heavy burden for him. This is because, in the aftermath of battle, he would search his soul to consider if the excessively high level of casualties was caused by his failures and his lack of judgement.

However, Erich feels that this time it's different. This might well be the day that he has been dreading because the colonel is staring directly at him. He struggles to stand, his movements hampered by fatigue and nervous anticipation. Colonel Friendrich places a hand on Erich's shoulder and almost forces him to sit back down. 'No,' he says, 'please sit down, my friend.'

Erich struggles to ask the question. 'Kurt is dead. That is what you are here to tell me, isn't it?'

'Probably, I'm sorry to say,' replies the colonel.

'Probably?'

Colonel Friendrich sits in a vacant seat next to Erich. 'After the first British assaults, we were unable to find him. We weren't able to find many of our men in what was left of our trenches. I thought, I hoped, that he had been taken prisoner but then there were very reliable reports that told me that he had died.'

'But not confirmed?'

'Not confirmed as yet, but it would be wrong of me to give you false hope, Erich, the reports are pretty reliable. Now we have recovered more of our lost ground, we may be able to find him.'

Colonel Friendrich stands and smooths down his tunic. 'I will of course keep you informed, Erich, but you know that you must prepare yourself.'

Erich remains seated and he bows his head. 'How long will this madness continue, Colonel? How many more must we lose?'

The colonel takes out a rather ornate-looking case from his inside pocket and removes two cigarettes. He puts one in his mouth and offers the other to Erich. Erich gratefully accepts it and when the colonel ignites a lighter and places it in front of his cigarette, he draws a deep breath. Once it's lit, he leans back and inhales the addictive smoke. He slowly blows it out and stares for a moment at what is obviously an expensive cigarette. 'Now that is what I call a real cigarette, real tobacco,' he looks at the colonel. 'You spoil me. How can I now smoke the rubbish that I have had to become accustomed to?'

Colonel Friendrich savours the taste of his cigarette for a moment. 'In answer to your question, Erich, it is difficult to see an end to it and now the Americans are in the war with new blood and their industrial power, well. I think and I fear the worst. Now we are taking older men and younger boys, it cannot go on, and as you know our people at home are starting to suffer from having little to eat. I am certain that we will lose this war.'

Erich looks at him. 'And if we are defeated, who will remember our dead?'

The colonel offers a reassuring smile. 'You, me, their families and comrades who survive. Now you must excuse me, Erich, I will visit my men, and I will of course tell them that the sacrifices that they are making will end in victory. I have been telling them that for almost three years now and I think that they are starting to doubt what I am telling them. Well goodbye, Erich, my thoughts are with you and your wife.'

Erich nods and thanks the colonel. As Colonel Friedrich strolls away, Erich stands and walks towards the senior commander's office to ask if he can apply for compassionate leave. With the wounded from Passchendaele flooding in, it is not a good time to think of returning home, but when is it ever a good time? He knows that his place now is to be with his wife and his surviving son.

Chapter Twenty-Three

11 November, 1918 – Blackburn

John carefully goes about his work, meticulously and skilfully threading the needle through the cloth and pulling it tight. He looks at the large clock at the end of the room. It displays the time of a quarter past nine in the morning and it's the fourth time that he's checked it since he arrived at work at eight. John normally has the ability to apply himself to his craft with a level of dedication that's reflected in a consistent performance of concentration. However, today it's different, the twelve men working in the workshop feel it, they struggle to contain their excitement and are clearly distracted. They've heard the rumours that the war will end on this day, it's been well publicised in the press that the government has been negotiating a ceasefire resulting in the surrender of the German forces.

Suddenly, a phone bell rings out, all the men stop what they're doing and look towards the frosted glass window of Mr Webster's office. They can see the shadowy figure of Mr Webster pick up the phone, and although the image is defused the men can see that he's holding the phone in one hand and the hearing piece is held at his ear. 'Right,' he says loudly. Mr Webster always speaks at such a volume when on the phone because he's aware of the long distance that his voice has to travel. 'Right,' he repeats, 'that's it then, right-o, right-o.' He puts the phone down and clearly writes something on a paper on his desk, opens the door of the office and walks into the workshop.

The short and elderly Mr Webster stands for a moment

and addresses his employees, 'Now then, men, stop what you're doing and gather round because I've something important to tell you.' The men do as they're told and eagerly move closer to their boss. Mr Webster places a pair of small, round-rimmed spectacles on his nose and unfolds a piece of paper. 'I've written it down so that I don't get it wrong,' he says. 'As you know, my youngest boy is with the Blackburn Times and he's managed to get a bit of information on events and on what's going on.'

He then reads from the paper that he's holding. 'As you know, negotiations have been underway for some time, an agreement was reached this morning at five o'clock, well, ten past to be precise, as far as my boy knows.' The men start to get a little impatient and wish that their boss would hurry up with the information, although they know that this is Mr Webster's way because he will not be rushed under any circumstances. A careful and measured approach is applied at all times. 'Now,' he continues to say, 'we're waiting to get confirmation from Manchester but it's now clear that all hostilities will cease at eleven o'clock this morning and the guns will finally be silent.'

This news is met by an unusual silence. The men are thoughtful and take a moment to consider the enormity of what they've heard. Mr Webster continues to read from the paper, 'The mayor has called for the council to sit shortly after eleven to decide on what to do with events and holidays and such like.' He folds the paper and removes his spectacles, thinks for a moment and says, 'That's it, men. Now, this war has taken its toll on most of us, we've lost lads, my son Tom as you know went with the Pals to the Somme and never came back.' Mr Webster looks around the room. He's aware that some of his workers can tell a similar story and he looks directly at John. 'There's your Herbert, John.' Then he scans the rest of the faces of the men. 'And your brother Richard, Mons weren't it?' Mr Webster is careful not to forget any of the sacrifices that his employees have had to make. All of them are affected; it may have been a son, a daughter, a brother, a sister, a cousin or even a good friend.

'Now,' Mr Webster says, 'this is a time for your families, go home and spend time with them. I'm going down to the Town Hall, no doubt there'll be something going on. I don't want to see you tomorrow, day off, it'll be paid.'

The men thank their boss for his generosity, put on their coats and leave the workshop. Little is said, there isn't much to say. They bid each other farewell and head off in different directions. John has the company of Jim Stanton for his walk home because his house is in the street next to where John lives. Jim lost a son at the naval battle of Jutland and as they walk both men reflect on how they feel about the news.

The time is approaching a quarter past ten. Annie brushes the hairs from the shoulders of John's suit jacket while he adjusts his tie with the aid of the hallstand mirror. He turns around and looks at this wife. She makes a further minor adjustment to his tie.

'Will I do, Annie?' he says. 'Would our Bert be proud of me?'

Annie smiles at him. 'You'll do very nicely, he'd be very proud, John, very proud indeed.' They leave the house and stroll slowly towards the tram stop, there they wait as the first tram goes by. The conductor waves to indicate that there's no room and it certainly looks to be as full as it can be with many having to stand. After a few minutes another tram stops and although it's also very full, there's space for John to stand and Annie to sit. The conductor tells them that as the rumours of the ceasefire spread, most of the population of the town is now heading to the town centre to hear the news. He also tells them that because of the demand, extra trams are to be put on.

Once off the tram, John and Annie head towards the Town Hall, and the closer they get, the busier it becomes. John does his best to make sure that Annie is protected and shielded from people who are pushing past. 'Steady on, slow down,' he says, 'take it easy.' When they reach the square, John looks up at the Market Hall clock, which reads almost five minutes to eleven.

'Five minutes to go or thereabouts,' he shouts at Annie, 'not long now.'

The mayor, dressed in his dark blue robe and proudly wearing his shiny chain of office, briefly stands on the balcony at the front of the Town Hall. He's joined by other members of the council who stand and wave at people they know and recognise, and also at people they think they know.

The mayor disappears and slowly the council retires from the scene. Suddenly, the bell of the clock tower on the Market Hall strikes, one, two, three and so on until finally everybody has counted eleven chimes. Then it falls silent. The crowd is stunned for a moment, it's the first time that the bell has been heard since the war began because the council had decreed that it would not be heard again until victory was achieved. Slowly, many in the crowd start to cheer and the volume increases until it becomes almost deafening. Small union flags are being waved. John looks towards Annie and indicates that the best thing to do is to move to somewhere where it's quieter and less hectic.

Once away from the square they make for the Boulevard and on the way they pass the White Bull Inn. John looks through the window and is somewhat relieved to see that there are vacant seats available. Once Annie is seated in the lounge bar John goes to the counter to buy some drinks and returns with a pint of ale and a half of milk stout for his wife. He takes off his trilby hat and sits next to Annie. 'It's only Dutton's brew but it'll do,' he says. 'Any port in a storm and all that.'

They enjoy their drinks and start to talk. Their conversation is interrupted when they become aware of the presence of a familiar figure who's standing in front of them. 'Aye up, Stan,' says John, 'I thought you'd be set on council business, haven't you got a meeting with the mayor?'

Councillor Stanley Smith sits next to John and takes a long drink of his ale. Being a plump and stocky middle-aged man he quickly perspires when doing very little. He takes out a handkerchief and dabs his forehead. He puts his beer glass on the table. 'I got the understanding of what was being said and I made my excuses, I needed a drink I were thinking.'

'Well,' asks John, 'what were decided like?'

'A lot,' replies Stan. 'The Cotton Employers' Association has said that its members can have a day off and needn't go back until Wednesday morning and that's the start of it. The mayor has said that his mill workers can have till Thursday, which is good of him and very generous.'

'What about the schools, Stan?' asks Annie. 'I'd heard that they might be shut for a day or so.'

'A week off,' replies Stan. 'A whole week.'

'Blimey,' says John, 'they're not doing things by halves. I don't need to go in until Wednesday myself.'

Stan finishes his ale, stands up and puts on his bowler hat. 'If you're thinking of going to the picture house or the theatre, you'd better go early to be on the safe side, they're all getting booked up already, mind there'll be extra trams on.'

'Well, that's a thought, Annie,' says John, 'it's a long time since we went to the picture house, I wonder what's on?'

Annie smiles at him, 'It doesn't matter what's on at the picture house. When I went to St Mark's yesterday, the Reverend Bourne told me that if the armistice came today, there'd be a service of remembrance tonight at half past seven. That's where we'll be with the children.'

Stan bids the couple farewell and leaves. 'He didn't mention his daughter,' says John. 'Beth were her name, is that right?'

'It were Beatrice,' replies Annie. 'She were with the Army Nursing Corp.'

'Aye that's right, she were killed in France when those buggers lobbed a shell into the hospital where she were working.'

'And she were going to get married the following year, that were sad,' adds Annie.

'That's it, to that lad who lived on Revidge Road, Gordon he were called.'

John stands and puts on his hat. 'I'll come to church on one condition, Annie.'

'And what's the condition?'

'If I'm allowed a pint in the Lion afterwards. I need to get rid of the taste of this Dutton's beer.'

John gets ready to leave.

'Just sit down please, John,' Annie says. 'We've avoided it all day.'

'Avoided what?'

'Thinking of our Bert. It's almost as if he's been forgotten, in all this celebration.'

'Aye,' says John as he sits back down, 'you're right, Annie, look at this lot, all over the place, singing, cheering and being a bit silly like.'

'And a lot of these folk will have lost boys.' Annie looks around the bar. 'There's Sam Longhurst over there, his son were killed in Belgium, then there's Sarah Leighten, her lad were blinded, and Mr and Mrs Derby lost two boys, didn't they?'

'Aye they did, within a week of each other at Ypres, I think it were in the year of sixteen, and there's young Jack Smeaton, his twin brother were never found after Passchendaele.' John moves closer to Annie, puts his arm around her and holds her tight, he kisses her on the cheek and keeps his head next to hers. 'We won't forget our boy, Annie, we never will.'

The couple sit in silence for a moment while they remember their son; they remind themselves of the good days and not so good times, they recall images of when Bert was a very small boy to when he became a young man. After a time, they leave the pub and walk arm in arm towards the Boulevard to catch a tram home.

'All this happiness, Annie, well it's like a wake at a funeral. Have you noticed how folk get a bit high-spirited and loud when they should be a bit sombre? It's a front, a release and that's what everyone's like now. Glad it's over, relieved that we've won, but in the days, weeks and months to come, there'll be a lot of sadness. We'll never have our Bert back, but he'll always be with us, Annie.'

As they stand and wait for the tram to Billinge End, John looks at Annie. There's a bit of a twinkle in his eye. 'Do you know, Annie, I think we'll go over there.'

'Over where?'

'To Belgium, to see our Bert. Not immediately, but when things will have settled down like and got back to normal.'

'Are you serious, John, do you think it's possible?'

'Well, Kitchener sent a lot of chaps over there, can't be too difficult, there's only two of us. Yes, I'll look into it and make a plan.'

Annie smiles at him. 'Well, John, it sounds as if it could be complicated, but I'll leave it to you. If anybody can do it, you can.'

'You know me, Annie, I like it when it's complicated and when it requires a lot of thought and planning.'

The Reverend Bourne stands in the pulpit of St Mark's church. His frame is short and he's somewhat on the plump side in build, he has a large white moustache and a full head of white hair. Many liken him to the Prime Minister, Lloyd George, in manner and looks. As he looks down at the congregation he smiles. It pleases him to see that his church is full, all the seats are taken and many are standing at the back. A hymn is in progress and the minister waits until the start of the last verse before climbing the steps to the pulpit, which is his platform of authority and where he will deliver his sermon. Knowing that the signing of the armistice was due to be delivered, the content of the sermon has been written and considered for some days. The congregation continues to sing:

> *'While I draw this fleeting breath, when mine eyes shall close in death, when I soar to worlds unknown, see thee on thy judgement throne, Rock of Ages, cleft for me, let me hide myself in thee.'*

At the last note, the people sit, and when they're seated and finally settled, the Reverend Bourne pauses for a moment and begins his deliberation. 'My dear friends, children of our loving God, you are welcome to join with me in celebrating this wonderful day.' He looks down again at his audience; many are faces that he immediately recognises, some look familiar and there are a few he doesn't know.

Sitting with Annie and John are James and Emma. Harold has failed to attend as usual. He'd been out with his friends and although he'd promised faithfully to be back in good time for the service there was no sign of him when they left their house. Annie leans nearer to John and says quietly, 'Mr Bourne's looking at you, John, and he's wondering who you are.'

'What an exaggeration, Annie, I were here last month,' he whispers. 'I told him that there were some parts of his sermon that I could take issue with.'

Reverend Bourne continues with his oration. 'In the summer of 1914, we said goodbye to many of our boys from the town and some we didn't see again. They were good boys who'd answered the call to defend their country, to fight for a just cause and secure a rightful and a just victory. For *King and Country* was the call, and lads of Lancashire were at the front of the queue, proudly marching forth, *with the cross of Jesus,* as our great hymn pronounces. Those words were written by Sabine Baring-Gould in 1865 and they're as relevant today as when they were first written. Our brave soldiers have won the physical war, now we have to defeat Satan in the spiritual battles that lie ahead.' He raises his arms up and in a very loud voice says, '*Onward Christian Soldiers, marching as to war,* as to war, no longer, *marching off to war.* We all prayed for the victory that the memory of our dead sons demanded, and the Lord listened and gave us what we asked for because we were on the side of righteousness and light. Now, without the gun and the instruments of war, we must continue the fight, this is not the end of our struggle, the greater test is about to begin, *onward Christian Soldiers.*'

The minister pauses for a moment and scans the hall. 'Have we destroyed evil, were the sons of our enemies doing the devil's work? Many times I stood here before you and talked of the evil that had to be destroyed. I believed it then and I believe it now. We prayed and God listened to us, he had to decide who was worthy and he chose us.' Again he pauses, bows his head and thinks for a moment. Then he gives the congregation a meaningful and intense stare. 'What I'm about to say now, some of you may find difficult to understand. I do believe that the dark forces drove the Hun on to commit the most hideous of crimes against the innocent. But, and this is the important thing, although not without blame and now having to bear the guilt of their actions, the young men who were seduced into taking up arms for the alliance of evil were used and ultimately betrayed by their masters. Now is the time for forgiveness, to forgive our enemies. This is the greatest test that we have been given. We are now Christians, we are now soldiers without guns, the words of Christ are our weapons, *we forgive them that trespass against us.* When we say the Lord's Prayer and we say those words, we must mean it. Again he raises a hand and forms a tight fist. '*Onward Christian Soldiers, marching as to war.* We must show by example, it will be the way we talk about our former enemies and when needed, to welcome them to us, this is the way we show that forgiveness is in our hearts.'

'Now we are relieved to put away the gun,' says the minister. He picks up a bible and holds it up above his head. 'This is now our weapon; the good book, forgiveness and kindness will win the coming battles.'

The congregation is for a moment mainly silent and then a ripple of a hum of muttering is heard as they digest what Reverend Bourne has said. While his hand is still raised, he opens up his fingers and the clenched fist softens as he asks the congregation to cease talking and to continue listening.

'The last four years have been a trial for us all, we have had to make sacrifices, and now comes the greatest test that we could ever have been given, we can hate, but can we forgive? *Onward Christian Soldiers*. Our enemies must be returned to the Lord, no longer by the force of arms but by our compassion and our understanding.'

John speaks quietly to Annie, 'Think on, Vicar, he's changed his tune, and if he thinks I'm going to forgive those...'

'Careful, John, remember where we are.'

'Well, he's talking nonsense.'

The sermon continues until finally the minister says, 'Remember what Jesus said, *and forgive us our trespasses, as we forgive them that trespass against us.*' The service is concluded by the singing of *Abide with me* and at the end of the hymn the Reverend Bourne gives his final blessing before the worshippers depart. As the congregation leaves the church the minister shakes the hand of each parishioner and bids them farewell. John has deliberately stayed at the back of the queue so that he can seek clarification on the main points of the sermon. Annie has already left the church and waits with the minister until John eventually emerges from the doorway. Reverend Bourne shakes John's hand and smiles warmly at him. 'Did you approve of my sermon, John?' he says, knowing that it's very likely that he didn't.

'Well,' says John, 'you expect a lot of us, Vicar. In fact the issue that I have with the church at times is that they, that's educated chaps like you, are out of touch and not really living in the real world. My view is that a thanks for victory would have sufficed and done very nicely and it should have been left at that.'

'Oh, John, if only it was that simple. It's not what we the clergy, the ministers of the Church, ask of you, it's what God demands.'

'Perhaps it's God who's out of touch then, Vicar.'

Reverend Bourne laughs. 'I don't think we're in a position to criticise or question our Lord, it's not our place. We may have been granted the freedom of choice, but there're some things that can't be negotiated. God's plan is not up for discussion.'

'Sounds like he's got a closed mind, Vicar.'

'When God sent his son to us, the message was clearly understood, it wasn't ambiguous, or vague, *let he who is without sin, cast the first stone.* We may have won the war, but can we win the peace? We're all sinners in the eyes of the Lord and we need to repent. We'll curry much favour with our creator by admitting our weaknesses and this can start by us forgiving those who we feel have wronged us. Our Lord expects a lot from us, as I said, it's a test and it's a difficult test for many.'

John thinks for a moment, he starts to slowly walk away, stops and turns to say one final thing, 'Next time you have a talk with God, you can tell him from me that he's not got it right and he'll lose some of us because it's asking too much.'

Reverend Bourne holds up his hand to say a final farewell and watches as John and Annie exit the churchyard. As the couple walk down the road Annie says, 'He's a good man, he's only concerned about our well-being and our spiritual lives, our souls, that's what concerns him.'

John stops and looks at her. 'Aye, I understand that, Annie, but I wouldn't like to work for his boss, we'd fall out in no time and I'd soon get the sack.'

Chapter Twenty-Four

3 August, 1932 – Poperinge

John and Henry sit outside a bar located on a busy street in the centre of the town. They're smoking their pipes and drinking lager beer. Both are relaxed and have eagerly taken the opportunity to spend a quiet time together. They discuss how Blackburn Rovers faired last season and what the prospects are for the coming campaign. Like most supporters they know what needs to be done to improve the team's chances of success. There have been rumours that the landlord of the Lion, Frank Bennet, has been considering retiring. This is very worrying news because Frank has always been concerned about the needs of his regulars. He manages the quality of his ale to perfection, it's considered to be the finest in the area and second to none. After calling time at the end of a Friday or a Saturday evening drinking session, Frank will bolt the door after most of the drinkers have left. However, John and his companions remain seated because they know that Frank considers them to be the favoured and trusted few and are invited to stay.

Annie and Mary take a very dim view of this disregard for the licensing laws and when both their husbands admit to not feeling particularly well the next morning, their complaining is not treated very sympathetically. John and Henry hope that Frank's son Peter may be persuaded to take on the tenancy and being *a chip off the old block,* normal service may be resumed.

Henry takes a long drink and holds up the large tankard to examine it and to make a visual analysis. First he observes the light-coloured drink one way and then positions the glass so that the sun filters through, highlighting the clarity of the beer. 'Not a bad beer really. A bit yellow, second best compared to what we're used to at home. It's not ale though, is it?' Henry looks again at his drink. 'Well, being experts as we are, we're good judges and we know a good pint. But we've been spoilt really, having three breweries in't town like.'

'You're right, Henry, but I'm the first to admit it's what you're used to and brought up with. I'm not sure what these Belgium folk would make of our ales. Mind you, once they've tasted it, they might turn their noses up at this lager beer when they get back home. Perhaps it's better that they don't know.'

'Well, while we're here, it's all right for a time, but…' Henry stops talking because something catches his attention.

'What's up?' asks John.

'Aye up, John, look o'er yon, could be trouble, I can see it.' Henry points towards the street. John follows his brother-in-law's directions and spots Erich Lehmann who's walking by on the other side of the road. Erich catches sight of them, stops and after waiting for the passing traffic to go by, crosses the road and approaches them. Clearly he's determined to engage them both in conversation.

Henry bows his head and out of the corner of his mouth says, 'Oh heck, John, here we go.'

John leans back and folds his arms in a gesture of steadfast defiance. 'Stand your ground, Henry, and finish your beer, we'll not be retreating or withdrawing.'

Erich stands before them; his stance presents him as a man who's almost standing to attention. He nods his head slightly. 'Good day, gentlemen. May I join you?'

John looks across the table, it's unfortunate but a vacant chair is obviously available, he reluctantly nods to grant his begrudging approval. 'Help yourself,' he says, deliberately avoiding eye contact. 'It's a free world, thanks to the British Army.'

Erich removes his straw boater hat and places it on the table. He sits down opposite the two men and turns to try to attract the attention of the waiter. Henry noisily pushes his chair back and stands up, he puts on his cap. 'I'm going John, better things to do, are you coming with me?'

John stares at Henry in disbelief. 'No I'm not and you shouldn't be leaving either, we were here first, now sit down and finish your beer.'

In an unusual gesture of self-determination and in attempting to act on his own authority, Henry disregards his brother-in-law's instruction. 'No I'll go, I don't feel comfortable, John, I've got better things to do and I'm fussy about the company I keep.'

Henry leaves. John watches his departure, shakes his head and stares directly at Erich. 'You see what you've done now? We were having a nice quiet drink together.'

Erich shakes his head. 'I'm sorry, I did not wish to upset you and spoil your day.'

'Well you have, you've spoilt it.'

The waiter approaches and produces a pad ready to take Erich's order. 'Just a beer, bitte,' he points at John's glass tankard and adds, 'like this, danke.'

The waiter leaves to get the drink. Erich turns back to speak to John, 'You said thanks to the British Army but you forgot to include the French, the Canadians, the Australians, the Americans and...'

'All right, all right, the Allies if you like, but the point is that our chaps came from all over the Empire, even from India, they came to support us because we were in the right and you were wrong.'

'Whatever their nationality and country of birth, all these young men gave their lives, all these sons, brothers and husbands made a sacrifice, gave their lives.'

'Aye, all these sons on our side gave their lives for a just cause. You don't seem to understand, you can't understand it, no wonder the French called you the Bosche, it means stubborn and obstinate. Ours were a just cause, not like your lot.'

Erich sighs long and deeply, he searches for a strategy to make his point. 'Let me if I may put something to you, you will first think that it is absurd and I fully understand.'

John takes a quick drink and slams his tankard onto the table, some of the frothy liquid splashes out. 'I've no time for this, no patience with it.'

'Imagine if you can, Mr Williams, that you are a German citizen, it is 1914 and your son is eager to enlist, to fight for his country.'

John shakes his head and stares at his foe. 'You what? How could I be a bloody German?'

'Why not? You are from the Anglo Saxon community. Many of your ancestors came from Northern Germany.'

John spots a flaw in Erich's preposterous reasoning. 'Well that's where you're wrong,' he says with a triumphant look on his face, as if he's about to trap the king and declare *checkmate*. 'Caernarfon,' he announces.

'Caernarfon?'

'Aye, Caernarfon, North Wales, that's where my ancestors come from.'

'And how is this relevant?'

John leans forward to deliver the final blow and down his opponent. 'The Welsh are pure blood, the real British, none of this Saxon contamination, none of your pollution flows through our veins.'

Erich is becoming increasingly more frustrated. 'Well, please can I make a point? Imagine and picture yourself as a citizen of Germany.'

John's disappointed that Erich hasn't accepted his argument and withdrawn, he prepares to attack. 'Right, this is how it is, if I were as you say a German and my boy said that he were joining up, I'd soon put that daft idea out of his head.'

'Why, why would you do that?'

'Because your bloody country was in the wrong, everyone knows it.'

Erich leans back and looks up to the ceiling and sighs. 'I accept that we were the aggressors in the first place, but does that make us in the wrong?'

John senses victory. 'Look, it's obvious, Belgium gave us the land where our boys are buried, you've got to pay rent for yours, that's because you were in the wrong.'

Erich again shakes his head. 'It is not a case of who was right and who was wrong. We must respect our dead, young men who gave their lives, cut down, with their lives before them.'

John chuckles in a sarcastic way, 'I'll respect my dead; you do what you like.'

Erich is now clearly becoming more irritated. 'I think that you have a closed mind, Mr Williams.'

'The thing is, I'm proud of what my boy did and I loved him. You can't feel the same about your son, you couldn't possibly feel the same.'

Other customers at the café stare at the two men because Erich's voice increases in volume. 'You don't think that I loved my son?'

John's face is now a deep red colour, he's starting to shake with rage. 'How can you love a murderer, a bloody assassin? That's what your lot were.'

Erich is outraged. He stands abruptly and in doing so pushes his chair over and it clatters onto the stone floor. He adopts an aggressive stance. 'A murderer? You call my son a murderer, why, because he fought and killed the enemy as your boy did?'

John is seething. 'I heard the stories, I heard the stories about your lot bayoneting children and raping women and...'

'What stories?' shouts Erich, oblivious to the fact that he is the focus of attention by the other customers. 'Propaganda and you believed it.'

'Aye, I did believe it, still do, and I expect that your son being an officer was responsible for it, being in charge, giving his orders, his murderous orders…'

Erich looks down, he attempts to compose himself and regain some dignity, his voice is a little softer, 'That is a despicable thing to say. I would never say such a thing about your son.'

John strikes what he believes to be the final decisive blow. 'Well you wouldn't be able to say anything like that because my boy wouldn't have done things like that.'

Erich picks up his hat and turns to walk away, it's clear to him that there's very little point in continuing the argument, nothing is to be gained from further confrontation.

A triumphant John shouts after him, 'You know what I hope? I hope your boy was killed by a bullet that came from my Bert's gun, I'd like that, I'd like to think that.'

Erich stops, turns around and quickly walks back towards John. He throws down his hat, leans over and violently seizes the lapels on John's jacket. He's shaking and is extremely angry, his face now so close to his adversary's face that he can feel the warmth of John's breath. He struggles to find the words, all reasoning is now lost. 'You… you stupid man!' he shouts. 'You are the most ridiculous person I have ever met!'

John's shaken and when Erich releases his grip and steps back, John brushes down the now creased material of his jacket. He adjusts his tie and smooths down his ruffled hair and, although stunned, deliberately puts on an expression that portrays smug satisfaction. He looks pleased with himself. 'Oh yes, here we are, here comes the Hun out of the bunker with his machine gun, what happened to the respectable doctor, eh?'

Erich tries to compose himself, he's sweating and still shaking with rage. He takes a further moment to collect his thoughts and compose himself. He looks around the café and for the first time becomes aware of the other customers' interest in their distasteful and embarrassing performance. 'The respected doctor, as you call me, has been pushed to the limits of his reasoning.'

'You can't hide it can you? It's in there, the bully the tyrant… the assassin…'

Erich walks away, then turns to make another comment, 'Congratulations, Mr Williams, you have succeeded in making me act in a way that I never thought was possible. In that, you are victorious. I'm sorry I cannot confirm to you that your son could have taken my Kurt's life. He was killed by a shell and I know that there was little of him left.'

John takes a long drink of his beer and watches as Erich puts on his hat and walks into the café. The waiter approaches him. Erich takes out a bank note from his wallet and hands it to him. The waiter opens his own wallet to find some change. Erich waves his hand to indicate that a generous tip is in order, which is given as a form of apology for his unacceptable behaviour and conduct. A thoughtful Erich leaves the café and deliberately avoids eye contact with John. He walks down the road and doesn't look back.

Chapter Twenty-Five

1 November, 1918 – Etreux, France

The burly German soldier wielding a large stick aggressively and forcefully strikes the back of the struggling and distressed horse, which is clearly a pale shadow of the fine, proud animal that was brought into service two years before. Years of abuse and ill-treatment have taken its toll. The outline of the animal's ribcage is very visible, its eyes portray fear and terror, the nostrils are flared and in the coldness of early morning, steam rises from its shiny coat now dripping with sweat. 'Pull, you lazy, fucking beast!' the soldier screams.

On the muddy road, the cart that the horse is attempting to pull slides and slithers, then slips down a slope into a ditch. There it rests for a moment, the horse breathing heavily and gasping for air, it rests on its side and the pitiful beast's situation is now hopeless. It's clearly impossible for the horse to stand, even though the brutal soldier thinks otherwise. Again the stick comes down onto the stricken animal's bleeding and scarred back. 'Fuck you, you old useless nag, get up you bag of shit.'

An officer shouts at him and quickly steps forward to wrench the stick from the soldier's fist. He pushes him so that he falls back against the bank of the ditch. From his holster, the officer takes out a revolver and fires one precise shot into the horse's head. He glares at the soldier, shakes his head and climbs out of the ditch to join the other troops that are marching along the road, although staggering would be a more appropriate description of their slow advance. Like the horse, the soldiers are unrecognisable in comparison to the well-disciplined, proud and smart troops that marched through Belgium in the summer of 1914. Now they look ragged and unkempt, their patched-up, grey uniforms are stained with mud. Some hold rifles while others carry blankets and sacks containing the few provisions that they have managed to scrounge and find. Shellfire and the unmistakable repetitive reverberation of machine guns being fired can be heard in the distance, and the soldiers fear that the sound of death is getting closer.

Further down the line there's a motorised ambulance. It travels as quickly as it's able to but, due to the congestion on the road, its pace is very slow. Sitting alongside the driver is Erich Lehmann. He's very tired because it's been a difficult and demanding few days up till now. When he was given the opportunity to escort seriously injured soldiers back to Germany, he jumped at the chance. He's heading towards his home, back to his family and very importantly, back to his Martina. It's now clear that the government is seeking to achieve a ceasefire, to surrender, and when this happens he wants to be with his wife. His commanding officer has assured him that once he's safely delivered his wounded men to a hospital near Bonn, he'll be given leave so that he can go home.

The convoy moves slowly towards the Belgian border. At the village of Boue, the combat troops are mustered to make a stand to slow down the enemy. Here, the ambulance is joined by some other hospital wagons, motorised and horse-drawn. A colonel halts Erich's wagon and approaches the passenger side door. Erich leans out to speak to the officer. 'Why have we been stopped?' he snaps. 'It is important that we get these men to a hospital for treatment, as soon as possible.'

The colonel, short and stocky in build, wearing the traditional peaked cap with the badge denoting his rank, looks at the line of transport carrying the wounded. 'We will erect some tents for the men, then you will hand over your wagons for our use. This is now your order.'

Erich slams his fist down on the panel in front of his seat. 'We have been given orders to take these men home for treatment,' he says in a raised voice, the tone of which plainly expresses his frustration. He reaches into his tunic and produces some official-looking documents. Erich sifts through the papers and finds the order that confirms his course of action. He hands the paper to the colonel and waits for the officer's response.

'Stupid, stuck-up bastard,' mutters the driver.

After a careful inspection of the document, the colonel hands it back to Erich. 'This is meaningless,' he says in a dismissive way. 'Things have changed. The Americans are breaking through just to the south and my orders are to get these soldiers back to the front and to push the enemy back.'

Erich looks back at the line of bedraggled, scruffy and dishevelled men who were once a fighting force. 'You mean these men? They can hardly walk, let alone fight, this war is lost and it is time to go home.'

The colonel leans closer to the window of the truck, he's becoming increasingly angry. 'As far as I know, the German army has not surrendered. With more spirit and once we regroup, we can win this war and push on to final victory. If you disagree, you can explain your views to a panel of a Court Martial Assembly. Defeatist's talk will not be tolerated, it spreads like a disease.'

Erich shakes his head and looks at the driver who shrugs his shoulders. He leans close to the driver and says quietly so that the colonel can't hear him, 'Stay here, I will sort it out. Don't abandon the trucks till I come back.' The driver nods and then starts to worry about how he's going to avoid complying with the colonel's orders.

As Erich climbs down from the cab, a car pulls up alongside the truck. Seated on the back seat is a senior officer and from the insignia of a gold leaf on the red collar on his coat, Erich recognises that he's a lieutenant general of a Prussian Regiment. The general calls the colonel over and talks to him for a moment, then he waves his hand at Erich to summon him to discuss the situation further. Erich approaches the slim-built and elegant-looking general who stays seated in the car. Erich salutes and the senior officer acknowledges this by tapping his regimental cane on the front of his cap. As he strokes his large, drooping moustache he asks, 'What is this all about, Medical Officer, or whatever your rank is, are you disobeying orders?'

'Sir,' answers Erich, 'I have been given orders to take these severely wounded soldiers back to the Fatherland so that they can get the treatment that they need. They have given so much and I believe that they deserve to be helped.'

The colonel argues his case and talks of possible victory. The general shakes his head. 'If I thought that this small number of transport trucks would turn the tide for us then I would say, take them colonel, but I do not believe it to be true.' He looks at Erich. 'You have opinions and views which are not tolerated in the army, but I can see that you want the best for your men. Carry on with your journey.'

The colonel starts to protest and the general raises his hand to indicate that the debate is at an end. Erich thanks the general and climbs back into the cab of the truck. The general calls after him, 'You will not have an escort from here, I will take your armed men, make sure that you have red crosses on top of all your transport. There are a lot of enemy aircraft up there and they will shoot at you, but if they know that you carry injured men even the British will respect that.'

Erich sits back in his seat, his earlier feeling of fatigue has lifted, he now feels invigorated and rejuvenated, the driver grins at him. 'Right, driver, let's go home, shall we? Now where can we get some more white sheets and red paint?'

Chapter Twenty-Six

3 August, 1932 – Poperinge

Martina walks alone along the pavement on a very pleasantly located tree-lined avenue. She's enjoying the afternoon sunshine and is holding a small, cream-coloured parasol that matches the floral-patterned, summer outfit that she's wearing. Major and Mrs Aspinal are also taking a recreational stroll down the same avenue. They too look the part; Major Aspinal in a light-coloured cotton suit and Mrs Aspinal wearing a white floral dress and a cream jacket with a matching hat, displaying well-crafted and delicate silk flowers. When they meet Martina, Major Aspinal touches the brim of his Panama hat and nods his head slightly. 'Lovely day, Mrs... sorry, Frau Lehmann,' he says.

'Delightful day,' replies Martina, 'although I think we could do with a small cooling breeze, do you not think?'

'Still, we can't complain too much,' replies the major.

'Your husband's not with you this afternoon, Frau Lehmann?' observes Mrs Aspinal.

'Oh, he is somewhere, he went to buy a hat and I know he had seen a... boat hat, is it?'

'Ah, a straw boater, I think you mean,' says the major. 'Just the thing for this warm weather and suitable for the occasion.'

'Yes, that is it, a straw boater, he is not much of a hat person normally, but this just seemed to appeal to him. I think you say *it took his fancy*.'

'Well said, Frau Lehmann,' laughs Major Aspinal, 'and if something takes your fancy, you have to act on it and it has to be done.'

'Please,' protests Martina, 'in the English way, call me Martina.'

'Well, if informality is the order of the day,' says the major, 'we are William and Georgina.'

'Georgina,' says Martina, 'what a charming name, so agreeable.'

The three new friends stroll slowly down the avenue.

'How do you find the hotel, Martina?' asks Georgina. 'Is it to your liking?'

'My Erich found it. He contacted an agency that was able to give him some details of suitable accommodation.'

'No,' says Georgina, 'when I say find it, I mean, what do you think of it?'

'I see what you mean,' replies Martina. 'It is clean I think, the food is good and Madame De Vos is very helpful, do you agree?'

'Well, William was billeted in the hotel for a time in the war when it was officers' quarters, he just felt that he wanted to stay there again, didn't you, William?'

'Well I did, you see,' adds William. 'Wouldn't have bothered otherwise. Not really our cup of tea, so to speak, but as a base, comfortable enough.'

'You don't like the tea in the hotel?' says Martina.

William and Georgina both laugh. 'Isn't it strange,' says William, 'we say these things always assuming that the recipient of our conversation is fully aware of the idiosyncrasies of our complicated language and how we phrase our views with a degree of flippancy, you might say.'

Martina stares at William for a moment. Clearly she has some difficulty in understanding William's explanation regarding his comments about tea.

'William wasn't talking about tea as such,' explains Georgina, 'he means that when we travel, we look to stay in accommodation of a certain standard. Madame De Vos's hotel is acceptable, but won't be memorable.'

Martina smiles. 'I see, like tea, the better the quality, the more you remember it. It is probably about the price that you pay.'

'Exactly,' replies William, 'it's what you're used to at the end of the day. Now, how do you find the people of this pleasant little town and at the hotel?'

'I find the local people to be very friendly and as I said, Madame De Vos and her staff are very agreeable,' says Martina.

'Still, bit unfortunate, I mean you bumping into that John Williams and his family,' adds William. 'People like that never quite see the bigger picture. Not bad people really, salt of the earth and all that, but lack some education and it's about breeding you know. Their sort, well, they'll always bear a grudge, always be bitter, I say forgive and forget.'

'It is as you say, unfortunate,' says Martina, 'but, I understand it in some way. Like us, they lost a son, and that will never be forgotten. It is always in your mind. The day before, I talked with Mrs Williams and her sister and after a difficult introduction, we were all right, I think. We had as you say something in common.'

'Of course,' says William, 'I don't know what it's like to lose a son in a war, must be quite dreadful, but that's no excuse for bad manners you know.'

Georgina stops and places her hand on Martina's arm. 'Is that your husband, Martina, standing over there by that gate?'

Martina looks in the same direction and sees Erich standing with his hands in his pockets and he appears to be kicking something like a pebble into the gutter.

'Yes, it is,' confirms Martina. 'I see that he has been successful in buying his straw boater. He will be pleased, I think.'

'Well, I'm not sure that he looks that pleased, on the contrary, he looks a little anxious, don't you think?' says Georgina.

Martina looks at him. 'You're right, Georgina, I rarely see him with his hands in his pockets and his manner is strange, will you excuse me please?'

Martina leaves the Aspinals and goes to talk to her husband. As she approaches, Erich puts up his hand, indicating that he wishes to be left alone.

'Leave me, Martina, I am not good company at the moment.'

'Erich, what is the matter?' says Martina. She holds Erich's arm and directs him towards a bench, that's close by. 'Please, Erich,' she says, 'sit and tell me what it is, please.'

Erich sits down and sighs deeply, he bows his head and shakes it. 'Am I an unreasonable man?'

Martina smiles and shakes her head. 'No, not at all.'

'Am I belligerent, hostile, aggressive...?'

'Of course not, not the Erich that I know.'

'Then why, why does that man bring out the worst in me?'

Martina sighs deeply. Things are becoming clearer. 'Now I see, I think you mean Mr Williams.'

'You call him Mr Williams, you give him the respect he does not deserve.' Erich stands up and walks around, he clenches his fists and stands in front of Martina. 'That small-minded man. Rarely have I felt such hatred and been so violent.'

Martina takes hold of one of his clenched fists and attempts to open his hand. 'Violent, did you hit him?'

'No, I grabbed his coat, shook him and threatened him, but strike him? No, I didn't hit him.'

'Well, that is a relief, but hatred, Erich, I've never heard you say this before.'

Erich sits back down next to Martina, takes her hands in his and looks into her face. 'We must all have some hatred in us, Martina, much or little. I realised at that moment that I had more hatred in me than I knew.'

'And you hate the English, the enemy?'

'They killed our son, Martina.'

'That is true, Erich, somebody or some people in their army killed our son and some soldier from our country, in our army, killed their son.'

Erich looks at his wife and considers what she has said. *Thank God for Martina*, he thinks, *she always talks with such common sense.* Erich answers by saying, 'When I was with the army, we always referred to the British as the enemy. But you know, I never really felt it or hated them. If their wounded came into our hospital, I just saw them as young men, in pain and dying. I didn't treat them any differently. I didn't, I couldn't hate them, I'm a doctor for God's sake, I believe in healing and caring.'

'And now?'

'Today, I saw that Mr Williams as the enemy. Perhaps that hatred has always been in me and in that moment my anger revealed itself.'

Martina stands and offers Erich her hand. He stands and together they walk hand in hand down the street.

As they walk she says, 'The day after tomorrow we will go home. This has been very emotional for us, when we are home, perhaps you will feel different.'

Erich stops his wife and stares directly at her, he has a questioning look on his face. 'Martina, do you resent the way the British war dead are respected and honoured, and wish that our son was treated the same? That ceremony in Ypres, and the bold and proud cemeteries.'

'I'd never thought of it,' Martina stops and looks at Erich. 'Or, perhaps I have. It is a situation that I accept, we have little choice, we have to accept it. In time I'm sure it will change, I hope it will change.'

The couple continue their walk. Erich begins to feel a little more relaxed, although he still regrets that he lost his composure and feels ashamed of how he behaved.

Chapter Twenty-Seven

11 August, 1917 – Mainz

Erich Lehmann can't put off the visit any longer, it should have been done the day before, now is the time, it's a trip and a duty that he has to perform and it is now overdue. He walks through the hallway of his house and places his felt, trilby-style hat on his head. As he inspects his appearance in the hall mirror he's joined by Martina who looks over his shoulder and stares at her husband's reflection. 'Would you like me to come with you, Erich?'

He turns and gives Martina an affectionate smile. 'No, Martina, it will be too upsetting for you both, I will try to be as strong as I can, and hopefully give Mariel some of that strength. Of course, I would appreciate your company, but I do feel that this is something that Kurt would have wanted me to do, it is my responsibility.'

Erich leaves the house and walks down the path of the front garden. He holds an umbrella and wears a smart, full-length raincoat because he senses that rain is in the air. His mood is dark and it matches the dark colour of the grey clouds in the morning sky. He opens the gate, steps out onto the pavement and slowly walks down the leafy avenue. He's in no hurry to arrive at his destination and his pace is very slow. As he walks he considers how he's to tell Mariel Schneider that the future that she had planned with Kurt has been destroyed and will never be. On the main road he stands by a motor bus stop. He knows that a limited service is in operation although he's not too sure when transport will arrive. After a time he studies his pocket watch and sees that it's a quarter past nine, he looks at the sky, the threat of rain is clearly receding, and at that moment he decides that he would prefer to walk. Again, he plans his approach; he practices what he's going to say. Whichever strategy he uses, he knows that, as soon as Mariel sees him, the look on his face will betray him because he won't be able to hide the sadness and despair that's in his heart.

By the corner of the street, where the Schneider family lives, he pauses and lights a cigarette. He composes himself and after taking in two or three long draws on the cigarette, throws it down on the pavement and extinguishes it by stubbing it out with his foot. He walks round the bend of the corner and arrives at the gate to the Schneider's family house. The opening of the catch on the gate takes the attention of Franz Schneider who's carrying out some gardening work in the front garden. He's dressed in a jacket and a pair of trousers that are clearly reaching the end of practical use and soon to be discarded. His working outfit is completed by him wearing an old battered straw hat that Franz has become very fond of. He smiles as he walks down the path to greet the person that he now calls his friend. However, as soon as he's close enough to study Erich's face, Franz's expression changes to something more sombre.

'Something has happened to Kurt?' he says. 'I can see it in your face, Erich.'

Erich can only nod. He's yet to come to terms with the news himself, if he ever will. Franz closes the gate behind Erich, invites him to come into the house and directs him into the front study. Once seated, Erich says, 'I need to see Mariel in person, if I can please, Franz.'

Franz leans back in his chair. 'Unfortunately or for you, my friend, fortunately, she and her mother are visiting my sister in Frankfurt because she hasn't been too well lately. Now, I must ask you, Erich, what have you to tell me about your Kurt?'

'Missing, Franz, presumed dead, my only hope is that he

has been taken prisoner, but I have to say that there are some very reliable reports that he was killed in an explosion.'

'Then we must think the worst and hope for the best,' says Franz.

Erich leans forward and realises that he's still wearing his hat. He removes it and runs his hand over his head to ensure that his hair is neatly laid and looks tidy.

'There is little hope, Franz. I, I mean we, Martina and I, are prepared, it is wrong to hope for life, the only hope that we still have is that they will find his remains and that there is enough of him to bury. I would like to visit his grave one day.' He looks out of the window. 'Will Mariel be long? I tried to telephone but I couldn't get through, so I took a chance, I'm sorry.'

'Out of order, has been for some time, Erich, domestic telephones are not a priority these days and that is as it should be.'

'Perhaps I should arrange another visit. It could be tomorrow at the same time.'

Franz walks over to where Erich is sitting and puts his hand on his friend's shoulder. 'You know, when we first met, I wasn't that sure that we would get on, but since that wonderful day when our children became engaged, we have become good friends; you, me, Martina and my Helene. You have suffered enough. I shall lift the burden of the responsibility from you if you wish. I shall tell my daughter of the news that she has been dreading to hear.'

Erich sighs deeply, he's relieved, very relieved. 'I was prepared to tell her, you know that, that is why I came here.'

'I know, you did the right thing, I respect you for that.'

Erich stands and picks up his hat. 'Now I will leave you in peace. My place is now back with Martina and Peter.'

As he walks towards the front door Franz says, 'Where are my manners, I haven't offered you any refreshment, would you like to have something to drink?'

Erich puts up his hand. 'No thank you, Franz, perhaps next time, I will speak to you soon and I'm sure that Martina would like to visit in the near future.' He shakes Franz's hand, leaves the house and walks down the path towards the gate. Once on the road, he slowly walks in the direction of the district where he lives. His mind is full of mixed and contradictory emotions; he feels great relief at not having to inform Mariel of Kurt's death and yet, he also feels that he has been given a coward's way out. Had Mariel been at home, he would have accepted the responsibility of telling her himself because, as he saw it, this was a duty that he was honour-bound to carry out. He also knows that he would have had to witness, first hand, her despair and anguish. However, deep down, he knows that Kurt would have wanted his father to carry out the painful duty in person.

Later in the morning, Erich opens the gate to the front garden of his home. He studies the detail of his large, detached house, smartly clad in white weather-boarding. The building, that's positioned in sizeable and well-kept gardens, reflects a status that's supported by inheritance and a thriving and profitable medical practice that Erich's father had worked hard to establish. However, at this moment, the trappings of success mean nothing to him because this is the house and these are the gardens where Kurt would have brought his family. Kurt and Mariel will not be bringing their children to feed the fish in the pond, play ball games, play on the swings and climb the trees. It's a house, just a house, with an empty garden.

He enters the hallway, carefully places his hat on the hall stand, removes his coat and hangs it on a peg. His attention is taken by the sound of voices coming from the front living room. Clearly, Martina is entertaining someone or some visitors. When he walks through the door he recognises a very familiar person; it's Father Josef Ehrlichmann, the priest from their church. His heart sinks a little and he's disappointed. The priest, dressed in a dark ankle-length cassock that exaggerates his slim frame, stands and walks towards Erich. He smiles and holds out his hand. When Erich offers the priest his hand, Father Ehrlichmann embraces it with both of his hands and looks directly into the face of the grieving father. The expression on the priest's face displays genuine and sincere concern. His eyes seem to be grotesquely enlarged as a result of him having to wear a pair of glasses with very strong magnifying lenses. The glasses are the dominant feature on a face that is thin and quite grey in colour.

'Erich, how are you?' he says.

Erich asks the priest to sit back down and he sits next to Martina. 'Father Ehrlichmann was asking when he will see you at church again,' she says.

'We have missed you, Erich,' adds Father Ehrlichmann. 'When did I last hear your confession? Some time ago, I'm sure.'

Erich is somewhat irritated by the priest's comments. 'I have been rather busy, Father, working in the hospitals, doing what I can to help.'

'Of course, I realise that, Erich, but you must understand that I'm here for you and Martina, for the both of you and it would be delightful to see you once again at St Joseph's. I feel sure that it would be good for you, my friend. God has not forgotten you, I can assure you of that.'

Erich starts to feel angry but looks at Martina and considers how to temper his response. 'Perhaps, if I have time. I have a few days before I have to return to my duties.'

'It would be good if you could come with me to a service,' says Martina. 'I know I need it and I think that you do as well, it would be good for the both of us.'

Erich sighs and puts up his hands as a sign to say that he surrenders. 'Yes, you're right, Martina, I will do as you ask.'

'That would please me very much, Erich,' she says, then she turns to Father Ehrlichmann. 'You must be very busy these days, Father, many families to visit and to care for.'

The priest smiles at her. 'I do what I can, it is a duty that I have to perform, it is my calling after all. I'm needed.' He pauses for a moment. 'Shall we now pray, to ask for forgiveness and to commend Kurt's soul to his father in heaven?'

They stand and bow their heads. After a moment of silence

Father Ehrlichmann starts to quietly recite the prayers and when he finishes, he crosses himself, and Martina and Erich do the same. Martina holds the priest's hand and thanks him for coming to see them. Erich walks with the priest into the hallway, takes a coat from the stand and holds it open for Father Ehrlichmann to feed his arms through the sleeves. Erich hands him his hat, the priest takes it and puts it on. By the door, he offers his hand to Erich to bid him farewell. 'No, Father, I shall see you to the gate, that is my duty.'

As they walk down the path, Father Ehrlichmann says, 'Never think that God has deserted you, Erich, he watches over all his children. We must pray for a victory that our people want so much and deserve to have, for a victory that will honour the memory of your son.'

Erich stops. 'May I ask you something, Father?'

'Of course, what is troubling you?'

'You pray for victory, for a German success.'

'I do, when I conduct a service, I look down and I see many young men dressed in the grey uniform of our country. I see families who have sons serving at the front or have lost their children. For their sake, I ask for victory.'

'Victory or peace?'

'Victory will bring peace. I desire to see an end to all hostilities. My congregation longs for peace through victory.'

Erich thinks for a moment and slowly shakes his head. 'The thing is, Father, in Britain and France and in the other countries of our enemies, they pray for victory. What does God decide to do, who does he support, where do his loyalties lie, with them or us?'

'God does not take sides on a whim, we can only ask. There is a purpose to this war, it is beyond us to understand, we must only obey. If we are right, we will win.'

'I see the results of what happens when soldiers obey the orders of their superiors,' says Erich, clearly becoming increasingly more exasperated. 'They are killed or mutilated;

you have no idea what it is like in this war. We have been killing each other for as long as man has lived on this planet, and now we have perfected the art of slaughtering one another.'

Father Ehrlichmann gently puts his hand on Erich's shoulder. 'This is still too raw for you because you have suffered a great loss. Trust in God and he will help you.'

Erich shakes off the priest's hand and speaks with an angry voice, 'Don't patronise me please, Father, I have had these thoughts for some time. Yes I've lost a son, but many people have lost their sons. I'm not angry for myself, it's for all the dead and the families that grieve for them.'

'But, my son...'

'Please let me finish, I cannot think that what is happening in the war is part of a plan. I know what you're going to tell me, you are going to say that when God made us, he granted us the freedom to make our own mistakes...'

'That's exactly what I would say to you and with that freedom, well, I have to tell you, my son, that there are going to be some mistakes, it is inevitable.'

'A mistake, is that what you think this war is, a mistake?'

The priest puts his hand on Erich's shoulder again. 'I don't think that we will agree. If I can ask you my friend, was it the war that started to make you feel this way?'

Erich is now calmer. 'The truth is, Father, the horrors of war have only accelerated the thoughts that I had started to develop in my mind before the hostilities began. When I started practising medicine I experienced depressing times when I could do little to save a dying child, for example. I accepted it because, in many ways, death is a natural state at any age. But this war is evil and as it continues I have become convinced that we live in a Godless world. If there ever was a God, he has given up on us and you can't blame him for that. If he made us, he created a monster.'

Father Ehrlichmann opens the gate, steps out onto the pavement and closes the latch. He rests on the gate for a moment. 'Come to church, Erich, come with Martina. You may have given up on God but I can assure you, he has not given up on you.' He smiles, turns and walks slowly down the road.

Erich looks at the back of the priest. He starts to think that he has perhaps been a bit too hard on him. He also knows that Martina will be helped by her faith. 'Thank you for coming to see us, Father,' he shouts.

Father Ehrlichmann doesn't look round but raises his hand to acknowledge what Erich has said. He smiles and says to himself, 'We won't give up on you, Erich.'

Chapter Twenty-Eight

3 August, 1932 – Poperinge

Annie and Mary have enjoyed their day out and return to the hotel in good spirits. In the foyer they meet Madame De Vos and although she's busily attending to some new guests who are booking into the hotel, she's eager to talk with Annie. The two sisters stand by as Madame De Vos goes about her business. Once the new guests have been dealt with, she returns to speak with Annie and Mary.

'Hello, Madame De Vos,' says Annie. 'My goodness it's warm today.'

'It is, Mrs Williams, it is a little too hot I think. There is a fan in the reception room and it was not working before but my cousin came to deal with it, I will try it, I feel sure that it will make a difference.'

Mary complains, 'I find it a bit oppressive, rather unpleasant. If the fan does work, it will be very welcome.'

'Is that what you wanted to talk about, Madame De Vos?' asks Annie. 'I'd like to go upstairs to freshen up now.'

Madame De Vos speaks quietly and indicates by tilting her head that Annie needs to go into the reception room. 'Mr Williams is sat in there. I don't think that he is himself and he has been very quiet for some time. I am rather concerned.'

'Oh, thank you, Madame De Vos,' says Annie as she looks into the reception room. 'I'll see to him. I'm sure it's nothing, he gets a bit moody from time to time.'

Madame De Vos walks ahead of Annie and Mary into the

reception room, pulls a lever and the large fan located in the centre of the ceiling slowly turns and starts to gather momentum. She claps her hands and says, 'Voila.' Annie and Mary smile and thank her. John doesn't move and remains seated in the corner of the room. He's obviously in a sombre mood, his head's bowed and he appears to be deep in thought.

'Hello, John,' says Annie, 'all by yourself, I see.'

John continues to look down and doesn't really acknowledge them with any form of greeting. 'I'm thinking, Annie,' he mumbles. 'I just need time to think.'

Annie becomes concerned. It's rare for him to appear to be so downcast. 'Whatever's the matter, John? You're not right are you, what's happened?'

John looks up. 'I've gone a bit too far, overdid it like, overreacted I think.'

'Have you been drinking, John?' asks Mary.

John responds to his sister-in-law's accusation, 'No, I bloody well haven't.'

Annie immediately chastises him, 'No need for that, John, I don't want to hear that language.'

'Well, I only had the one,' admits John. 'He said I could be a German.'

'Who said that?' asks Annie.

'That bloody German, the doctor.'

Annie is starting to lose patience with him. 'I don't want to have to tell you again about your language, John, now what were you saying, how could you possibly be a German?'

'That's what I said, Annie, that's exactly what I said, what a daft idea, isn't it?'

Annie is mystified, 'Why would he say that?'

'He said that I could be a German and if I were, our son would have joined their army and fought for them.'

Annie thinks for a moment. 'Well that's right, I suppose he would have, I suppose.'

John stares at Annie. 'What... what do you mean?'

'Well, we were born in England,' explains Annie, 'but I can see his point, we could have been born in Germany, or anywhere. We don't have a say in where we're born, could have been in another country.'

John becomes indignant and very defensive. 'So you're taking his side, I might have known it.'

Annie sits down next to John and sighs deeply. 'Dear me, John, it's not a question of sides. The fact is, if you'd been born in Germany you wouldn't know any different and our son might now be buried in a German cemetery.'

'Our son would now be buried in a German cemetery. Is that what you'd like, Annie, really?'

Annie takes hold of John's hand. 'Oh, John, I don't want our son to be buried in any cemetery, not while we're alive, I don't want to be coming here every year. I'd like it if like other folk we went to Blackpool or Southport or somewhere like that. I wish that our Bert and his family were coming round to us for their dinner on a Sunday. I'd love to see you and him go off to the pub for a drink and a catch-up while I settle down to read to his children and then have a chat to his wife.' Annie can see that John is becoming increasingly upset and tries to change the mood. She looks at John and then at Mary. 'Mind you, Mary, looking at John in this light I think that there's something of the Kaiser about him.'

Mary senses what Annie is up to and joins in with her game. 'Of course, yes, you might be right, Annie, a bit more work on that moustache, yes I can see it now, you're right, Annie.'

John stares first at Annie and then at his sister-in-law. 'The bloody Kaiser, me?'

Annie starts to enjoy teasing him. 'If he were to wear that helmet, you know the one with the spike on the top, don't you think, Mary?'

'Definitely, I can see it now,' agrees Mary, 'it's a good likeness.'

John refuses to become involved in the humour of the

conversation. 'This is rubbish. I'll not be made fun of, Annie, it's not a laughing matter.'

'Well what else can we do, John?'

'I'll not be an object of ridicule and made fun of.'

'You're not, John, you're a caring, loyal and respected man.'

John stands up and walks over to the window, looks out into the street and shrugs his shoulders. 'What do I do now? I can't face him again, I said that his son were a murderer.'

Annie's shocked. 'John, you didn't, is that what you said?'

'Aye,' he admits, 'I did, and worse.'

Annie stands and walks over to him. 'I think that an apology is in order.'

John shakes his head. 'No chance, he's too arrogant, you'll never get him to apologise.'

'Not him, John, you… you should apologise.'

'But…'

Annie holds his arm for a moment. 'I'm going to our room to freshen up before dinner. I don't want an atmosphere in the dining room, I want to feel comfortable, if you see what I mean. Please sort it out.'

Annie walks out of the room and Mary follows her. Before leaving she turns and says, 'Don't take on, John, some people thought that the Kaiser was quite good-looking. A bit, well, rather distinguished like.'

Annie and Mary walk through the foyer and climb the stairs. John is left alone. He looks in the mirror, holds his head back and strikes a pose. He's disturbed when Henry walks into the room.

'Henry,' says John.

'What's up John?'

'Do you recall how the old Kaiser looked?'

'Who, Kaiser Bill?'

'Aye, what did he look like?'

'Aye, I do recall what he looked like, ugly bugger if I remember right.'

Chapter Twenty-Nine

11 November, 1918 – Mainz, Germany

Martina Lehmann looks at the clock in the living room of their home. It tells her that it's nine minutes to the ceasefire, the armistice, the surrender of the German forces and the defeat of a nation. Erich walks into the room carrying a bottle of wine. He sits down next to his wife and puts the wine next to two fine crystal glasses on a small table in front of the settee where they're seated. They sit in silence for a moment and both look out into the garden. Both have in their minds images of Kurt playing on the grass.

'Do you remember,' says Martina, 'when Kurt was really small, he was not even one, when he started to walk and he was so determined to be independent, he fell over so many times.' They smile at each other. 'Can you see him as an older boy?' she asks. 'And then when he was much bigger, with Peter.' They can both hear the laughter and remember when it was Peter who would fall over and his elder brother would rush over to pick him up and make sure that he wasn't hurt.

'Do you recall,' says Erich, 'that June day in 1914, it was our wedding anniversary, twenty years.' Together, they remember that warm sunny afternoon when they sat in the garden and were joined by other family members; Martina's sister, Gertrude and her family of husband Albrecht and sons Bernhard and Sebastian. Also there, were Erich's brother Dieter, his wife Ebba, son Maximilian and daughter, Greta. Later in the day Erich's parents, Dr Rolf Lehmann and Erica, came and were also joined by Martina's parents, Winifred and Heinrich. Although rumours of war were gathering pace, the family made every attempt to push the reports of potential conflict well into the background and when the men started to debate the latest intelligence, Erica Lehmann reprimanded them.

'My mother would not hear of it,' says Erich. 'She was determined to make it a very special day for us.'

'And it was, Erich, it was a delightful day and a time of joy.'

Erich nods in agreement, then his mood changes, he becomes very serious. 'Poor Maximilian,' he says, 'killed at the Somme. I think of Ebba and Dieter, my poor brother.'

They sit in silence and Martina looks again at the clock, it tells her that it's five to eleven and there are five minutes to go. 'I am not sure why we are having a drink, Erich.'

'To the future, Martina, and to the memory of Kurt and Max. I think that it is the right thing to do.' He pours the red claret into the glasses.

He hands Martina her drink and they wait for the hand on the clock to move into position. Suddenly, the clock starts to chime, and Erich and Martina silently count down the hours. When they reach eleven they both raise their glasses. 'To Kurt,' says Martina.

'To our Kurt and to Max,' says Erich.

Their solitude and the moment of quiet contemplation are disturbed when the bell cord at the front door is pulled. For a moment Erich is slightly annoyed at a possible intrusion on a very private moment, then he reminds himself there will be many who don't know that the armistice is to begin at eleven o'clock on this day. He walks through the hallway and opens the front door. There on the steps are his brother Dieter and his sister-in-law Ebba. 'This is right,' Erich says, 'it is good for you to come here today, please come in, you are very welcome.'

Dieter and Ebba accept Erich's invitation and enter the house. Dieter is without doubt Erich's younger brother by two years, similar in build and facial features, but because his eyesight does not require assistance, he doesn't need to wear spectacles. Ebba is short, slim and dark-haired, she has a pleasant face and is generally described as being pretty, rather than handsome. Erich kisses his sister-in-law's cheek and shakes his brother's hand, then he guides them through to the front living room. Martina greets them. 'Get two more glasses, Erich.'

'Are we celebrating?' asks Dieter.

'Yes, we are,' replies Erich. 'We are toasting the future, the future for our children.' He hands their guests a glass each and raises his own. 'To the future.'

'To the future,' they all repeat.

The four family members sit in silence, they're quiet and thoughtful. After a time Erich stands and says, 'I think I will take a walk, will anybody join me?'

'I will come with you, Erich,' says Dieter. He turns to Martina and Ebba, 'Will you ladies care to take the air with us?'

'Not for me thank you, Dieter,' replies Martina.

'You must keep away from the centre of the city,' says Ebba. 'I have heard that there are communists there and they have guns. There are also deserters who are trying to make trouble.'

'No,' says Erich, 'there is trouble in some places but that is in the north. We will be safe here, you can rest assured.'

'I shall sit with Martina,' says Ebba. 'Enjoy your walk and be careful, just in case. Communists are not very nice people.'

Both men put on their homburg hats and leave the house. At the bottom of the steps they each light a cigarette and walk on. 'So the guns are finally silent after four years,' says Dieter.

'Most of them,' replies Erich. 'There will be some who have not received the order and a few others who choose not to obey the command. However, today, tomorrow and the day after, the killing will stop and then the hard work will begin. I must start by helping the wounded, the blinded and the crippled. I will leave the Medical Corp as soon as I am able to, then I will need to rebuild Father's practice. I'll need to earn my living. What about you, Dieter, what plans do you have?'

'After I have finished at the War Department, I shall return to teaching, to try to shape the young minds of the future.'

The roads that the two brothers walk down are strangely quiet, there's little sign of any form of activity. However, there's more sign of life the closer they get to the city centre, shouts can be heard and there's the sound of motor vehicles somewhere. As they walk along the main street, past the timber-framed, medieval houses, bars and shops, they recall when the thoroughfare was a scene of vibrant commercial activity, with street markets that offered an abundance of fish, meat, fruit and vegetables. Stalls and shops were laden with gifts, fabrics and garments. The café bars used to be full of people dining and drinking, laughter and music could be heard coming from the beer halls. In fact, everything that was needed to sustain life and provide enjoyment was available for purchase in the rather well-to-do city of Mainz. Now the shelves in the shops are practically empty, most of the bars are shut and the market, even in a much reduced and modest condition, has not been seen during the past year.

Slowly, the streets start to become busier. News of the ceasefire is starting to filter through and people are gathering to find out if the rumours are true. Citizens of the city and travellers stand and talk, they stop and question passers-by to ask if they have any updated information. Those who are fortunate to still have employment down tools and enter the street, eager to seek confirmation of the armistice. The few remaining shopkeepers that still have goods to sell, however meagre in either quality or quantity, also congregate in clusters. The mood is strange; relief that the killing and maiming has all but now stopped, sadness when remembering those who will not return and thinking of those who will come home, but bearing the very visible scars of conflict and destruction. Then there are those who talk of betrayal and treachery.

As the two brothers turn to walk down towards the river, they hear a voice, 'Can you help a soldier, Sir, who has had it bad, really bad, Sir, if you can?'

They look down to see a legless soldier who's sitting on a small cart. He's dressed in a rather shabby Prussian Guard's uniform, he looks dirty and in his grubby hand he holds a metal cup. Erich reaches into his trouser pocket and feels for some money. By touch, he recognises what he feels to be a three mark coin. Although he knows that this would be over-generous, he gladly drops it into the man's begging cup. Dieter also places some coins in the cup but he's not as generous as his brother, his gift comprises of two ten pfennig coins. The man smiles and thanks them; tonight he will eat.

As they continue their short journey, Dieter says, 'That was very lavish of you, Erich, you gave him three marks.'

Erich stops and looks at him. 'It might seem like that, but for all I know I could have helped to remove his legs, which I would have had to do, to save his life. If he knew that I may have been responsible for condemning him to life as a beggar, would he thank me?'

The two brothers continue their walk. When they reach the river they turn and stroll along the wide path that runs alongside. The city is becoming populated again, more people are walking and taking in the air. A large industrial barge chugs its way up the river, black smoke bellowing from the chimneystack. The grinding and pounding sound of the well-worn steam engine indicates that it's seen better days and the unpleasant noise intrudes on the thoughts and the quiet contemplation of the walkers. The people who stroll past Erich and Dieter don't speak to them, but acknowledge them with a nod and a polite smile.

'What now, Erich?' says Dieter. 'What immediate plans have you got?'

'I shall contact my unit to find out how long I will have to continue serving and how long it will be before I can return to the practice.'

'Perhaps,' says Dieter, 'Father can finally retire.'

'Yes,' laughs Erich, 'like two women in the kitchen, a mother and daughter, it would not be advisable for us to share a surgery. He would tell me where I am going wrong and how I need to do things in the tried and trusted way. I shall of course enjoy spending more time with Martina and Peter. My son is now our future.'

After a time they stop and because they've been so engrossed in their conversation they're surprised by how far they've walked. 'My word,' says Dieter, 'we had better return to your house or our ladies will be sending out a search party.'

'A search party,' says Erich. 'I remember once organising a search party for a wounded soldier.'

'What, you lost a patient?' Dieter laughs. 'That was very careless of you, Erich.'

'It does sound odd, doesn't it? We had this young soldier in the hospital with a bad arm injury, he was very confused and in some distress, which is normal in many cases. I looked at his wound and wondered if we could save the arm so I went to get another officer's opinion. When we returned, he had gone and run away. We looked all around the hospital, we looked everywhere and we didn't find him, he had vanished. I asked an orderly to form a search party to go and look for him. I know that my commanding officer wasn't that impressed, he told me that we were far too busy to deal with one deserter.'

'I suppose he had a point,' says Dieter.

'You see, Dieter, I didn't see him as a deserter, I just saw him as a frightened and bewildered young man who perhaps thought that I was going to take his arm off.'

'Was he found?'

'No, I never saw him again. I don't know what happened to him.'

Erich looks at his brother, he looks serious. 'The thing is, I don't know whether we could have saved his arm, but in time, he would have adjusted to his disability. But I was concerned about his mind; would he be able to cope with visions of horror that probably will never leave his head?'

Dieter sighs. 'Come, brother, this is very depressing, now is the time for optimism and hope, we must look to the future and deal with what we have to.'

Erich thinks for a moment. 'You are right, like all people in Germany we must rebuild, we owe it to our surviving children to help them create a world that is fit to live in.'

Dieter laughs. 'My God, Erich, can you hear us, this is very profound, we sound as if we are politicians who are electioneering. Let us get home and have a good drink. I do not know about you, but I could do with getting a bit drunk, in fact, I feel that I would like to get very drunk.'

Chapter Thirty

3 August, 1932 – Poperinge

Erich and Martina walk into the foyer. They stand for a moment and discuss how they're going to spend their evening. Peter and Emma have been sat in the garden and enter the foyer. A menu is displayed on a small stand on the reception desk and the two couples read it to see what's on offer.

'Have you enjoyed your day, Mrs Lehmann and Dr Lehmann?' says Emma. 'We, that's Peter and I, have had a very pleasant afternoon.'

Martina smiles at her. 'I was having a good day, very relaxing, but it changed.'

'Why, what happened?' asks Emma.

Martina puts up her hand. 'It is not important. May I call you Emma?'

'Please do,' replies Emma. She would ask if she could call the doctor and his wife by their first names but remembers what Peter told her about the formalities in German society, so she doesn't request permission. Instead she says, 'Peter has been telling me about where you live in Mainz and how nice it is.'

Erich gives his son a knowing look. 'Peter, is it? Things have developed very quickly.'

Emma's a little embarrassed, while Peter laughs. 'I have explained to Emma how we do things and perhaps how things may change.'

'One day, perhaps,' says Erich. 'And where do you live, Emma? I'm sure it is very nice.'

'We live in Lancashire, a place called Blackburn, have you been there, heard of it?'

'Yes, I have heard of it,' says Erich. 'I have never been there. It is well known for cotton I think and because you live in the Red Rose County, you do not appreciate the white variety, is that correct?'

'That's right,' laughs Emma. 'It's a thing we have with Yorkshire people. How did you know about that?'

'When I worked in London,' answers Erich, 'two colleagues I worked with were from the north, one from Lancashire and the other from Yorkshire. They used to have fun with each other, it was very entertaining. David, that is the doctor who came from Lancashire, Bolton I think it was, said that Robert, who was also a doctor and came from Leeds, was very reluctant to spend some money and was careful with it.'

Emma laughs again. 'My dad would say that they're tight.'

'Tight?' asks Martina.

'Tight with money,' replies Erich, 'not wanting to spend too much money and looking after it, or as I remember, they call it brass. Robert would say that Lancashire people, I think he called them folk, were very nosy.' He looks at the puzzled look in his wife's face and before she asks, he adds, 'It means that they want to know other people's business.'

Emma is enjoying the conversation. 'This is a question that my dad would ask,' she pauses for a moment. 'What is the best thing to come out of Yorkshire?'

Erich thinks for a moment. 'Ah,' he says, 'perhaps the Yorkshire pudding?'

Emma shakes her head.

Erich thinks again. 'Hmm, not the pudding, then beer, or ale as you call it?'

Again, Emma shakes her head.

'Then,' says Erich, 'it must be the wool? They are very good at making wool.'

'Not even close I'm afraid, Dr Lehmann,' says Emma.

'Then I must admit defeat,' says Eric. 'What is the best thing to come out of Yorkshire, according to your father?'

Emma laughs. 'It's the road to Lancashire!'

All four of them laugh, Emma looks at the clock by the desk and excuses herself to go to her room and prepare for dinner. Peter leaves his parents alone to go to his room. Before he leaves them he says, 'She's nice, isn't she?'

'Yes, very pleasant and I have to say, extremely attractive,' say Martina.

Erich raises his finger and says, 'Slowly Peter, think of her father, he would not like it.'

Peter leaves them and walks up the stairs. Martina looks at Erich. She's pleased to see him smile and hear him laugh.

All this time, John had been sitting by himself in the reception room and he had listened to the conversation that had taken place. He couldn't be seen from the foyer, which meant that Emma and the Lehmanns had been unaware of his presence. He wasn't deliberately eavesdropping but he couldn't avoid hearing what was being said without making himself known. John steals himself. He walks out of the room and approaches the couple. At first they're surprised by seeing John and immediately wonder if their conversation with Emma has been overheard.

'Good afternoon, Dr Lehmann, Mrs Lehmann,' says John, nervously.

Erich turns and raises his hand. 'Please, Mr Williams, no more heated exchanges, enough is enough, there is nothing more to discuss.'

Martina looks at her husband and realises that it's important for the two men to talk, especially because Peter and Emma seem to have formed a very strong friendship.

'Erich, I'm going to our room and I'll leave you and Mr Williams to talk.'

Erich shakes his head. 'I'll come with you, Martina, there's no point in this.'

Martina puts her hand on Erich's arm and looks directly at him. 'No, Erich, you need to do this.'

Martina walks up the stairs and leaves the two men together. Erich sighs and prepares himself for another confrontational discussion and a heated argument.

'What is it, Mr Williams? Is there something that you wish to add to our earlier conversation? I have just calmed down and if you like, I have recovered from the disagreement and the quarrel that we had earlier…'

'But,' protests John.

'Let me finish please and don't shout me down,' he pauses for a moment. 'I have just had a very pleasant conversation with your daughter…'

'I know, I heard.'

'You heard us?'

'Aye, I did.'

Erich again shakes his head and half smiles. 'Then you will have heard us having a very civilised and enjoyable talk. It is possible, you know, despite who you are and where you come from.'

'I know,' replies John. 'I'd like to apologise, Dr Lehmann, I really would like to say sorry.'

Erich stares at him. 'You would?'

'Aye. I talked to my wife and, well, I went a bit far. I know I did.'

Erich puts his hand on the back of his neck and moves his head from side to side, he looks up and then at John. 'We were both very emotional, I understand, we both said things we now regret. I would like to think that I acted and spoke completely out of character, in fact I know that I did.'

'Me more than you, I think,' replies John.

Erich sighs deeply. 'Then I accept your apology and in turn, offer you mine. I am also sorry about what I said.'

'Oh no. There's no need for that, on your part. I was to blame, well mostly.'

Erich says, 'Let that be an end to it then. We are to leave the day after tomorrow and I doubt if we will meet after that, although you never know.'

John thinks for a moment. 'Oh, you mean our Emma and your boy.'

'How old is your daughter?'

'Oh, let me see, she'll be twenty-one now.'

'My Peter has just become twenty-three. How old were you when you got married? If I might ask.'

'I were twenty-two, why?'

'Our children are not children anymore, they will now make their own way in life, decide what they want to do and who they are to take their journey with. We can advise, but we also have to accept. Your Emma and our Peter may make a life together, or they may not, it is their choice. I wish them well.' Erich nods to John, turns and walks towards the stairs.

John is left alone with his thoughts. He stares at the floor and considers what Erich has just said. Erich puts one foot on the first step, stops and turns round. He walks back to speak to John again. 'Mr Williams, I have a thought, it may help both of us.'

John looks up. 'What's that then?'

'I must ask you, would you care to come with me to see where my son is buried? As I told you, we leave for home the day after tomorrow and before that, Martina and I wish to say a final goodbye to our son.'

John is somewhat taken aback. 'Well I don't know about that, it would be a strange thing for me to do. Go against the grain a bit like.'

Erich smiles at him. 'No, you're right of course, I shouldn't have expected it.'

John thinks again. 'I'd never have thought of doing that, or anything like it.'

'Mr Williams, I haven't been to the cemetery where your son is buried and so I have not seen his grave, but I have visited some British and Allied war cemeteries. I know what they are like. They are all honourable and well cared for places of rest.'

'So, you've seen what our places are like and you approve of them?'

'I have, and with our war dead you would see something very different, I think. But if you feel that by coming with me to my son's place of rest is too much for you, then I fully understand.'

John feels challenged and responds positively. 'Do you know, Dr Lehmann, I might, I just might. Mind you, I'll have to tell Annie what we plan to do.'

'Of course, Mr Williams, it should not be a secret.'

John looks at Erich and as if he has had a deep and profound thought, says, 'It's just come to me; it's fate that's brought us here today. I'm not that spiritual but I can feel our Bert's guiding hand on this business. I'll tell Annie, she might want to come.'

'Your wife would be very welcome. It would be some company for Martina.'

'You know, I think we will. I'm sure Annie will think it's the right thing to do.'

The two men walk towards the stairs, John stops and puts his hand on Erich's arm. 'What I just said then, when I came over a bit funny like.'

'Funny, like?'

'Aye, it's not like me to talk like that, best not say anything, I shouldn't think it'll happen again.'

'Good, says Erich, 'we are agreed. After breakfast, shall we say?'

Chapter Thirty-One

4 August, 1932 – Langemark, German Military Cemetery, Belgium

The Lehmanns' motor car pulls up outside the cemetery gates, Erich and John get out of the vehicle and both men assist their wives in stepping down from the rear seats. John looks at the entrance to the cemetery; iron gates are held in position by two large, square pillars constructed of grey and dark red stone. It's all very neat and uniform in style.

The four recently acquainted companions walk towards the gate and pass over large stone slabs. The theme of grey and red stone is continued all around the perimeter of the burial site in the form of a shoulder-high security wall that establishes the boundary. Once inside, they pause and view what they can see. The landscape is mainly of healthy and established grass and has the appearance of a garden lawn that has been well-cut and carefully looked after. In the distance, crosses can be seen, some still constructed of dark wood but many have been cut from grey stone. Dark, flat, granite square stones have been placed on the ground in a regimented and uniform pattern that has the look of soldiers on parade.

Numerous small trees that have obviously been recently planted populate the area, they are at different stages of growth and are in full leaf. They're already starting to create a very distinctive atmosphere and the strategy is clear to see. When the trees are at the height of their growth, they will provide a protective canopy and shield the burial markers from the elements, although, it will mean that the cemetery will become a dark and hidden place. Here, there is no statement of resolve, no declaration of victory, just a poignant memorial and a reminder of the futility of war.

John stares ahead. 'Blimey, this is something different, very different, all these trees, oaks aren't they?'

'Yes,' answers Erich, 'they are oaks, it is the German national tree.'

'Where's your boy buried, Doctor? asks John.

Erich looks around and tries to get his bearings, he looks a little confused. First he steps one way then another. 'Now, let me see, I didn't find it too difficult to find his grave the other day.'

John's a little confused. 'I suppose it changes a bit, you know, with these trees growing. It's quite a big place isn't it?'

'Well, where he was before, the cemetery was a lot smaller and he was easier to find,' replies Erich.

'Where he were before, what do you mean, how long has he been here?'

Erich realises that he needs to provide an explanation. 'You see, he has been here one year only. In 1917 he was buried in another cemetery. That place is now being closed, his body was exhumed last year and now his place of rest is here with more of his comrades. The authorities wrote to us and told us what they planned to do.'

'So, dug up and moved here?' says John. 'Where were he before, then?'

Erich continues to scan the area. 'He was in the Passchendaele burial ground and he now shares his grave, with his comrades.'

'Blimey, why did they shut the other place?'

'There is an ongoing plan to consolidate all these sites, so that the cemeteries can be better managed and well looked after. This place was inaugurated early in July; that is why we came here this time.' Erich looks ahead and then appears to be relieved because he thinks that he has identified a possible place where the grave could be.

'Ah, I think that this is it, please come, Mr Williams, it is over here, I'm sure of it.'

Erich and John march off and they talk as they walk.

'You didn't mind them moving him like, did you? Did you say that they told you what they were planning to do, and that they kept you informed?'

'Of course we were kept fully informed of the plans that the commission were putting into practice. It is a typically German practical solution, you see, Mr Williams; your war dead are appreciated, ours are tolerated. In many ways it is right that he now rests here. You see, when he first joined the army in 1914 he was a student. Many of his fellow students joined up with him at the same time, in fact so many that they were formed into their own battalions. They were called the Student Volunteers. In October and November in the first year, many of them were killed and three thousand of them now rest here, and this place is also known as the Student Cemetery.'

'Like the Pals.'

'The Pals?'

'Aye, the Accrington Pals, they were called. Near to where we live, there's a town called Accrington, you'll never have heard of it. Well, to encourage recruitment, the government had this idea; if you're going to join up, bring a friend along. This was just before we had conscription when lads were made to join up.'

'And this worked, did they join up?'

'Oh aye, it did work, they came to join up mainly from Accrington but from all over East Lancs as well. That's part of the county where we live.'

'That will be the east part of Lancashire?'

'That's it, well, it seemed to be a good plan; if you're going off to somewhere new, to a life that you're unsure about, it helps to have a pal with you. They were called the 'Accrington Pals'. It weren't just round us, other places did it, I remember there were Pals from Sheffield. Seemed like a good idea, but they soon stopped it.'

'Why did they stop it if so many joined?'

'The Accrington Pals, as I said, who were mainly from the one town, climbed out of the trenches at the Somme in 1916, on the first day. I think there were about six hundred of them in the first attack and hardly any of them came back. Every road and street had lost sons, brothers and fathers. It were too much in one go.'

Martina and Annie have no wish to match the men's pace. They prefer to walk more slowly and the slower, more leisurely walk allows them to talk. 'Well, this is a turn up for the books,' says Annie.

'A turn up, what is a turn up?'

'Well,' explains Annie, 'it means it's strange, out of the ordinary, for our John, to be in a German cemetery. I have to say that I never thought I'd see it.'

'So, you have never been to a German cemetery before?'

'Oh, no, some years ago a couple from England, Kent I think it were, were visiting their son's grave. We got a bit friendly with them and they said they were going to visit a German cemetery and asked us if we'd like to go with them. Oh, I asked John what he thought of that, and he said that he didn't think it would be appropriate and that was the end of it.'

Eventually, Erich and John reach the grave, stand by the flat gravestone and take time to study the detail inscribed on it. Erich points to his son's name. 'He is here with five of his comrades. There is some comfort in that I suppose.'

'Six of them down there?'

'That's right,' replies Erich.

John looks up and gazes around the cemetery, he sighs deeply. 'This place is very quiet, nice in its own way mind, but very different to our places. Sort of blends in, I suppose.'

'Deliberately so, so different.'

'Aye, so different, though it's not as... what would you call it?'

'Less triumphant?'

'Aye,' says John, 'that's it, triumphant.'

Erich looks directly at John, and he sighs. 'It is about victory and defeat.'

John thinks for a moment. 'This Hitler chap, he won't get far will he, what do make of it?'

Erich smiles and laughs a little. 'Mr Williams, I have never heard him referred to as a *chap* before. Now, what do I make of him? The Nazi party is a party with a vision, offering a proud and honourable future.'

'You're all for them then?'

'The rise of a defeated nation,' replies Erich, 'pride restored and poverty banished. You can see the attraction; it will appeal to many.'

'And does it appeal you?'

'I see a different future; I see violence, brutality, persecution and the end of freedom and compassion. So the answer is no, it does not appeal to me and it never will.'

'And war, do you think there could be another war?'

'I think it is a possibility. I'm afraid to say that Adolf Hitler is a dangerous man, you should read the book he wrote, it is called Mein Kampf.'

'If there's a war what would you expect your son Peter to do, fight for Hitler?'

'Do? Do as we all must do. I expect him to follow his conscience, he must do what he thinks is right.'

'And what would you do?'

'Care for the dying, try to mend the minds and do what I can to repair their broken bodies. It will be the same as last time for me and that is why I dread it. The last war cost me my son and my faith.

'It doesn't seem right in here talking about another war. This was supposed to be the Great War, the war to end all wars, the finish of it, weren't it?'

'A war to end all wars, I think that there is no such thing,' replies Erich. 'War, it is in man's nature, to make war, to destroy and annihilate.'

'When our boy joined up and went off to war, I were as pleased as punch, couldn't be happier. I could hold my head up, eh, I were that proud.'

'I suppose I felt something of that when Kurt joined up.'

'As it went on and the number of casualties went up, the worst time was when they posted names of the casualties from the Somme. As time went on, I became fearful, dreaded seeing the message boy.'

'Message boy?' asks Erich.

'Aye, that's what he were called, he were a bit like a postman but moved quicker, he rode a bike. Mind you, there were more women doing the job than men at that time.'

'This message boy, as you call him, could be giving you a letter you did not want to receive.'

'Aye, or a telegram, officers' families mainly got telegrams. Deaths and the wounded of other ranks were usually told by a letter, it were called a Death Notice. The postmaster in the town decided that if anything came in from the War Office, it were to be sent out as quickly as it could. So the message boy delivered the notices with the telegrams. Good chap, our postmaster, he were very sensitive to our needs. When I saw the boy riding his bike up our road, I'd say to myself, 'Keep going, postie boy, go on by.'

'Postie boy?'

'Aye, that's what I called him, bit of a nickname like.'

'We had something similar to the *postie boy* in Germany.'

John continues with his story. 'One day, he parked his bike outside our house. I swallowed hard and called to Annie, *postie boy's outside* I said. Annie came through to me, she were as white as a sheet. Then the boy must have realised he were on wrong side of the street. He went over to the other side and knocked on the door of the Ainsworth's house. Jack Ainsworth took the telegram, or it might have been a letter, his wife came and stood by him and they held each other for a bit. Poor Jack and Hilda, I thought.'

'You must have felt some relief.'

'Aye, I were sorry for them but pleased for us. I'm a bit ashamed to say it now.'

'But it was understandable.'

'Annie said *what a terrible shame, nice lad John, he were with the Royal Lancs weren't he?*'

'*Aye*, I said, *he were, different battalion though*. We carried on, postie boy came and went, then one day, in August it were, around the middle of the month, the boy parked his bike outside our place. This time he hadn't got the wrong side of the street.'

'This was the news you were dreading?'

'It were. I had three pennies in my pocket and when I took the envelope I handed him the money. *For your trouble lad,* I said, *there'll be no need for a reply*. I knew what it were, it were the end of our Bert.' John looks down and shakes his head then turns to Erich and speaks directly to him. 'Is that how you heard about your boy, with a telegram like?'

'It was fortunate that Kurt's senior officer came to see me at the hospital where I was working. When he told me, I was given leave to return home so I was able to tell Martina in person. I had time to get used to it and was able to offer her some comfort.'

'That visit from his senior officer, was it because your boy was an officer?'

'I suppose it was. Anyway, that was how it was for us. Our Kurt was engaged to be married and I went to tell her the news.'

'She must have been really upset.'

'She was of course but I did not see her on that day to tell her the news myself, she was not at home. Her father told her but it was my responsibility to carry out that painful duty. A few years later, she married and had three children. She would visit us from time to time and bring her children with her. We would sit in the living room while her children played in the garden, and both Martina and I would think that they could have been our grandchildren.'

Both men are quiet and thoughtful for a minute.

'We had a letter from a senior officer from Bert's company,' says John. 'It were a few weeks later. I thought that were nice and good of him to take the time.'

'These things are important, to know that he did his duty to the end.'

'Aye, that's right, important to know.'

John bows his head, overcome by his thoughts, and he remembers what has passed. 'And yet at one time his duty didn't matter to me.'

'How do you mean?'

John shakes his head; clearly he's started to recall events that he would have preferred to forget.

'After the Somme he came home. He had a bit of a wound, nothing serious like, it were a bit of shrapnel in the shoulder.'

'He soon recovered, then?'

'Too soon. I asked him if he could play on it a bit, make out it were worse than it was, tell 'em he'd lost some feeling in the arm like.'

'So that he didn't have to go back, you wanted to keep him at home?'

'Aye, that's it; go back, hopefully stay in England and be given light duties, back home and safe.'

'It's hard to exaggerate an injury. It might not have worked, Mr Williams.'

'Probably not. But you should have seen his face when I suggested it. He said that I were being selfish and he couldn't let his mates down. I'll never forget that look on his face, it were awful, I'll never forget it.'

Erich smiles at him, he understands exactly what John's saying. 'You are only human, Mr Williams. I might have done the same. My boy was never wounded in three years, until he was killed.'

'I know, but I think our Bert thought that I had let him down, betrayed him somehow. We never mentioned it again, but I still regretted that I said it. Trouble is, once you say something like that, you can't take it back.'

'Nobody can blame you, you were thinking with your heart and not with your head, as they say.'

'I can only blame myself, Doctor. I just hope he didn't think too badly of me.'

Martina and Annie join Erich and John. Martina leans over and places some flowers on the stone, then she steps back and bows her head. 'Rest now, my son, till we meet again. God bless you.'

Martina and Erich stand arm in arm and look down at the headstone. Annie looks at John, and by moving her head and looking away, she indicates to her husband that it's time to leave the couple on their own. They don't say anything and walk slowly away. At a discrete and considered distance away, they stop and look back.

'God bless you she said, do you think he's blessed by God?'

'I don't know, Annie, you're the religious one, not me, that's your territory, you're the keen churchgoer.'

'Well, what I can say, John, with some certainty, they're all God's children, I believe that, I do.'

'Aye, look at this lot, Annie, sons, brothers and fathers, just like at Dozinghem.'

Annie turns to John and smiles at him, then she looks back at Erich and Martina as they stand in silence.

'Look at them, John, they're probably doing what we do, remembering as many things about their boy that they can still recall, the good times and the not so good things.'

'Aye,' adds John, 'the things we said to our boy and the things that we wished we'd said.'

'That's it, John, things that made us laugh, things that made us angry and, well, things that made us cry.'

Annie looks thoughtful. 'Do you know, John, when we were talking to Mr and Mrs Aspinal the other day.'

'You mean the major and his wife.'

'If you like,' Annie pauses for a moment. 'I thought then, these people aren't like us, we've nothing in common with them, they live in a different world.'

'Oh, I don't know, Annie, they were polite like, he seemed to be more interested than her.'

'Polite in their way, I suppose, humoured us I think, more than anything.'

'Why are you talking about them?'

'We've come to a foreign land and met a couple from another country, who come from a very different background to us…'

'I know what you're going to say, Annie, we've more in common with the Lehmanns than we'll ever have with people like the Aspinals.'

'It's what we share, John, that sense of loss, it doesn't matter where you come from, you shouldn't live longer than your children, it can't be right.'

Annie takes out a handkerchief and carefully dabs her eyes, puts her arm around John's back and holds him tight. 'I'm glad we came here today, John, I really am.'

John looks at her and smiles. 'Aye, well so am I, Annie. I just hope that their boy is allowed to rest in peace and stay here in his final resting place like.'

'What do you mean?'

'I'll tell you later, Annie, it's complicated.'

'I'll have that put on your gravestone, John.'

'What?'

'It was complicated.'

John laughs. 'It's always complicated, Annie, always is.'

Eventually, the couple are joined by Martina and Erich. 'I think that it is time to leave,' says Erich. 'We have done what we wished to do.' He then sweeps his outstretched arm towards the gate. 'Come, your carriage awaits.'

As they walk slowly towards the exit, Martina and Annie lead the way, while Erich and John discuss the plans for the continuing development of the cemetery.

'My Kurt will be joined by many more of his comrades in here, I am sure of it.'

'You mean,' says John, 'when they close the other cemeteries?'

'It's the new plan. It makes sense I suppose.'

'Though it doesn't seem right, digging them up and moving them.'

'In many ways, this is the price we pay for losing the war, I don't know if it would have been different if we had won, but when they are finally laid to rest here, they will be well cared for and respected. The trees will grow and under the shade and the protection of the branches, Kurt and his friends will sleep. I think it will be a good place, if there has to be such a place.'

'Aye, that's right I suppose.'

Erich points back at the cemetery and looks at John.

'My son's remains, his broken bones, are here in the ground.' He then taps his forehead. 'But Kurt is in here. What is in the ground is not as important as what is in our minds and in our hearts, it is here where he lives.' As they leave through the gates Erich turns to take one last look, there is a thought in his mind that he'll not visit again. He puts his hand on John's shoulder.

'Two sons, two graves, this is what we share.'

'And two families,' says John. 'We've been separated by where we come from, divided by a war and, although I don't think we'll ever see eye to eye on some things, we're united in grief. No doubt about that.'

Chapter Thirty-Two

5 August, 1932 – Poperinge

John applies the finishing touches to his smoothly-shaved face. He dips the cut-throat razor into the bowl of warm water and sets about removing the final soap from under his chin. At all times he's keen to avoid any contact with his moustache; he considers it to be a handsome feature, which is usually well-trimmed and groomed. He hears the sound of a motor vehicle that's pulled up outside the hotel.

'That'll be our Paul, did you hear, Annie?' he says while still peering into the mirror. 'Right on time as arranged, good lad.' Annie stops putting their clothes into the suitcases and walks over to the window. She's able to confirm that John's correct and that their transport to Ostend has arrived on time.

Annie walks back to the bed and continues with the packing. She sits on the bed and looks at her husband. 'Do you think we'll come again, John, I mean every year as we have?'

John wipes the last of the soap from his face and turns to look at Annie. He's yet to finish dressing and is wearing his braces over his undershirt. 'Why do you say that, Annie?'

Annie thinks for a moment. 'Well, all this business with Dr Lehmann and his family, in a way it's sort of brought things to an end. I almost feel that we've finally laid our Bert to rest.'

John sits next to her. 'All these years, Annie, we can't stop now, we're in the habit of it. If we were sat on some deckchairs on't North Shore at Blackpool, well I wouldn't mind betting that I'd look at you and you'd look back at me and we'd think the same, Annie.'

'And what's that, John, as if I don't know?'

'We'd wish we were in Belgium, I think you know I'm right.'

Annie stands up to finish the packing. One case is full and she closes the catches. 'I'm nearly done, John. Now, shift yourself and get your shirt on and yes, you're right, it wouldn't be the same if we didn't come again.'

John takes down his braces, puts on his shirt and starts to attach the removable collar. Annie comes to his aid and helps him with the stud, once in place she feeds through a tie and makes sure that it's level before tying it together.

She smiles at him as he looks her in the face. 'Mind you, Annie, it'll not be the same again, it's been a funny old time, I feel as if I've been on one of those big rides at Blackpool, up and down, side to side, all shaken up like.'

Annie finishes adjusting John's tie, puts her hands on his shoulders and look directly into his eyes. 'They call it a rollercoaster and when you saw it you said that they'd never get you on a contraption like that, so how do you know what it's like?'

'I can imagine it, Annie. I've seen the looks on the faces of the folk as they get off, and paid good money to be shaken about and feel all ill as a consequence.'

Annie shakes her head and laughs; she finishes filling the second case and closes it. 'Right, that's it, now as I said, shift yourself and put your coat on, we don't want to keep young Paul hanging about, and that ferry certainly won't wait for us.' There's a knock on the door and John opens it to see Hugo who has come to give them a hand with their luggage.

He grins at them and walks in to pick up both cases. 'Service with a smile,' says John.

The couple follow Hugo down the stairs, through the foyer and out onto the veranda. There, they pause for a moment and

John takes out his pipe. 'Yes,' says Annie, 'you'd better do that now before we get on the coach.'

They're joined by Mary and Henry. 'Another nice fine day,' says Mary. 'I hope the crossing's going to be all right, nice and smooth.'

She sees that Henry is following John's lead and is starting to fill his pipe. 'Get it over with,' she says, 'before we set off.' She turns to Annie. 'The things we have to put up with. Did your Bert ever leave a gas mask at home? I could do with it now.' Annie laughs and sets off down the steps and Mary follows her.

John and Henry stay behind and stand on the top of the veranda steps and smoke their pipes. 'Have you enjoyed your time here, Henry, found it interesting like?'

'Oh yes,' replies Henry, 'very educational, learnt a bit. Not sure I'd like to live here though, or be here for any more length of time. It's a very different place, suits the folk round here mind, but it's not for me.'

'Each to their own, Henry, each to their own.'

The two men are interrupted by the approach of Erich and Martina who are also leaving the hotel. John and Henry politely stand aside to allow them to pass by. Martina thanks them, smiles and walks down the steps. Erich stands with the two men. 'Will it take you long to get home, Doctor?' asks Henry.

Erich thinks for a moment. 'We are going to call in to stay with some friends in Cologne, so it is difficult to know how many hours. Your journey is more problematical I think, with the Channel to cross.'

'Well,' replies Henry, 'just as well it's there, to keep you lot out.' As soon as he says it, the look on John's face tells him that his remark is out of place. However, he's relieved to see that Erich is smiling at him. 'I'm sorry, Doctor, it was my attempt at a bit of humour, making light of it you might say.'

'That's quite all right, Mr Reynolds, if we can't laugh or as you say, make light of it, what else can we do?' His expression changes and he looks serious. 'I only hope that you'll not need it again, but you might.'

'Amen to that,' says John. Henry bids Erich goodbye and walks down the steps towards the coach. Erich offers John his hand. John looks at the outstretched hand, raises his own hand, then thinks better of it and pulls back.

'Too much, I'm not ready for that,' he says. Erich nods and slightly bows his head.

'I understand,' says Erich, 'perhaps at some time.'

John looks down the steps and sees that Annie has been watching him, and the slow shake of her head tells him that she disapproves of his refusal. She feels that when they are at home he might well come to regret his stubbornness. Erich starts to leave the veranda and John calls to him to stop for a moment. He walks down the steps and holds out his hand.

Erich smiles and gladly shakes John's hand. 'You know, we may meet again, Mr Williams, and I wish you and your family well. Have a good future.'

John wishes the same and walks over to meet Annie. 'I saw you looking, Annie,' he says. 'I knew well enough what you meant. Hope you're satisfied, I had to swallow some pride there.'

'Poppycock,' says Annie, 'I knew you wanted to finish it nicely and you did, I'm pleased with you.'

John and Annie walk arm in arm to the coach, and they pass Emma and Peter who are saying their goodbyes. As they walk by the young couple, John quietly speaks to Annie out the corner of his mouth, 'I suppose you can tell Emma he can visit, if he's passing by in Lancashire like.'

Annie chuckles and says to Emma, 'Your father is not against a visit from Peter and I would welcome it.' She then looks at Peter, 'He did add if you happened to be passing by.' Emma and Annie laugh; it's typical of John to add this proviso almost as some form of a disclaimer.

'Thank you, Mrs Williams, I appreciate that,' says Peter.

Emma puts her hand through Peter's arm and smiles at him. 'And so do I.'

Madame De Vos and Hugo come to say goodbye. Paul has been asked by Erich to check the water and oil levels in their car. The bonnet is open and Herbert looks in. He beckons to Hugo to join him and this he does. Both boys stare in at the engine and point at some of the detail of what seems to be a very complex and intricate piece of machinery. They ask Paul a number of questions which he does his best to answer, although he admits that some of the complicated workings of a sophisticated Daimler engine are beyond his knowledge.

Henry carries a large suitcase and puts it by the door of the luggage compartment of the coach. He takes out his handkerchief and mops his brow. Mary and Madame De Vos walk by him. 'That case is heavier now than when we came,' he complains. 'We haven't used half of the stuff in it, you know, weighs a ton, heavier than the barrels I shift about.'

'Oh give over, Henry,' says Mary, 'you've always got to have a moan at something, there's only a bit of lace that's extra.'

Madame De Vos laughs. 'It is always the way of it, Mr Reynolds, I hear it all the time from my guests.'

'Oh ignore him, Madame De Vos, the day that he stops moaning I'll book him in at the doctors and have his head looked at, then we'll have him put away and I'll have some peace.'

Paul has finished his work on the car. He produces a map and he and John study the route they are to take. Annie stands by them and Martina takes the opportunity to approach her to say goodbye. Annie holds out her hand, smiles at her and holds Martina's hand for a moment.

'Goodbye, Mrs Williams,' says Martina.

'It's Annie, you must call me Annie.'

'Yes, of course, this can be difficult for me, if I have your permission to call you by your Christian name, you must call me Martina.'

'Well, goodbye, Martina.'

'Have a good and safe journey, Annie.'

'And you,' replies Annie. 'Just when I get to know you, we're saying goodbye.'

Martina looks at Emma and Peter who are in conversation. It seems that they are developing what appears to be a very close and intimate relationship. 'We may meet again, you never know, perhaps.'

'Well, my John would say, I'm sure he's a nice boy, with prospects, but it's complicated.'

Martina looks a little puzzled. 'Complicated?'

'With problems,' explains Annie. 'It's John's way, just his way.'

'Well, I think that your Emma is a nice girl, with prospects.'

Emma and Peter walk towards the coach, now they're holding hands. They talk more and laugh, and it's plain to see that they're well-matched and are at ease in each other's company.

'Will you write to me?' asks Peter.

Emma is pleased to be asked. 'I shall put pen to paper as soon as we get home.'

'But you will have little to tell in such a short time.'

Emma smiles at him. 'Well, Peter, I think that you will find that I will have a lot to tell you. Sometimes it's better to write about things than say them in person.'

The couple embrace and steal a quick kiss, Emma climbs up into the coach and sits by a window, which she opens so that she can continue talking to Peter.

Annie sits next to John on the coach, leans towards him and speaks quietly, 'That's good of you to say that, John, about Peter being invited to visit us.'

'Well I had to didn't I, Annie, I wouldn't like to see our Emma feeling sorry for herself and being in a bit of a mood like.'

'Mind you, it would be peculiar if he just happened to be passing Blackburn, wouldn't it?'

'Well,' says John, 'let's hope nothing comes of it. I wonder if that Robert Shaw's fixed up now?'

All the family is seated on the coach. Henry stands and

carries out an exaggerated head count. 'All aboard now, driver!' he shouts. 'Here we go again, next stop, Ostend.'

Paul looks round, taps the peak on his cap, engages first gear and the coach moves slowly and noisily away from the hotel. Because the vehicle has been standing with the engine running for some time, a large amount of smoke bellows out of the exhaust, much to the annoyance of passers-by.

'Listen to the intrepid world traveller,' says Mary. 'He'd never been further than Morecambe before. Course there was that cup final once.'

Annie speaks quietly again to John. 'Seriously, John, if anything came of it, you know with our Emma and Peter, would you be that unhappy?'

John thinks for a moment and says, 'Unhappy would be the wrong way of looking at it, Annie, I mean where would they live, I can't see Peter being content to live in Bromley Street, can you? It would be complicated, Annie, very complicated.'

'Now, how did I know that you would say that?' replies Annie. 'Anyway, there are other places to live, other than Bromley Street, there are some nice houses on Means Road.'

'Means Road?' says John. 'He'd have to do a lot of doctoring to afford to live on Means Road!'

The coach travels down the road, and the occupants wave at the hotel staff who are standing on the steps and waving back.

Hugo looks up at his mother. 'Do you think they will come back next year?'

'Yes certainly. Mr and Mrs Williams,' replies Madam De Vos, 'find it difficult not to, but not Herbert perhaps, although you never know.'

Chapter Thirty-Three

30 July, 1952 – Poperinge

The heavy, torrential rain hammers down on the steps that lead up to the veranda of the hotel. A taxi pulls by the kerb close to the bottom of the steps and a couple wearing raincoats get out of the vehicle. Brenda Williams opens a large umbrella and tries without too much success to create a shelter for her and the man who's accompanying her.

The couple begin to climb the slippery, drenched steps, the water cascades down onto their shoes and they move as quickly as they can, being careful to avoid any mishaps. The man is Herbert, Brenda's husband, and he's carrying two small suitcases. At the top of the steps they shelter for a moment under the glass canopy of the veranda. They shake off as much of the water as they are able to. Brenda opens and closes the umbrella quickly, with a violent and aggressive action, to ensure that a limited amount of water is taken inside. Herbert looks at the sign that reads 'Madame De Vos, Hotel'.

They enter the foyer and Herbert removes his trilby hat, walks up to the desk and caresses a round-topped bell; it's a familiar object, which he remembers from many years before. With the flat of his hand he strikes the bell and a loud chime is heard, audible even above the sound of the rain that continues to crash down onto the canopy outside.

A young, dark-haired girl in her late teens, slim and short in height, rushes out from a back room. She quickly positions herself behind the desk and presents the couple with a well-practiced, warm and welcoming smile.

'How are you?' she enquires. 'Well, I hope. My name is Agnes, how can I be of assistance?'

'Thank you, we are well. My name is Mr Williams, Mr H. E. Williams and this is my wife. I wrote some weeks ago to book accommodation for us, for two nights, we're from England.'

The girl looks down at the book and is pleased to announce that all is in order, they are expected. She turns another book to Herbert and asks him to sign and this he does.

Then she says, 'Oh, you are Herbert Edward Williams.'

Herbert nods. 'That's me, but why do you say my full name like this?'

'Madame De Vos,' she answers. 'She saw the booking and gave me instructions to tell her as soon as you arrive, this is important.'

'And she's still here?' asks Herbert.

'She is. If you would like to remove your damp coats, I will take them for drying and you can go into the reception room where we have prepared a nice fire to warm you, I will bring you some tea.'

Herbert and Brenda remove their coats, hand them to Agnes, and enter the reception room. Herbert is immediately familiar with the room. Although it has obviously been redecorated, the style and colour scheme are identical to the memory that he has and most of the furniture is the same. They sit by the fire and warm themselves. Agnes brings in the tea and the couple help themselves. There are also two large slices of cake for them to enjoy. Agnes leaves them. She takes the two small suitcases upstairs, and tells them that their room will shortly be ready.

The couple, warmed by the roaring fire, sip their tea and start to feel relaxed. Suddenly there's an announcement from the door that leads from the foyer.

'Mr and Mrs Williams, you are here at last.'

Herbert and Brenda look round to see a woman who's a stranger to Brenda but easily identified by Herbert because it's without doubt Madame De Vos. Herbert stands and approaches her, she takes his hands. 'Herbert Edward Williams, so good to see you.'

Herbert introduces Brenda. 'Madame De Vos, this is my wife Brenda.'

Madame De Vos looks at the slim, attractive woman who has a fair and delicate complexion set off with an abundance of dark brown hair. She smiles and then looks at Herbert. She sees the man and remembers the boy. She can start to see his father in him because she remembers John well. In comparison, Herbert is somewhat slimmer and his moustache is smaller and more suited to the modern age. The hair that was blonde and fair is now light brown in colour and slightly wavy. Madame De Vos sits with them and they immediately start to reminisce.

'I recall that when you last came,' Madame De Vos says, 'the weather was very warm, nice, with plenty of sunshine, different from today but they say it will improve.'

Herbert finishes his tea and analyses the appearance of Madame De Vos; apart from grey hair, little has changed in her appearance and her still smooth skin belies her advancing years. 'Madame De Vos...' he says.

He's interrupted by Madame De Vos. 'We have known each other for, let me see... twenty years. I think that you can call me by my given name, which is Emma.'

'I remember, it's the same as my sister's name,' says Herbert. 'So, how are you keeping, Emma?'

'I am well, but importantly, how are your parents?'

'Father died three years ago, but Mother is still well and apart from some arthritis, enjoys her life. She has grandchildren who she adores.'

'And you, have you contributed to her happiness by having children?'

'Yes,' replies Brenda, 'two boys, Philip who is five and Steven, he's three.'

'Your mother and father last came here in 1937. I could see

that it was becoming too much for him and I wasn't surprised when your mother wrote to say that they wouldn't be coming again. Then of course we had the war.'

'Well, Dad saw the end of the war which pleased him. It kept him going I think.'

'Did you fly the aeroplanes, as you wanted?'

'Yes, I joined the RAF in 1938. I became a navigator and served with Bomber Command for most of the war. My brothers fought: Jim joined the navy and Harry went into the army, and we all came through it. Dad used to say that the Williams' boys had all the services covered and yet again they were doing their bit. Jim was wounded but he got over it and now works as an engineer. Harry was a prisoner for the final months of the war after being captured at Arnhem and now he works as a newspaper reporter. Emma's war work was with the intelligence service. It was a bit hush-hush and even today she doesn't talk much about it.'

'And what is it that you now do, Herbert?'

'I work in the new world of television. I've a feeling that it might provide me with a good future, although my Uncle George would disagree, *flash in the pan*, he says and *it'll never catch on*.'

'And what of Mary and Harold, no sorry, I mean Henry?'

'Auntie Mary, much the same as you probably remember. Only one of her daughters had a child, a boy, and Mary said it was a very poor return. She, that's Liz, married an American soldier who had been stationed in England and he now works in London.'

Madame De Vos claps her hands and laughs. '*A poor return*, this is the Mary I remember, and how is Henry?'

'Sadly, Uncle Henry died last year. He enjoyed his retirement, spent a lot of time fishing, but missed Dad a lot.'

'Your Emma,' says Madame De Vos. 'I know she never met Peter Lehmann again, did she have children?'

'She did,' answers Brenda, 'a boy. She's also a good teacher now and really enjoys her job.'

Herbert pauses for a moment. 'You said that you knew that Emma and Peter never met after 1932. How did you know that, did my mother write and tell you?'

'No. Martina Lehmann writes to me occasionally and keeps me up to date as you might say.'

'The Lehmanns, how are things with them?'

'Well, I know that Peter and Emma wrote to each other for a time and then Peter met and married a girl called Marlene, that was in 1939, or was it a year later? They had a baby boy, I can't remember what he is called, no doubt I'll remember later. Or perhaps I could find one of Martina's letters, now let me see…' Madame De Vos looks up, raises her eyes and thinks for a moment. 'It will come to me later.'

'So Martina told you about Peter and Emma, in her letters?' asks Herbert.

'No, I actually met Peter Lehmann during the war.'

'Peter visited you? He came back to Poperinge?'

'We had not been evacuated in the second war and Hugo and I ran the hotel together. By that time my mother-in-law had passed on and Hugo insisted that we keep the name of 'Madame De Vos' on the hotel sign. It was in the spring of 1942, one of the girls at the desk called up the stairs where I was cleaning and told me that two German officers wanted rooms for the night. We often had German officers staying and I couldn't understand why she had told me. You see, it wasn't good to turn German soldiers away; they could have made things difficult for you. At the same time it was important not to be seen as being a collaborator, it wasn't easy. Most of them were polite and well mannered.'

'Peter was one of the officers booking in, I presume?' asks Herbert.

'As I came down the stairs, I recognised him immediately. He looked so smart in his uniform, he was a medical officer. He smiled at me and I invited him and his friend to sit with me and have some tea. His friend's name was Wolfgang. I thought that

that was a typical German name, if ever I heard one. It was Peter who told me about he and Emma and his life as it was then. The next day Peter and his friend left and I never saw him again. Now what is Martina's grandson's name?'

Herbert interrupts her. 'Please, Emma, it's not that important, but it's good to know that Martina had a grandchild. From time to time my mother would think of her and as each of her grandchildren were born, she would say, *I hope Martina Lehmann is feeling as happy as I am.*'

'Well,' continues Madame De Vos, 'there was only the one, he must be eleven or twelve now and the last I heard was that he was, how would you say... in good condition.'

'We must be thankful for that,' says Herbert. 'At the end of the war we flew over many of the German cities in the daylight and the amount of devastation was hard to believe.'

'They paid a high price, a very high price,' adds Madame De Vos. 'When peace came I was so pleased to get the first letter from Martina, but the news was not so pleasing.'

'Was this about Peter?'

'Yes, it was. Sadly it was. He went to the east, to Russia, and it was assumed that he died in Stalingrad early in 1943. Martina never saw or heard of him again.'

'And her husband, the doctor?'

Madame De Vos sighs deeply and looks out of the window. 'Dr Lehmann was killed during an air raid as he went to his work in a hospital in Frankfurt. That was in the January of 1945. Now, Martina has her grandson, ah, I remember, it is Klaus. She also has the company of her daughter-in-law, so she is not alone and this makes me feel happier. But it is true that she has lost two sons in the two wars and no mother can give more.'

There's a moment of silence as Madame De Vos remembers and Herbert reflects on and considers what he has heard. Eventually, Herbert stands, and stretches his legs by walking slowly to the door. He stops and looks at Madame De Vos, clearly wishing to say something but the question that he wants to ask may well provide an answer that he doesn't want to hear.

'Emma, I have a story to tell you.'

Madame De Vos senses Herbert's feelings of unease and discomfort. 'Please, Herbert, tell me your story, I am intrigued, but I would be surprised if I did not know what it is about.'

Herbert sits next to Madame De Vos. 'As you know, I was in the RAF and like many who served, I made friends and still keep in touch with many of them. One friend, a chap called David Clark, was a rear gunner on a Lanc, sorry, a Lancaster Bomber. In 1944, his plane was shot down and although he bailed out, he was badly injured. He and two other airmen were found by members of the Belgian resistance and hidden from the Germans. One young man, a member of the resistance, did all he could for Dave, and the medical help that he managed to obtain without a doubt saved his life.'

Madame De Vos smiles, 'I know where this is leading, Herbert, but please continue.'

'When Dave was well enough to travel, the resistance group, with the help of the French, got him to the Channel and from there a fishing boat smuggled him out of France and home. Dave always wanted to find the young man who helped him, but because the resistance members didn't use their real names, he didn't know who he was. The only clue that he had was a memory of being hidden in a safe house, a farm cottage near Lille in Northern France.'

Herbert is distracted momentarily by the expression on Madame De Vos's face. It looks as if she's anticipating the end of the story.

'Emma,' he asks, 'have you heard this story before?'

'No,' she replies, 'but I know of your story. Please let me allow you to finish.'

'Dave and a friend of his travelled around the countryside near Lille and eventually found the farmhouse. Fortunately, the farmer and his wife had survived the war and were able to reveal the identity of the man who Dave was searching for…'

Herbert is interrupted by Madame De Vos, she raises her hand as if to stop him. 'His name was Hugo.'

'That's it, Emma, Hugo De Vos. That was your Hugo, wasn't it?'

'It was.'

'Dave also discovered that later in 1944, Hugo was caught by the Gestapo and executed. I'm sorry but I have to ask, was that true?'

Madame De Vos nods, takes out a handkerchief and dabs each eye. 'Yes, it was in July that year.'

Brenda takes hold of her hand and holds it for a moment. 'I'm sorry that we have upset you, but Bert needed to know.'

A quiet moment follows, then their attention is taken by the sound of two children, a girl of about twelve and a boy who could be two or three years older. They're standing in the doorway of the reception room and the boy is holding a football in his hands. Herbert looks at the boy. He's somewhat taken aback, because the youth's face is a face that he recognises.

'Hugo, it's Hugo,' he utters.

Madame De Vos composes herself. 'That is my grandson, Christian, and behind him is his sister, Maria. Children, say hello to our guests, Mr and Mrs Williams.'

The two children politely say hello and Christian begins to talk in Dutch. Madame De Vos stops him. 'Christian, we have guests from England, please speak English.'

'Grandma,' says Christian, 'can I play football in the garden please? Maria will be in goal.'

Madame De Vos looks out of the window. 'It may have stopped raining but the ground is very wet and you will damage the grass.'

'But,' protests Christian.

'That's the way it is, Christian,' Madame De Vos replies in a firm voice. 'When it is drier, you can play, and when you play, you must mind my flowers.'

Christian nods in reluctant agreement and the children leave the doorway. Herbert shakes his head. 'When I saw Christian, I thought I was looking at Hugo. I well remember that day when Peter and I played football with your son. I remember it as if it were yesterday.'

Madame De Vos summons up the memory of that day. 'The other day I was in the garden and Christian scored a goal, which is easy I think because Maria doesn't really like to play in goal, in fact she doesn't want to play football at all. Then, I heard Christian shout 'Blackburn Rovers one, Eintracht Frankfurt, nil!''

Herbert laughs. 'How... how on earth did he know that?'

'He must have only been five, playing football with his father, and I clearly heard Hugo say that several times. It has stuck with Christian since and I know that when he plays, he wishes that he could play football with his father.'

Herbert stands up and offers his hand to Brenda.

He looks at Madame De Vos. 'Now, if you don't mind, Emma, if our room is ready it would be nice to relax and freshen up before dinner.'

'Of course, Herbert, you must be tired Brenda, I will see you at dinner, or is it tea, as your father once said, tea at teatime.'

Herbert and Brenda laugh and they walk towards the doorway, then Herbert turns to Madame De Vos. 'If it's not too upsetting, Emma, may I ask, were you fortunate, if that's the right thing to say, to be able to lay Hugo to rest as you would have wished?'

'Yes, I pleaded with them and I have to say that I used Peter Lehmann's name and talked of him as being a friend of the family, which in many ways he was. I went twice to Brussels. When I was there for the second time and while I was pleading with the sergeant at the desk, a young officer was leaving. He recognised me and came over to see what the fuss was all about, it was Wolfgang, Peter's friend. When I told him what I wanted, what I needed, he took the sergeant to one side and talked with him. Wolfgang then left and the sergeant then made arrangements for me to collect my son's body, I was so grateful. So Hugo was returned to me.'

Herbert looks around the room, many memories come flooding back, he looks at Madame De Vos once again. 'Where is Hugo now, Emma?'

'I will show you,' Madame De Vos stands and invites Herbert and Brenda to follow her. They go into the garden and the couple follow Madame De Vos to the far side of the lawn. They stand by the well-tended and carefully nurtured, impressive display of colourful flowers.

Madame De Vos points to the flowerbeds. 'Here, this is where my Hugo rests and this is where, one day, I will join him.' After a moment of contemplation and respectful silence, they walk slowly back towards the hotel. Madame De Vos stops and asks one last question, 'You said that your Emma had children?'

'A boy,' replies Brenda, 'he's called Peter.'

'So, she married, I presume. Did she marry well?'

'Yes,' answers Herbert, 'she did. She's married to a chap called Robert, Robert Shaw.'

'Then this is a happy ending,' says a smiling and contented Madame De Vos.

The clouds start to clear away and the sun shines through, picking out the rich colours that the well-tended garden presents. After the rain, a fine hazy mist is seen as it rises from the ground. The air smells sweet and as it mingles with the scent of the flowers, it creates a fragrance that is so strong that it can almost be tasted. Herbert looks around at the tranquil and almost idyllic scene.

'When I came here in 1932, I came to see a grave with my name on it. When I left, I realised then, and it's more true today, that there are many in the world who can say, *there's a grave in Belgium, with my name on it.*'

The End

Author's Note

There are many British and Commonwealth cemeteries in the Flanders region, ranging from the very small containing a few dozen graves to the very large where thousands of service personnel are buried. The cemeteries are impressive, with a large white cross memorial as a centrepiece located in a prominent position. Regimental headstones displaying the name and date of death are in most cases kept in immaculate condition.

In July 1917, in readiness for the forthcoming Third Battle of Ypres, groups of casualty clearing stations were placed at three positions. One of these sites was at a place called Westvleteren which was outside the main area of hostilities, yet was close to the front. The proposed cemetery was named Dozinghem, The 4th, 47th and 61st Casualty Clearing Stations were posted at Dozinghem and the military cemetery was used by them until early in 1918. At the end of the war, 3,174 Commonwealth soldiers lay in the cemetery along with sixty-five German war dead.

The Belgian and French communities recognise to this day the sacrifice that the Allied soldiers made. However, as visible as the Allied fallen are, the German dead seemed to be almost invisible. The German cemeteries are very different places; they are very understated and this is where many of the forgotten dead of WW1 are buried.

At the end of 1918, German military burial sites were spread over 678 Belgian parish districts. In the district of Langemark, northeast of Ypres, there were many German burial sites of different sizes. As well as these sites, thousands of German soldiers had been buried in individual burial plots in fields and woods. German soldiers were also buried in civilian cemeteries or in British, Belgian and French military cemeteries.

The German and Belgian governments reached an agreement in 1925 to set up the Official German Burial Service in Belgium. In co-operation with the Belgian authorities, the French Service de Pensions and the Commonwealth War Graves Commission authorised the exhumation and reburial of German military dead took place.

During the 1930s, approximately 10,000 war dead were brought to the Langemark cemetery from eighteen German burial sites around the region, and the total number of burials reached about 14,000. Approximately 3,000 of the graves were those of the Student Volunteers who were killed in the Flanders region in 1914 and because of this, the cemetery became known as the *Student Cemetery*. The Belgian government was reluctant to give up any more land for German burials after the war and in the need to consolidate and manage the sites without too much expansion, eight soldiers on average were buried in each plot. Where known, the dead soldiers' names are inscribed on a flat square stone. Today, the total number of soldiers buried or commemorated in Langemark stands at 44,234, of which 24,916 are unidentified.

In the Flanders region around Ypres, including Hill 60, Passchendaele, Lys and Sanctuary Wood, over 1,700,000 soldiers on both sides were killed or wounded. This figure does not include a large number of civilians. For some family members of the dead, there's some consolation in knowing where their dead are laid to rest. But countless numbers of soldiers simply disappeared into the fields of Flanders without a trace and many of those perished in the mud at Passchendaele.

Passchendaele
Also known as the Third Battle of Ypres, Passchendaele typified in this one struggle what the Great War is renowned for; senseless slaughter and little or no real gains. The battle began in the early hours of the morning of 31 July, 1917. Ypres was the main town

within a salient or bulge in the British lines and the site of two previous battles.

An intense artillery barrage lasted two weeks, with 4.5 million shells fired from 3,000 guns. The intensity of the bombardment served as a warning to the German army that an attack was imminent. Unfortunately for the Allied forces, it failed to destroy the heavily-fortified German positions. When the infantry offensive began, the troops, mainly from British and Commonwealth regiments and supported by the French, came under severe and intense machine gun fire and mortar attack. The Germans had learnt some valuable lessons from their experiences at the Somme; they retired to the safety of their deep and fortified bunkers. The constant shelling churned up the clay soil and destroyed the drainage systems. Within a few days, the heaviest rain for 30 years had turned the soil into a quagmire, producing a heavy thick mud that clogged up rifles and immobilised tanks. The water in the shell-holes became so deep that men and horses drowned in it.

After the initial attacks that lasted for four days, few of the objectives had been achieved. While the left wing of the attack had some success, the right wing completely failed. What followed was a pause in major hostilities to assess and regroup. Then, on 16 August, the attack was resumed and again, to little effect. A stalemate was established for another month until the weather improved and the British Command felt confident enough to launch another attack, which began on 20 September with limited success. However, further attacks in October failed to make any real progress. Eventually, the capture of what little remained of the Passchendaele village, by British and Canadian forces on 6 November, signalled the official end of the campaign.

In securing Passchendaele village, commander-in-chief, Douglas Haigh, could claim that one of the main objectives had been achieved. The truth was that the village lay barely five miles beyond the starting point of the initial offensive. A decisive blow had been promised; it had taken over three months, cost

325,000 Allied and 260,000 German casualties and did little more than make the bump of the Ypres salient a bit larger. At the time, the British Command was of the opinion that the German army could not afford to lose such a large amount of casualties. It was felt that the Allies, who were being reinforced by America's entry into the war, could sustain such losses.

Passchendaele became known not only for the scale of the carnage and the high level of casualties, but also for the mud and the creation of a desolate landscape. The armies on both sides fought hard, showing immense bravery and displaying an unquestionable sense of duty and commitment. It's right that today we should continue to recognise, remember and respect the sacrifice that they made.

Many men from Lancashire fought and died in Flanders along with Allied soldiers from other British and Commonwealth regiments. However, there was no regiment called *The Royal Lancastrian Light Infantry*. I chose to use a fictitious regiment to avoid any reference to the possible identification of soldiers who actually served at Passchendaele.

Acknowledgements

My grateful thanks to: Jessie Owen, Tom Owen, Cat Webb and Lindsey Payne, The Commonwealth War Graves Commission, The Imperial War Museum and to Thwaites Brewery for producing excellent ale that's very easy on the palate.

THE NEXT BOOK IN THE SERIES BY STEWART GILL OWEN:

White Sands

3 September, 1939
Livingston Road, Blackburn, Lancashire

John Williams sighs deeply. He leans forward and with some difficulty raises his rather portly frame from his favoured easy-chair. He steadies himself and walks slowly across the room and switches off the wireless. Now in his sixty-fifth year, John is suffering from some very irritating, age-related, health disorders that are common ailments in a man of his years. Problems with his joints, although not totally restricting his mobility, have nevertheless curtailed his long and energetic walks in the park. He rubs the open palm of his left hand over the top of his head to smooth down his light grey, thinning hair. At the same time, he caresses his large, droopy moustache with the thumb and index finger of his right hand.

He looks at his brother-in-law, Henry Reynolds, who is of a much smaller build. Like John, he wears a moustache, although it is tightly cropped and therefore small by comparison. Henry has looked the same for many years due to his hair, which always seems to have been white and is still wiry and curly. Both men have taken to wearing bowler hats, particularly at the weekends, and at the Red Lion public house they have been nicknamed Laurel and Hardy, after the popular film comic duo.

John sighs again. 'Well, you heard what Chamberlain said, Henry, *unless we heard from Germany that they were prepared at once to withdraw their troops from Poland, a state of war would exist between us.*'

'Well, it couldn't be plainer could it, John?'

John turns and looks directly at Henry, slowly shakes his head and repeats the most chilling part of the broadcast.

'I have to tell you now that no such undertaking has been received and that consequently this country is at war with Germany.'

'At war with Germany,' repeats Henry.

'Aye, I saw it coming Henry, I always said it.'

www.ingramcontent.com/pod-product-compliance
Lightning Source LLC
LaVergne TN
LVHW041540070426
835507LV00011B/837